D1233684

From *Brown* to *Meredith*

From *Brown* to *Meredith*

THE LONG STRUGGLE FOR SCHOOL
DESEGREGATION IN LOUISVILLE, KENTUCKY,
1954–2007

Tracy E. K'Meyer

The University of North Carolina Press / Chapel Hill

This book was published with the assistance of the
Thornton H. Brooks Fund of the University of North Carolina Press.

Set in Utopia and Aller types by codeMantra
Manufactured in the United States of America

The map on p. 8 is based on one prepared by Robert Forbes,
University of Louisville Center for GIS.

The paper in this book meets the guidelines for permanence and durability
of the Committee on Production Guidelines for Book Longevity of the Council on
Library Resources. The University of North Carolina Press has been a member of
the Green Press Initiative since 2003.

Library of Congress Cataloging-in-Publication Data
K'Meyer, Tracy Elaine.
From Brown to Meredith : the long struggle for school desegregation in
Louisville, Kentucky, 1954–2007 / Tracy E. K'Meyer.
pages cm
Includes bibliographical references and index.
ISBN 978-1-4696-0708-5 (cloth : alk. paper)
1. School integration—Kentucky—Louisville—History. 2. Busing for
school integration—Kentucky—Louisville—History. 3. Public schools—Kentucky—
Louisville—History. 4. Educational equalization—Kentucky—Louisville—History.
5. Louisville (Ky.)—Race relations. I. Title.
LC214.23.L68K64 2013
379.2'630976944—dc23
2012051383
17 16 15 14 13   5 4 3 2 1

For Colin and Norah

Contents

Illustrations and Map

A map of selected schools and neighborhoods in Louisville and Jefferson County appears on page 8.

Acknowledgments

Any historian incurs debts while producing a book. Because in this case oral history is the major source, I have more than the usual helpful souls to thank for their contribution to the finished product. First and foremost, this book would not have been possible without the generosity of the interviewees who shared their time and stories. I have benefited greatly from the work of the scholars who conducted the interviews, especially Darlene Eakin, Ethel White, Elizabeth Gritter, and David P. Cline. And I am very grateful to the Southern Oral History Program at the University of North Carolina–Chapel Hill for choosing Louisville as one of its case study communities and to Jacquelyn Hall for her encouragement of this book from the beginning. Last-minute interviews to fill gaps in the record were transcribed by Lee Keeling and Amanda Busch, with funding from the University of Louisville College of Arts and Sciences. Archivists at the University of Louisville main archives and photographic archives, Jefferson County Public School archives, and University of North Carolina–Chapel Hill helped me secure and document permissions to use the interviews and provided most of the photographs. My thanks also go to Sherry Jelsma for allowing me to use a photograph from her personal collection.

During the process of writing and revising this book I received helpful suggestions from a number of colleagues. Catherine Fosl and Kathryn Nasstrom read drafts of every chapter, sometimes more than once, and gave me insightful feedback. As the editor of the *Oral History Review*, Kathryn Nasstrom also helped me conceptualize an article drawn from some of the same research as this book, in the process helping me refine ideas for the later chapters. I appreciate the comments of the anonymous readers, which helped me reframe and strengthen chapter 2 in particular. Finally, I am deeply grateful to John Dittmer, not only for the inspiration his *Local People* gives to all of my work but also for reminding me of the Howard Zinn quote that crystallized the theme in the conclusion of this book.

Finally, I want to thank the friends who listened to me talk about school desegregation endlessly, and enthusiastically cheered me on to finish this book. I hope it doesn't let them down. Most important, this, like all of my work was accomplished in partnership with my husband and colleague, A. Glenn Crothers. His enormous faith in me, and his close editing of my writing, made the completion of this book possible. I dedicate it to our beautiful children, Colin and Norah.

From *Brown* to *Meredith*

and had encountered much more complicated stories. In oral history projects conducted in Louisville throughout a period of thirty years, local people—black and white, students and teachers, administrators and community activists—shared memories that reached further back in time, reflected both good and bad experiences in desegregation, and both implicitly and explicitly assessed the results of the process. Most important, and seemingly absent from the 2007 public dialogue around *Meredith* and much of the scholarship on school desegregation, the interviews conveyed a story of blacks and whites coming together with a commitment to work for integration. This book explores the multifaceted memory of the long struggle for school desegregation, and my hope is that it will contribute to the contemporary dialogue on the future of diversity and equality in education.

For almost as long as communities have struggled with the problem of school desegregation, scholars have documented and analyzed the process and its results. Most studies of the early response to *Brown v. Board of Education* describe massive resistance and its powerful impact on southern politics and the civil rights movement.[2] Scholars who have examined the second wave of school desegregation after 1968 focus on crises in cities like Boston, but also on less dramatic though no more happy stories in places like Nashville, Buffalo, and Richmond, Virginia. Although these works explore legal wrangling and policy responses, they highlight the opposition to busing among white families and how the white response contributed to the rise of the modern conservative movement.[3] Because of the local nature of school policy decisions, many scholars have focused on one particular community, tracing the development of desegregation during the half century since *Brown*, including in border cities, whose experiences resembled Louisville's. These community studies reveal the consistency of elements of the story across geography and time, including initial resistance; begrudging, slow, and minimal implementation; the shift to busing and community conflict that resulted; white flight, demographic shifts, and resegregation; and the retreat from affirmative efforts to achieve integration.[4] Finally, around the fiftieth anniversary of the *Brown* decision, a number of new volumes assessed its implementation, focusing on legal philosophy, the development of freedom-of-choice policies that helped white communities evade change, the limited impact of desegregation, and the at times negative results for black teachers and communities.[5]

The interpretive emphasis of much of this scholarship, particularly on the second wave of desegregation, has drawn criticism from some scholars, including Jeanne Theoharis and Jacquelyn Hall, who suggest a need for a new lens through which to view the long desegregation battle. In a 2001 essay on the Boston conflict, Theoharis charges historians with validating the anti-busing forces' "racialized notions of neighborhood." By focusing on understanding the opponents of desegregation, Theoharis argues, scholars have rendered that position the normal one. More recently, Hall has argued that the focus on resistance and opposition has made it easy to assume, particularly since the shift to a more conservative court and political climate led to the reversal of desegregation plans, that support for desegregation never existed—at least among whites—and that resegregation was inevitable. Meanwhile, scholars have largely neglected the story of pro-integration activists in the 1970s and 1980s and of how they won access to relatively more equal educational resources for African Americans.[6] Community case studies, by examining the role of different groups in the process throughout a long period of time, expand the picture. Such local studies for example address what African American parents wanted and believed in Baltimore, or how and why moderate whites helped make busing go smoothly in Richmond, or how whites and blacks cooperated to create a relatively more equitable system in Charlotte.[7] This book follows these models by using individual stories to enlarge our understanding of the processes and results of school desegregation.

At several points during the half century after *Brown*, the struggle for school desegregation in Louisville and Jefferson County rose to national attention and significance. In 1956, Louisville integrated quietly by redistricting schools by residence without regard to race and allowing transfers out of assigned schools. The seeming success of that process earned the community national and even international praise as an example of a southern town that had implemented *Brown* with little opposition. Two decades later, however, when the city schools merged with those in surrounding Jefferson County into one system and underwent court-ordered busing to achieve metropolitan-wide desegregation, the violence and racist rhetoric of the opposition rivaled the ugly scenes in Boston, and the national media pointed to Louisville as an example of the turmoil caused by busing. Then, in 1984 and again in 1991, during a period when communities around the country were abandoning school desegregation efforts with federal court approval, Louisville bucked the national trend. In both years, civil rights advocates fought back against the school superintendent's efforts to limit busing and undermine desegregation and succeeded in reforming and preserving assignment plans aimed at achieving racially balanced student bodies. The success of the resulting "voluntary" desegregation program, with modifications to it throughout the years, helped Louisville and

Jefferson County make Kentucky the most integrated state in the nation.[8] In 2007, the Jefferson County Public Schools entered the national limelight again, when the Supreme Court heard *Meredith v. Jefferson County Board of Education* and determined that the schools could no longer use race as a deciding factor in student placement. The decision set off a prolonged debate about whether and how to maintain racial diversity in the classroom.

From Brown to Meredith tells the story of school desegregation in Louisville and Jefferson County in the spirit of two trends in recent civil rights scholarship. The framework of the long civil rights movement expands our vision by reaching back for roots and forward for enduring struggles, avoiding the trap of seeing the movement as a series of discrete moments in a narrow time frame. The history of school desegregation consists of more than the dramatic events at Little Rock and Boston. By tracing the struggle from the response to *Brown* to the aftermath of *Meredith*—from the Supreme Court order for districts to integrate to its prohibition of affirmative efforts to do so—this book emphasizes that desegregation was a long-term process of preparation, debate, renegotiation, and reform of school policies, one that often took place out of the limelight but that shaped students' educational experience. This book also takes inspiration from the "local people" approach, viewing the equal rights struggle through the perspective of grassroots actors.[9] This story does not focus on judges or lawyers (though they are mentioned), but rather on students, teachers, principals, Parent-Teacher Association (PTA) volunteers, and community activists. Their experiences reveal how desegregation worked on the ground: how people laid the groundwork for it, dealt with it inside the school buildings, and over time either challenged or defended policies, adjusting them to meet new needs. Their stories give life to the history of school desegregation by illuminating the expectations, hopes, and disappointments people felt during the process. Finally, individual experience reveals the diverse results of school desegregation and thus forces us to formulate broad and complex conclusions about its impact and significance.

This book differs from the traditional community study monograph by employing oral history interviews to convey much of the story. This approach tightens the focus on local people by using their words, takes advantage of the richness of the available oral sources, and reveals additional layers of information and interpretation. On the most basic level, oral history uncovers stories that have not been included in the written record. Without interviews we would know little about how principals, teachers, and PTA volunteers got ready for desegregation, or how many black and white teachers and students experienced it. Yet oral history by its very nature also illuminates the memory—individual and collective—of school desegregation and can demonstrate how people employ that memory in ongoing debates. In interviews narrators express how they understood events and, as important, what they want posterity to know about them. This allows them to give credit they think is overdue, critique shortcomings in past policies, and point in the direction they would like to see schools move in the future. Finally, oral history draws attention to the stories that are incorporated into shared public memory and those that have been largely communally forgotten. My use of oral history was sparked by curiosity about what is and is not remembered in Louisville and Jefferson County about the long struggle for school desegregation. These oral histories, I hope, will not only contribute to a more complete history but will also provoke consideration of why some stories are forgotten, and how their absence affects public dialogue about the schools.[10]

The oral histories collected here convey a complicated history of school desegregation in Louisville and Jefferson County through multifaceted individual stories. Evidence in the narratives confirms many of the arguments in the scholarly literature on the subject. Although Louisville did not experience much of the massive resistance that occurred in the 1950s, the interviews point to the persistent obstacles faced by black students, the violent opposition to busing in 1975, and doubts about whether it was all worth it. But a parallel and less well-known story also emerges. These interviews reveal a relatively untold story of how people in the community worked for school desegregation: how they saw it as the next natural step in civil rights, prepared for it, worked in classrooms and in the community to make the beginning of busing more peaceful, served on negotiating committees to reform the system, stood up to the school superintendent to keep it, and continued to defend it in the face of legal challenges. Ultimately, this book seeks to dislodge the story of school desegregation from the narrative of resistance and defeat by highlighting the voices of people working for and experiencing change within the schools. I hope that by placing this forgotten story alongside the memory of limited progress, tension, and resistance, this book will help pave the way for a more balanced and thorough scholarly evaluation of, and public dialogue about, school desegregation.

The interviews represented here resulted from five projects conducted between 1973 and 2011. The nature and scope of these projects necessarily shapes the content of this book, by determining what stories were recorded and thus are available as evidence. In 1973, Darlene Eakin, a graduate student at the University of Louisville, recorded fourteen interviews with principals, PTA officials, and civic leaders about the 1956 desegregation of the Louisville city schools. She wanted to document school leaders' preparation for desegregation and to allow the interviewees to assess and explain the success of the process. In 1988, an independent scholar, Ethel White, interviewed seventeen participants in the busing crisis of 1975, focusing on city and school officials and people who worked within the system as either employees or volunteers. Her work is particularly valuable for the in-depth conversations with opposition leaders and for identifying women who worked behind the scenes and received little attention at the time. Between 1999 and 2001, I conducted a larger project on the civil rights movement in Louisville. Although schools were not a focus of that research, thirteen of the activists interviewed discussed their youthful experiences in desegregated schools or their role in the busing controversy. In 2004 and 2005, the Southern Oral History Program (SOHP) of the University of North Carolina–Chapel Hill sent a team of researchers to Louisville to record stories with thirty-nine people about the desegregation of the local schools after 1970, focusing on the busing crisis but also including some material about later revisions to the desegregation plan. In 2009, one of the researchers returned to document the aftermath of the *Meredith* case with five additional interviews. This project was part of the Long Civil Rights Movement initiative, which uses oral history to understand more fully how the enduring black freedom struggle and its legacies have shaped the contemporary South.[11] Finally, in spring 2011, I completed eight interviews with participants in the debates of the 1980s and 1990s to fill in holes in the record. All of the interviews are available in full at the Southern Historical Collection at the University of North Carolina or the University Archives at the University of Louisville.

Before taking the form presented here, individual stories went through a process of filtering and shaping that began with the interview itself and extended through the author's editorial choices. The original interviews were created in a two-person process. The interviewers chose the narrators, selected the topics, and asked the questions. The interviewees responded to those questions based on their memories of the past, as filtered by their position and perspective in the present. My role was to mold the full interviews into a coherent narrative. To begin, I sorted all the material into chapter categories. I then selected stories seeking balanced representation by race, gender, and position relative to events. There is some disagreement among oral historians about the extent to which transcripts should be edited.[12] I leaned toward enhancing readability, coherence, and narrative flow. I eliminated verbal space fillers—ums, uhs, and the like—and in most cases false starts to sentences. I cut repetitive passages, digressions, and material that was unclear out of context. Meanwhile, I introduced paragraph breaks and added transitional words to connect or clarify passages. Faced with the sheer bounty of material, I selected the most compelling stories that represented central themes in the body of interviews.

The stories of school desegregation in Louisville and Jefferson County are presented here in four chapters. The first chapter covers the initial wave of school desegregation after *Brown* and the experiences of the first group of black students to go into the formerly white schools. Chapter 2 centers on the beginning of court-ordered busing and the crisis it sparked. It includes reflections from both those who opposed and those who supported integration, as well as descriptions of what principals, teachers, and students experienced inside the schools in those tumultuous years. The third chapter takes the story from 1981 to 2007, the period of challenges to and reforms in the student assignment plans. Here, participants in the debates of the time talk about their goals and actions in the 1984 and 1991 confrontations with the school superintendent about whether to reduce or eliminate busing, and during the court challenges to the desegregation plan. The final chapter contains the narrators' reflections about the meaning and impact of school desegregation in the community. Each chapter begins with an introduction that lays out key events to give readers sufficient context for understanding the narratives. The bulk of each chapter consists of the interview selections themselves. Finally, each chapter ends with a short analysis of the key themes in the narratives and conclusions about their significance.

The stories shared by the narrators are rooted in the mid-twentieth-century context of Louisville and Jefferson County and in the history of the two polities up to the eve of the *Brown* decision. At the beginning of this story, the city and county public schools constituted separate and very different systems. In 1950, the county still had a largely rural character but was rapidly undergoing suburbanization. As elsewhere in the country, the people moving to those suburbs were almost exclusively whites, and as the county grew, its black population remained about 4 percent. During the following decades the county's population would far outpace the city's, but its ratio of white to black would hold constant. The county schools educated black children only through the ninth grade. A handful of small, isolated all-black primary schools served the African American community, but once students reached high school they had to take the bus into Louisville to go to Central High School, or attend the private Lincoln Institute in rural Simpsonville, Kentucky. Meanwhile, on the eve of the *Brown*

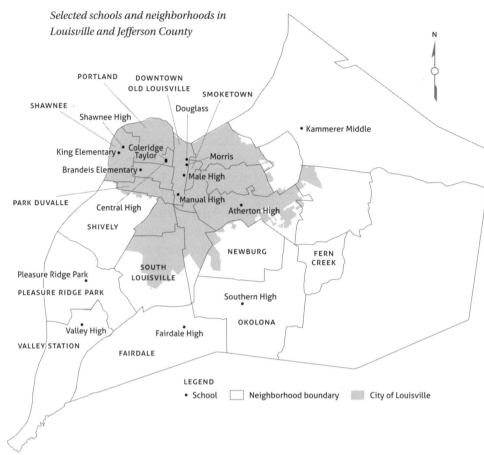

Selected schools and neighborhoods in Louisville and Jefferson County

N

PORTLAND   DOWNTOWN
            OLD LOUISVILLE
                        SMOKETOWN
SHAWNEE
            Douglass
    Shawnee High
                                    • Kammerer Middle

                • Coleridge
King Elementary•   Taylor
Brandeis Elementary•   • Morris
                    •• Male High
PARK DUVALLE
            Central High   • Manual High
    SHIVELY   Atherton High

                    NEWBURG   FERN
                                   CREEK
            SOUTH
Pleasure Ridge Park   LOUISVILLE
PLEASURE RIDGE PARK
                    Southern High
                    •
            OKOLONA

    Valley High   • Fairdale High
VALLEY STATION
        FAIRDALE

LEGEND
• School   ☐ Neighborhood boundary   ▨ City of Louisville

decision, the Louisville Independent district served a student population that was 74 percent white and 26 percent black. As whites continued to move out of the city during the following two decades, the ratio of blacks to whites in the Louisville schools hovered at nearly equal.[13] Because most African Americans lived in the city, and because the leadership for providing education to blacks—albeit unequally—and for challenging segregation was in the city, the story of school desegregation was largely centered on Louisville before the systems merged in 1975. Thus the first chapter of this book focuses on events only in the city, while later chapters deal with the merged city-county system.

At midcentury, Louisville was a segregated southern city with a self-image, and enough of a record, of racial progressivism to hint at potential support for school integration. In the late nineteenth century a system of Jim Crow segregation developed in the city that mirrored that of its sister communities in the South. This system developed gradually, but by the 1920s all public spaces, including theaters, hospitals, city offices, and parks, were racially segregated. Jim Crow also encompassed private space such as housing. In 1914 the city adopted a law banning anyone from occupying property on a block in which a majority of the other race resided. The Supreme Court in *Buchanan v. Warley* (1917) struck the law down, but that did not stop private entities—from builders to realtors to neighborhood associations—from securing residential segregation through other means. By the 1950s this separation had hardened, with the majority of African Americans restricted to two sections of the city: the area just south and east of downtown known as Smoketown, and parts of the west end. Meanwhile, employment discrimination restricted blacks to low-paying occupations. A separate black economy of retail shops, businesses, and professionals developed to serve the black community, but in 1940 more than 87 percent of African Americans who reported an occupation worked in service, common labor, or unskilled factory jobs.[14]

Pervasive segregation and inequality affected the educational system as well. Indeed, as the post–Civil War system of public education developed, at no point did city leaders consider letting white and black children attend school together. In 1870, the new Louisville city charter called for the building of separate black schools, and the first public classes for African American children took place later that year. The system expanded slowly, but it did include the first and for ten years the only black high school in the state, Central High, which opened in 1873. Black education received a small boost in 1882 when the federal circuit court ruled in *Commonwealth of Kentucky v. Jesse Ellis* that public funding for schools must be equally distributed. While this failed to result in truly equal funding for white and black education, money from general tax revenues, not just revenues raised from the black community, went into African American schools. The increased funding helped to spur the development in Louisville of the "colored" school system. By 1941 the city had fifty-seven white and nineteen black schools. In many ways, Louisville's black schools were better than those in the rest of the state. The high school included a pre-collegiate curriculum and there were junior highs. Most important, the system did not shorten the academic year as was common in rural parts of the state. Still, inequalities plagued the schools. Black institutions were more likely to lack a gymnasium, trade school courses and apprenticeship programs, and adequate heating and plumbing. And black teachers, regardless of their credentials, received less pay than their white counterparts. Finally, the Day Law, the 1904 state legislation that made it illegal for public or private educational institutions at any level to admit both black

Before Brown, *black and white students traveled on separate buses to segregated schools in Jefferson County. (Courtesy of the photographic archives, Special Collections, University of Louisville)*

and white students, inhibited challenges to the segregation at the root of these inequalities.[15]

Despite segregation in social, residential, work, and educational space, other factors gave Louisville more potential for progressive race relations. Most important, African Americans never faced large-scale disenfranchisement, and indeed they participated actively in political party organizations and elections. At a minimum, this encouraged elected officials to pay lip service to equality. In addition, after World War II the local economy became more industrial, with national corporations establishing branch plants in the city. Local white business people's interest in attracting more industry and their connections outside the city prompted some of them to promote an image of racial peace and progress, and to provide behind-the-scenes support for civil rights. Louisville was also more religiously diverse than other similarly sized southern cities, with relatively large Catholic and Jewish populations. Jewish organizations, particularly the National Council of Jewish Women, played a role in supporting desegregation at key moments. Moreover, the Catholic Church hierarchy was relatively forward thinking on school issues. The visibility of such white sympathizers in economic, religious, and civic life provided the basis for support for school integration and for interracial cooperation in achieving it.[16]

By the time of the *Brown* decision civil rights advocates had made some gains, giving Louisville a progressive self-image and providing activists a foundation for demanding more changes. In the 1930s political pressure from black voters had forced the city administration to hire African American police and firefighters, though they served only in black residential areas. Just before the war the local National Association for the Advancement of Colored People (NAACP) had succeeded in pressuring the school board to equalize black teacher salaries, employing precedents from elsewhere. In the postwar era, activists stepped up their efforts, amassing a list of civil rights achievements between 1948 and 1956. During these years, the city administration stopped advertising civil service jobs by race, hired a few black office workers, and desegregated space in government buildings. The largest campaign, the Interracial Hospital Movement, forced the governor and legislature to open public hospitals to all patients. Louisville NAACP lawyers also began a series of lawsuits to integrate the city parks, which led to some incremental change but did not really succeed until after *Brown*. Civil rights activists chastised the city for moving slowly beyond small symbolic steps that affected few people and barely dented the wall of segregation.[17] But they also used the litany of such successes and the white public's acceptance of these changes to argue that the next goals—including school desegregation—were a natural progression and could likewise be accomplished without turmoil.

Alongside these other campaigns, local civil rights leaders attacked segregation in education by attempting to amend or overturn the Day Law. The process began, as in the national NAACP effort, on the graduate and professional level. In 1944 sympathetic legislators introduced bills to open the state universities to blacks, but at that time concern about the fate of Kentucky State College, a historically black institution, divided African American public opinion and led to the bill dying in a state senate committee. After the war, the state allowed all hospitals to train black doctors and nurses. The major breakthrough came in 1949 when Lyman Johnson, a teacher at Central High School and an NAACP activist, sued for admission to the graduate program in history at the University of Kentucky and won. Shortly thereafter the legislature amended the Day Law to open all colleges and universities. The University of Louisville integrated in 1951, in the process closing its branch campus for blacks, Louisville Municipal College, and firing all but one of the latter's African American faculty. This turn of events raised concerns about the fate of black instructors as desegregation worked its way down to lower levels of education.[18]

With the universities slowly opening their doors, the next logical step was pre-collegiate education. Following the strategy of chipping away at the Day Law, supporters of integration moved to amend it once again. In September 1951, just weeks after the desegregation of higher education, the Committee on Education for Kentucky Youth, headed by Monsignor Felix N. Pitt of Louisville, recommended amending the Day Law to allow local boards of education to make their own policy regarding segregation. When that proposal stalled, Pitt tried another angle. In December, in his capacity as the secretary of the Louisville Catholic School Board, he proposed that parochial and private schools be allowed to desegregate. This time he got some support, including from the Mayor's Legislative Committee, which approved the proposal and recommended it to the legislature. However, the measure died without debate in the capitol.[19]

Two years later leaders of the Interracial Hospital Movement decided to try again to pursue legislation to integrate the public schools. In response to their demands, Senator C. W. A. McCann of Louisville in January 1954 introduced Senate Bill 6 to repeal the Day Law outright. To press for the measure, an interracial coalition organized a group of about two hundred people—"equally divided Negro and white"—from around the state to attend the Senate hearing. Only nine of the thirty-six members of the committee holding the hearing bothered to attend. Just days later Reverend

Felix S. Anderson, an African American legislator from Louisville, proposed a somewhat weaker measure that would allow school districts to choose on their own whether to desegregate, reasoning that this proposal would win more votes in the legislature. Yet neither bill moved forward. Legislators, with their eye on the Supreme Court calendar and with a decision in *Brown* pending, preferred to wait and let the court order them to change.[20] Nevertheless, the flurry of activity in the spring of 1954 demonstrated the existence of a coalition of blacks and whites ready to support school integration. They, and the rest of the citizens of Louisville and Jefferson County, awaited the Supreme Court's verdict.

CHAPTER ONE

School Desegregation in the Wake
of *Brown*, 1954–1971

In an oral history interview in 1988, Barry Bingham, the white publisher of the *Courier Journal* and the *Louisville Times*, remarked, "We did have a record here in Louisville which is worth remembering. I think the year was 1956 when the first integration of the Louisville schools came about, and that was done in such a peaceful way that President Eisenhower gave Louisville a citation for the integration of the schools."[1] The story he encouraged people to recall was of how the city had managed to implement the *Brown* decision with broad public cooperation and little of the furor seen elsewhere in the South, winning national and even international renown for its efforts. That story became for a time part of the city's identity, invoked by both blacks and whites, and many city residents still remembered the success of the school desegregation process two decades later. But other memories of school desegregation in the wake of *Brown*, especially those of the young pioneers that made it a reality, tarnish that reputation. Later, these young people did not remember the peaceful transition and praise, but rather the barriers to a fully equal education in the newly mixed schools. The narratives in this chapter thus illustrate how the past can be remembered through different lenses, and the way conflicting memories complicate interpretations of the history of school desegregation.

In 1954, when the Supreme Court announced the *Brown v. Board of Education* decision, African American leaders in Louisville responded with an enthusiasm tempered only by concern that the court's orders be implemented quickly. The editor of the *Defender*, the local black newsweekly, called *Brown* the culmination of a thirty-year fight. Expressing optimism for swift action on the decision, African American principal William H. Perry Jr. predicted that "Louisville is one city where desegregation will be accepted without any great problem" and would thus serve "as a pattern for other southern cities." In the coming months black spokesmen pushed for a rapid pace of change. For example, Charles Steele, the executive secretary of the local Urban League, told the *Courier Journal* that he hoped officials would make no effort to "dodge" the decision. Exactly one month later, the *Defender* began a series of articles to press school administrators to make quick progress on integration, calling on city and state officials to make Louisville a positive example for Kentucky and the entire South.[2]

White leaders in the city and state initially exhibited some inclination to do so. Louisville school board president William C. Embry announced that planning for desegregation would begin right away. Both the city's school superintendent, Omer Carmichael, and the county superintendent, Richard Van Hoose, replied that since the decision had been anticipated, their staff had already begun discussing how to accomplish it. On the state level, Governor Lawrence Wetherby asserted that "Kentucky will do whatever is necessary to comply with the law," and his attorney general, J. D. Buckman Jr., declared that the court's decision nullified the Day Law and provisions for segregation in the state constitution.[3] However, the momentum promised by these expressions of goodwill quickly stalled. The state school superintendent, Wendell P. Butler, praised the Supreme Court for delaying implementation pending its decision in *Brown II*, and signaled that Kentucky would put the brakes on for the immediate future. Soon thereafter, the Kentucky Board of Education ordered school districts to delay action on desegregation until at least after the 1954–55 school year. The Louisville Board of Education agreed to follow the state's lead.[4]

Despite this directive, in November 1954 Superintendent Carmichael asked principals, teachers, and Parent-Teacher Association (PTA) leaders to discuss possible problems that might come up in desegregation and how to avoid them. The *Defender* praised the move as a valuable first step. Then the superintendent visited a variety of civic groups to talk about desegregation. On one such occasion, a family fellowship night at a Methodist church, he promised to follow whatever the Supreme Court ordered for implementation without "subterfuge or sharp practices to defeat the purpose of the court." When *Brown II* was announced in late spring 1955, Morton Walker, the new president of the school board, concluded that they lacked the time to make a drastic change before the fall semester, but he and Carmichael promised that Louisville city schools would desegregate in September 1956. The local NAACP branch pressed the board that summer, announcing in July that it had twenty parents ready to act as plaintiffs if a suit became necessary. The group never filed the suit, however, because it accepted Carmichael's reiterated promised target date.[5]

In November 1955, Carmichael presented his plan for integrating the city schools to the Louisville Board of Education. The plan called for a complete redistricting of all schools in the city without regard to race, reflecting only the capacity of the buildings. Students would attend the school in their residential zone. Where two existing schools were close together, parents could choose between them. As the proposal developed, the board decided to allow open enrollment in the high schools, meaning that students could choose to attend any of them. The key feature of the program, and one that provoked the most debate, was a transfer option. Carmichael suggested that a student assigned to a school with a majority of the other race could transfer to one of his or her own race, subject only to the availability of space. He argued that this option would provide a safety valve, allowing hostile parents to opt out of desegregation. It would also achieve the court-ordered end of mandatory segregation without making "integration compulsory."[6] In this, the plan anticipated the reasoning behind the freedom-of-choice strategies that would become popular in the South during the following decade. This reasoning was upheld in 1955 by Judge John P. Parker of the Fourth District Court of Appeals, who established the principle that while school boards could not deny entrance to a school based on race they did not have to guarantee the mixing of the races.[7]

The African American community's reaction to the desegregation plan was mostly positive, with a few activists expressing doubts about the transfer option. Black leaders praised the approach for following the "letter and spirit of the Supreme Court decision" and avoiding the potential for friction as much as possible. Louisville NAACP president George T. Cordery generally approved the plan but wished the transfers had been left out. James Crumlin, the president of the Kentucky Conference of Branches of the NAACP, was more forceful, declaring "students must not be permitted to transfer from one school to another solely because of race." In contrast, African American politician Charles Anderson saw some benefit to transfers, believing they would reduce resistance by allowing parents to choose a school they liked. Even such a longtime champion of school desegregation as Lyman Johnson, who had personally integrated the University of

Kentucky, conceded that some transfers should be allowed for academic or curricular reasons. In the end, and provided no other option, most African Americans rallied around the plan, willing to give the board the benefit of the doubt on transfers.[8]

While Carmichael and the board developed Louisville's strategy for school desegregation, various local black, white, and mixed church and civic organizations worked to promote acceptance of it. These efforts began even before Carmichael initiated planning within the system. In September 1954, for example, the United Church Women of Kentucky passed a resolution praising the *Brown* decision and the "broad Christian principle" behind it. The pace of organizing accelerated in response to Carmichael's efforts to prompt a favorable climate. Youth Speaks, an organization of high school students, hosted events bringing blacks and whites together and reported no opposition from its constituency. The Eastern Council on Moral and Spiritual Education, a group of parents from the predominantly white and middle-class east end of the city, held forums and published a pamphlet to promote integration. On a more formal level, the Kentucky Education Association, the white teachers' professional organization, endorsed school desegregation, and the Louisville affiliate moved to accept black members. These and other statements and events welcoming school desegregation did not represent the majority of white opinion in the city. But along with the prominent news coverage they received from a supportive *Courier Journal* and *Louisville Times*, they helped create a climate conducive to a calm, quiet change.[9]

The public efforts to pave the way for desegregation contrasted with activities in most southern communities, which, with a few exceptions, geared up to resist *Brown*. A few other cities along the North/South border—Wilmington, Baltimore, and St. Louis—opened formerly white schools to black students beginning in the summer and fall of 1954. These communities phased in desegregation, depended on voluntary transfers, integrated relatively small numbers of students, and met little overt resistance.[10] Further south, state and local officials castigated *Brown* and the justices responsible for it. In Mississippi, the White Citizens' Council formed to obstruct desegregation through political and legal means, and the organization soon spread throughout the region. Parents and pundits expressed fears about the results of social mixing between the races and decried the violation of states' rights and overreach of federal authority by a tyrannical court. In the context of the Cold War, many opponents accused those who called for or condoned school desegregation—including Supreme Court judges and even President Eisenhower—of communist conspiracies. The rising tide of resistance climaxed in white mobs facing down black students and barring their entrance to the schools in places like Little Rock and New Orleans. This climate drowned out voices of moderation, and desegregation in the schools not only ground to a halt but barely even got started.[11]

Louisville saw some open opposition but on a small scale and without much impact on policy. As Carmichael and his staff began to plan for desegregation, they encountered some hostility from parents who peppered them with questions about socializing among students, hinting at the fear of miscegenation seen elsewhere in the region. Moreover, in the first weeks after the *Brown* decision a spate of letters to the editor of the *Courier Journal* decried the abuse of overweening federal authority and the resulting loss of parental control over educational decisions—themes that would reappear in almost identical terms in later school desegregation controversies in Louisville. However, these letters appeared alongside others that supported integration and urged people to give it a chance.[12]

As the start of desegregation approached, fervent opponents took more steps to try to disrupt it. Millard D. Grubbs, a Ku Klux Klan member from Georgia who had moved to Louisville in 1948, founded the Citizens' Council of Kentucky and filed an ultimately unsuccessful lawsuit to enjoin the local school board from integrating. The Citizens' Council also promoted a boycott of the school by white parents, though it garnered little participation. On opening day, the Citizens' Council picketed the offices of the school board, having been dissuaded from gathering outside Louisville Male High, the city's most prestigious white school, by the threat of arrest for creating a "clear and present danger." Yet the group only mustered five picketers, an indication of its dearth of popular appeal. After school started Grubbs and other opponents tried different tactics. In the fall, a young man from Detroit, Billy Branham, sued to get into Male as a student paying nonresident tuition and then sought to inspire youth opposition. Like those of Grubbs and the Citizens' Council, however, his organizing efforts fizzled. As the narratives that follow reveal, local leaders prepared for the worst, but they never took the organized opposition very seriously.[13]

Several factors contributed to the relative lack of agitation around school desegregation in Louisville. Simultaneous with *Brown*, segregationists' attention was drawn away from the schools to the specter of integrated neighborhoods when an African American family, Andrew and Charlotte Wade, moved into an all-white suburb. Anne and Carl Braden, white civil rights activists, helped the Wades to do so by purchasing the house and transferring it to them. The move sparked an anticommunist and segregationist furor that led to violence against the Wade home and landed Carl Braden in jail on charges of sedition. Anne Braden later theorized that committed segregationists spent their anger on the Wades and Bradens, while more moderate whites were determined to keep the community calm during school desegregation.[14] Moreover, the rigidity of the housing segregation that the Wades had threatened and that Grubbs and his associates had so ardently defended also contributed to a passive acceptance of Carmichael's plan. In a school system districted by neighborhood, and in a city in which blacks and whites lived in separate areas, most students would be assigned to schools that were overwhelmingly still of one race or the other. This reduced the number of people affected by the change in the schools, and thus with reason to oppose desegregation energetically.

Finally, the transfer option enabled parents to have their children opt out of desegregation, and many did so in the first couple of years. In March 1956 the school system sent out pupil assignment notices that gave parents the opportunity to list three alternatives for transfer to another institution. One month later, a review of the responses revealed that 45 percent of black parents and 85 percent of white parents requested a transfer. All the white parents in one district requested that their children be moved out of the previously black Virginia Avenue Elementary and DuValle Junior High schools and into nearby white schools. The superintendent promised to grant transfers as long as the buildings' capacity allowed it. Black civil rights leaders objected, arguing that transfers should be reserved for a small number of extreme objectors, and accused the superintendent of trying to limit desegregation. Regardless of the intent, the transfer option and the large number of parents availing themselves of it resulted in a lower than expected rate of desegregation in many schools. On registration day, for example, Phyllis Wheatley Elementary expected thirty-two white students, but only three or four arrived. Nearby James M. Bond awaited seventy-five whites and greeted only six or seven.[15]

Despite indications of quiet evasion, school desegregation began in Louisville in 1956 with little overt opposition and much fanfare. In part because of the threat of demonstrations and in part to watch his plan at work at the city's most venerable public school, Carmichael spent the morning at Male High. He witnessed black and white students mill about quietly before the opening bell and proceed without incident to their first class. As Benjamin Fine reported for the *New York Times*, "Children went to school, sat side by side," and "color differences seemed forgotten." In more grand

Students entering Louisville Male High School, September 10, 1956,
the first day of integration. (Courtesy of the Louisville Defender *Collection,*
Special Collections, University of Louisville)

terms he added, "When the history of this proud southern city is written, this day will undoubtedly go down as a historic landmark. . . . Even in the South, it was shown here, integration can be made to work without violence." Although completely segregated schools still existed, and others had only small percentages of the minority group in the student population, school officials boasted that 73.6 percent of all pupils now attended school with at least some members of the other race.[16]

The delay in teacher integration blotted this record, however. Black leaders worried about teacher job security from the start, and they had consistently pressed for simultaneous integration of faculties. Carmichael and other school officials had just as consistently resisted tackling what they saw as a separate and more difficult problem. The controversy came to a head in October 1956 when Carmichael made derogatory comments about black teachers in the national media, declaring them less fit than whites in stark terms. At a forum organized by black leaders to challenge him on the subject, Carmichael reiterated his views, saying "You just don't have as high a degree of competence among your Negro teachers." Upset black leaders pressed for an apology, prompting Carmichael to explain that he based his opinion on black teachers in other cities. But he also maintained that the subjective feelings of administrators could and should play a role in black teachers' assignments. Carmichael continued to fight teacher integration for another three years. Not until 1959 did he relent and begin to mix faculties. Only then could the *Defender* praise school officials for finishing the job and making Louisville deserving of the title of the South's most desegregated city.[17]

In the narratives that follow, city and school officials, teachers, principals, and students share their memories of early school desegregation in Louisville. The narratives begin with explanations of the process that paved the way for desegregation, in many cases emphasizing the reasons for its success. The second section includes reflections on some of the problems encountered in the process, including white opposition and the failure to integrate teachers. The remainder of the narratives concern life inside the schools after desegregation and reflect the very different perspectives of administrators and students.

Preparing for Desegregation

Many Louisvillians retrospectively credit the two years of preparation prior to desegregation for the extent of its success. Forums by school officials to educate the community and programs within the schools to prepare teachers, parents, and students made the public more open to integration.

Morton Walker, white president of the school board in 1956 (interview with Darlene Eakin, 1973). Walker explains why the school board waited until 1956 and the reasons he believed desegregation worked in Louisville.

We had what seemed to be two problems and we were caught between the two: one, we wanted to be sure that never at any time did it appear that there was any difference between the superintendent and the school board. We were putting up a united front. The next problem was not to move too fast or too slow because there were those, particularly the radical [segregationist] group, who wondered, "Ought you get into this, or can it wait until you actually have to?" I think most of us felt we ought to wait until we had the second ruling of the Supreme Court and some more details. Then that came out May of '55. Then we did not want to be pressured to move into immediate integration, by that I mean the fall of '55. So I made a statement in '55 that we would integrate in the fall of '56. The superintendent came in with the recommendation that we do that and the board instructed the superintendent to prepare plans for us so that we could integrate in '56.

We felt that we ought to make as much use of the time in between to get the community ready for it and the schools ready for it. I felt that if we'd gone in '55 we would not have had sufficient preparation and we could have had problems. I think preparing helped a great deal. I think most of us felt that we would not really have the problems in Louisville that other cities, say in the Deep South, had because Louisville was a pretty broad-minded city. We had integrated parks, the golf links, buses, street cars, all those things you see. I just felt Louisville would take it in stride. I really was never worried.

Roy Owsley, white administrative assistant to Mayor Charles Farnsley (interview with Darlene Eakin, 1973). Owsley highlights a point made by Walker: progress in the city in the postwar years enabled school desegregation to proceed without significant opposition.

I can say that along with the mayors I worked with, and heads of the various city departments, most of the members of the board of aldermen—there were some exceptions [but] I wouldn't like to single them out—it was a united movement from the very beginning. We were seeking to free the city of segregation, all of its attendant problems and evils and so forth. I am proud of the record personally, and I think all the mayors with whom I worked had a right to be proud of their records. I will say one other thing: I am sure that those accomplishments that took place between 1948 and 1956 paved the way, set the stage for the desegregation of public schools. I'm sure it made it much easier than it otherwise would have been the case. I don't say that the Board of Education would not have acted without this background, but without the accomplishments already made it would have been vastly more difficult to have successfully desegregated the public schools in 1956.

Milburn Maupin, African American teacher in 1956; later promoted to principal and first black assistant superintendent in the local school system (interview with Darlene Eakin, 1973). Here Maupin argues that the two-year wait proposed by the Board of Education facilitated desegregation. He acknowledges that local leaders' support for desegregation and the quiet steps taken to accomplish it created a climate for change in the city, but he also notes that teachers used the time to work within schools to prepare the students.

I feel that one of the geniuses that Mr. Carmichael had was careful planning and preparation. I felt then and I still do now believe that that was the right thing to do to take that amount of time [two years] to allow all this cross-fertilization of ideas and for people to gain acceptance of the idea. There were not a great many of my fellow black teachers that I knew who opposed that. Most people, I think, shared my feeling that it was much better to plan carefully as long as there was positive movement, not drifting, not aimlessness, not resistance, but careful planning to sow the seeds carefully to prepare people for accepting the inevitable rather than to boom go on and we're going to do it right now. I still believe basically that as a philosophy that that is the better way to get things done, rather than do it all now regardless of the consequences. I believe that is the best way to deal with change.

I was a teacher at the DuValle Junior High School. At the time I was working very actively with the groups that were way out front in preparing for integration and unity. It was a group called the Kentucky Council on Human Relations. In fact, I was even a part-time consultant for that group and went out through the state in biracial teams to try to help get blacks and whites talking together about student desegregation. What we saw was that there was a difference in the kind of leadership that Mr. Carmichael and his staff were exerting from people that were dragging their feet or resisting change. Part of what made it possible for Carmichael and his staff to do that was we have, and had then, a very liberal press that was helping to set forth the climate to continue in a positive way.

The people who were down at City Hall would confide privately with people like myself, who was just a classroom teacher but was active in integration, and would do things that would really be tipping toward desegregation. People like Mayor Farnsley; Roy Owsley, his administrative assistant; Dr. C. H. Parrish who was a professor of sociology; and people from the Urban League and NAACP would say, "Now, we're going to make certain [desegregation] moves and we are more or less going to let it happen."[18] So it will be a fait accompli before people realize that it happened and by that time it would be silly to react against it. And the newspapers cooperated. They got wind of it. They could have published a story that would have gotten the hotheads all inflamed. So it was a conspiracy toward a positive end. This helped to make what the school people were doing much more palatable and the easy thing to do.

Then, in 1954 and 1955, I was the chairman of the student activities committee at DuValle. We packaged assembly programs and we took some of the ones that we thought were pretty good and then we exchanged with white schools. I remember, for example, we took one of our assembly programs with the chorus and the dramatic skits and all that kind of stuff and went to [the all-white] Parkland Junior High School. Well, today, you'd say, "Well, what the hell is so great about that?" But then that was a big thing. You just never had black kids going into Parkland Junior High School for anything. Then they would come to us. To look back now we wonder why that was so great, but in those days when they'd come in our school they were nervous and they would have been drilled and coached about how you act when you go over there, and all this kind of thing. As the kids began to have these kinds of exchanges then they began to say, "Well, that wasn't such a big thing." That's why I think that there were blacks that opted to go to the previously all-white schools. One of the reasons was that these kinds of things that had been going on.

Josephine Trowel Patterson, African American teacher (interview with Darlene Eakin, 1973). Patterson emphasizes how black teachers tried to prepare their students to attend the white schools, giving them a strong sense of their own culture and advice about how to conduct themselves.

One of the things that we did to prepare was we tried to build up the students' self-image and we did this by bringing in literature on black contributions. We went back to the very beginning of the early civilization of this country, Crispus Attucks and his contributions to the freeing of this country from England. Then we moved out from there to familiarize the youngsters with the various contributions made by blacks in various fields. We drew heavily on the arts, beginning with Marian Anderson and persons like that. Then of course we moved out to sports, the sciences, and whatnot. We also taught them the Fourteenth and Fifteenth Amendments of the Constitution and about their rights. We taught them the National Negro Anthem which was called at that time "Lift Every Voice and Sing," by the two Johnson brothers. We realize that our national anthem is the "Star-Spangled Banner." But we simply called it the Negro Anthem at this point. We did teach them that particular song so that it gave them some background of the struggles of the Negroes. We tried to instill in them that black people had made some contributions, too.

Of course, we also talked with them about the conduct that they should exhibit. There were statements that every black child should be on guard, more or less, that certainly they should remember that I am somebody and I act no different to any other human being. I told them that they would have to go a little harder than that; that they're going to be on the spot, and all eyes are going to be on you. What you do is going to be misinterpreted maybe, because you are under pressure. The only way that they're going to really know you is by the way you act.

Ruth Higgins, white principal of Morris Elementary School (interview with Darlene Eakin, 1973). Higgins describes how she and Evelyn Jackson, the principal of the nearby all-black Douglass Elementary School, worked to prepare students, teachers, and parents for desegregation.

We spent about a year talking about [integration] at Morris. Each teacher was doing it her own way, but it was based on the idea of brotherhood. Teachers were saying: "We are in Morris school and the United States has decided that schools will not be separated according to color. Now we have been going to this school and we like it very much. The children who are coming in will be like all children going to a strange school and they will need to be welcomed. I'm sure they'll have a lot to tell us, a lot to give us, and we should have a lot of friendship to give them." I think it was along that line.

Now one thing that happened at the very beginning, Mrs. Jackson called me up as soon as we heard we were going to integrate and she said, "Will you come over to my PTA and give a talk on integration?" Well, I'm not a very good speaker and I had just been newly appointed, so that scared the daylights out of me. So I said, "Let me think about it." I called her back and I said, "Well, I won't have much to say on integration but let me talk on the United Nations and bring it down to our integration being the type of thing that the United Nations stands for." So that was the material I prepared. The whole Morris faculty and I were invited to the Douglass PTA meeting where I was going to give the talk. I invited my faculty and they split right down the middle. Half of them would go with me and the other half would not go with me. There may have been reasons other than the fact that they didn't want to go over to the school, but I'm sure that that was part of the reason they didn't want to go. But those who did go with me were quite impressed. The decorations were beautiful, the refreshments were beautiful; it was a very nice experience.

Evelyn Jackson, African American principal of Douglass Elementary School (interview with Darlene Eakin, 1973). The Douglass and Morris schools stood in proximity. Morris had served the Clarksdale housing project for low-income whites, while Douglass served the surrounding black community. After desegregation, redistricting swapped the schools' populations, and the two principals agreed to try to limit transfers and hold on to their new students. As a result, Douglass ended up with a black principal, black teachers, and mostly white students, while Morris had white staff and faculty and black students. Jackson explains the efforts of Carmichael and herself to prepare for desegregation and his concerns about potential problems at Douglass, which she insists never materialized.

Mr. Carmichael was a person who always discussed the moves he was going to make or anything he was thinking about with the principals. When he came to Louisville he broke down the segregation whereby the white principals met in the morning and the Negroes met in the afternoon. He stopped that and we all met at the same time. So we had become quite accustomed to meeting. He would discuss the issues with us, then he would proceed to go out into the community. He contacted the city fathers, he discussed integration in political groups, he discussed it in Lions and Rotary Clubs. He had quite a few meetings at the public library. He began to talk about it and to feel out the people to see how they felt about it. He kept saying it was going to be the law of the land. His premise was this: he was going to obey the law of the land.

To prepare my teachers I'd be very plain. I would say, "Now, suppose that in setting up the classes I give you all whites?" Of course, in those days we didn't say blacks, we said Negro. "I'll give you [only] a few Negroes. Would this disturb you?" And they said, "No." Then I said, "Suppose trouble came up and there was name-calling; then how would you handle it?" And they would say what they thought and I would say what I thought. Lots of times I was wrong. The secret of the thing I realized, as a beginning principal, is that shared leadership works for you. It really works for you if you turn your people loose and share your leadership with them. You're not always right. They would give me advice, many times they gave me advice.

We had to meet with our parents because a lot of the parents—I don't know what the white ones said about coming to me, but a lot of the black ones said they didn't want to send their children to Morris School. They were afraid they'd be mistreated and be outnumbered. I had to convince them that they were going to be in the majority there. I told them what we were trying to do and I hoped that they would go along. When it came to working with the PTA, I thought, "Well, now, this is where I'm going to have trouble," because there were undesirables in both races that I didn't think would be able to work with anybody, but they did. They came forth and they worked. I can honestly say that I never had one minute's trouble, never had any trouble, and Mrs. Higgins didn't have any trouble either.

Mr. Carmichael knew the situation that I would have, different from anyone else's, that I would have all white students. So, he called me on the day of registration, and he said, "Miss Jackson, you want me to send the police around in case something happens?" I said, "Oh no, Mr. Carmichael." I said, "Don't do that." I said, "Then you will kill what we are trying to do." I said, "Don't you send any police." I said, "No matter what happens, you let me handle it." And he didn't. We went smooth, didn't have any trouble at all.

Then on the morning in September when school opened Carmichael said to us, "Now, I want you to go in and I hope you won't have any trouble, but if you do have trouble you call and I'll be there." Well, he was expecting me to call and I didn't because I had no trouble. That morning we were very tense, the teachers and I. But when the students came in, why, we had good preparation, we were ready. As they walked in we registered them and ran them right through to their rooms, and their teachers tried to be prepared to talk to the parents and to start the classes and nobody had any time for anything else.

Obstacles to Integration

Despite school administrators' memories of a successful preparation and uneventful transition to desegregation, problems arose along the way, including debate over the transfer plan, some harassment by opponents, and, most important, a failure to integrate faculties simultaneously with students.

Anne Braden, white mother and civil rights activist (interview with Tracy E. K'Meyer, 2001). Braden opposed the transfer policy and believed that it revealed how Carmichael and the school system limited real integration.

So what happened was they redistricted the city schools. They sent out a letter to all the parents of students saying, "The Louisville schools will be desegregated next year. Your child has been assigned to such and such a school. If you would prefer he attend another school please list your choices, one, two, three on the back." So they encouraged a massive transfer, which happened. I think, to put the best face on it, that the school officials saw that as sort of a safety valve. If some parent was going to lose their mind, let them go on and transfer, which might have been all right if they had let them take the initiative. But doing that by letter really gave the impression the school board really wants you to transfer to where you're in a majority. And there was a massive transfer! I remember the figures because it was so appalling at the time. As I recall 85 percent of the white kids applied to transfer out of schools that had been black. I think it was something like 45 percent of the black.

I talked to people in my neighborhood, and that neighborhood was still, or my block was, mostly white then. I talked to people who had their kids in school and they said, well, they didn't care. They didn't mind their children going to school with Negroes, I guess they would say in those days. But it seemed like this was the way the school system wanted it to be. A little later in the '50s our son was in Virginia Avenue for the first grade. He was the only white child in that school! Everybody had transferred out. In that area back then there was enough racial mixture that if people had stayed put in the districts that they were assigned to it would have been about half and half. Some people probably really were repulsed by the idea, but mostly it was the psychology of, this is the way it's supposed to be, and they trans-ferred out. So very little desegregation actually happened. It was just sad.

Milburn Maupin, African American teacher (interview with Darlene Eakin, 1973). Maupin takes a more forgiving view of the transfer plan, though he hints at opposition to it among black leaders.

I can recall that there were some people, my colleagues in the teaching profession—Lyman Johnson comes to mind—who honestly felt things were moving much too slowly and should have been done with much more com-pleteness and much fewer options—less voluntary, discretionary kind of options available to people. I personally did not share that. I felt that the transfer plan provided the means so that the people who wanted to opt in for the integrated situation could do so, at the same time minimizing the trauma of people who were a little reluctant to put their feet in the water immediately. In other words, I genuinely felt that it was a good move to make. I believe, really, that that was a contributory factor to the smoothness with which integration got started here as opposed to some of the volatile, hostile kinds of things that happened elsewhere that were very much in the news at the same time.

Little vocal opposition to school desegregation existed in Louisville in 1956 compared to other cities. No interviews with public leaders of the opposition are extant. In the following excerpts, school and city officials describe their encounters with some opponents and their responses. The lack of overt trouble enabled these leaders to reemphasize the calm acceptance of change in Louisville and their own role in it.

Morton Walker, white president of the school board (interview with Darlene Eakin, 1973).

[Millard] Grubbs was the leader of the opposition. There were individuals who felt rather strongly that there was something wrong about mixing races, but there were no important citizens of the community that took such a stand. I received many letters from people and most of them were abusive in nature. "There's going to be a NAACP convention here, would you like to have so many Negroes stay in your home while the convention is here?" Or, I've had phone calls from people saying, "Well, I suppose you're going to have some niggers to come have dinner with you on Sunday." That kind of thing. I also received all sorts of publications and pamphlets showing that the black people were inferior people and the dangers of integration. I received calls after midnight with people saying, "You black, something." It wasn't a thing that was regular, not every night, but I had it.

Mrs. James Pate, white parent and PTA leader (interview with Darlene Eakin, 1973). All extant documentation on Mrs. Pate lists only her married name.

There was this man that came in here and he caused a lot of trouble; I think his name was Grubbs. He went into some of the schools and he enrolled students in some of our schools—Male and Manual and some of our downtown high schools—and he tried to create problems. He invited me to a meeting at the Earl Hotel, and I had heard of what type of program it might be so I sent someone, a representative, that wasn't as well-known as I was. They really wanted to cause a lot of trouble. They said bringing colored children in was illegal. He caused a lot of trouble for quite a while and somehow or another they got rid of him or he gave up. He even made open statements that he was going to have Mr. Carmichael arrested. He was trying to get me to protest bringing these children into our schools. I told him I wasn't going to do it. So for several weeks he had a group calling me every night, all night long, every hour, just exactly at one o'clock and two o'clock hollering "Nigger lover" into the phone. So that was quite a trying time.

Roy Owsley, white administrative assistant to Mayor Charles Farnsley (interview with Darlene Eakin, 1973).

In order to be kind to those persons who were not supporting the desegregation movement, or who, in some cases, were actually segregationists, you really had to have some kind of a feel for the background of the community, and that is, that while Louisville was not a southern city in the true sense of the word, its tradition was largely southern. Communities are hard to change, habits are hard to change, attitudes are hard to change if the creation of that habit or that attitude was a lifelong thing. Some of these persons came from that kind of a background and simply found it impossible to make a quick about-face. Some of them also thought desegregation just had no future. It just wasn't going to become a reality.

Generally the opponents of desegregation did not come out publicly. There were some exceptions, probably some extremists, but generally they did not come out, did not seek public confrontation. I think there were some letters to [the papers], but it's my memory generally that the confrontations with the opponents of desegregation were rare. They would confront you only on an individual basis or in a private office and private conference. Not openly, they didn't want to be quoted on it, didn't want any publicity. In response, you did what every good, alert public official does. You answered it with what appeared to be the best answer on your side at the time. Sometimes you say, "It's the law"; other times it's the proper and fair and humane thing to do; other times you might even try shaming him if he were a businessman and he was contributing to something less than the best quality of life in the city, and so forth.

For many African Americans, Carmichael's resistance to integrating faculty posed the most important obstacle to the success of school desegregation. Maupin tells the story of the confrontation between the superintendent and the black community on this issue, while Jackson follows with a critique of what happened to majority-black schools when faculty finally integrated.

Milburn Maupin, African American teacher (interview with Darlene Eakin, 1973).

In all candor, the first time I became aware of pretty widespread anxiety and insecurity among black teachers was when Mr. Carmichael was invited to Washington by then President Dwight Eisenhower. He was praised for the leadership, the smoothness with which the thing happened. He was interviewed by a battery of newsmen and said for the first time there, and then subsequently in *U.S. News and World Report*, statements that really infuriated us. At that time, I guess I would be considered a middle-of-the-roader, moderate, somewhere in between an Uncle Tom and a rabid militant, somewhere in the middle. But I quite frankly got very angry at the statements that he made. I even went to Lyman Johnson's house and said, "Shouldn't we do something about that?" We circulated a petition to question Mr. Carmichael and one of his assistants about these statements. The statements were such that it burned in me so that I almost memorized it and I never have forgotten it. "How can you expect anybody from a slummy, crime-ridden section of the city to be the equal of other people?" In other words, when the question was, "Why have you not moved into faculty desegregation at the same time that you moved into pupil desegregation?," he revealed his biases that blacks couldn't be the equal of whites as teachers and whatnot. "How can they, they've got poor instruction, they've got poor churches, they come from poor families, they come from slummy areas of the city with crime," and all this kind of thing. "How can you expect for these people to be accepted as teachers?"

I personally was disappointed that teachers were not desegregated right away. I expected Carmichael to be an honest person. During this period of time leading up to the student desegregation he started making a lot of moves that I thought would lead almost simultaneously to changing staff. For example, he was the first superintendent to have black and white principals meet together. Under Carmichael was the first time that they ever had black and white teachers on a curriculum committee. I was one of the first ones to get involved in that. I really feel that at the same time that they were trying to reach student desegregation, there were enough moves that were also being made, I think, that it could have happened all at the same time. I felt then, and I still do, that it would have been much better for the kids if they could have seen some familiar faces in 1956 when they did desegregation, as opposed to going into a completely strange field as far as the faculty was concerned.

Evelyn Jackson, African American principal of Douglass Elementary School (interview with Darlene Eakin, 1973). She refers to her transfer from Douglass to being the principal at Virginia Elementary in the west end, the school Anne Braden's child attended.

I felt that when they desegregated the student body they should have done the faculty at the same time. Mr. Carmichael's thoughts were against it. He moved slowly, a step at a time. We'll do the children first, then later we'll come back and do the teachers. He always said, "Move cautiously and slowly," and this is the reason he didn't move faculty. He felt that if you do too much at one time you're going to have people just kicking up their heels and being dissatisfied. So he went slowly with it.

I haven't been entirely satisfied with the way the teachers were moved. Teachers should have been moved the same way the children were moved. When they did move the teachers they began to take our cream off and put them in the white schools and leave us with the ones that were mediocre or slow. This was one thing that I voiced my sentiment about. I didn't like it at all. I had been asked who is your best teacher, and then I lose that teacher. That weakened the foundation of my faculty. When I left Douglass School I wanted to take most of these teachers with me and they wouldn't let me because they were teaching up there and they knew the whites, so they kept them. In fact, I didn't even get to bring one teacher with me. I was able to bring one clerk, that's all. The rest had to stay there.

The View from Inside the Schools

This final section consists of stories about how desegregation worked within the schools. It begins with administrators but consists primarily of the voices of black students.

Ruth Higgins, white principal of Morris Elementary School (interview with Darlene Eakin, 1973). In Higgins's memory, Morris School made an easy transition to integration. Her perspective was reinforced when her school and Douglass Elementary were featured in a national news documentary about Louisville's success in implementing *Brown*. She shares her recollections of the good relations between white and black students and parents.

Our children were quite happy that black children were coming to our school. When the black children came the white students practically spoiled them they were being so nice to them, for the first year anyhow. Far from not wanting to touch them or anything like that, the children wanted to touch each other, wanted to feel each other's hair and wanted to be friends with each other and brag about their friendships and things like that. Later on, I got the impression that it leveled off, but I never did have the feeling that there was any racial feeling there. There were plenty of fights, there were plenty of disagreements, and it was a rough school, but I didn't think it was lined up on racial lines.

In general, the relations between parents were very good. The thing that keeps the PTA happy is if it's making money. I remember that we were having chili suppers and one of the colored women had baked a beautiful cake and everybody wanted to buy her cake and sent her word how wonderful it was. They were getting on very well together, I thought, at the time that I was there. In such a transient school it was such a hard thing to have a PTA at all. I can't recall that they integrated in a very formal way, but they did talk about it and I did not have the feeling that they were prejudiced, openly anyhow. It just seems that these people were very nice.

I only recall one incident that I had in which the Negro family was very resentful over a misunderstanding. There was a little boy who was very hyperactive in first grade and one of the things he did was when a teacher wasn't looking he'd jump out the window. It made her very nervous because it got to where he not only jumped out the window but he was running out of the yard. Chestnut Street ran right in front of there and it was very, very busy. I tore around the front of the building and saw that he was just dashing out in the street. So I ran and grabbed him and he bit my hand and bit it so hard that it went right through the skin and bled. So I sent word to his parents. Without giving me a chance to say anything at all except that I was just trying to save his life, the parent said, "Well, it's just like Arkansas, you just hate us," and so forth, and so they transferred right quickly back to Douglass school. But people had not mistreated that child. I actually went out to get him because I thought surely he was going to get hit.

Now I won't say that there wasn't prejudice on the part of the faculty against some of the Negro children because there was and I think it would be unrealistic to think that there wouldn't be. There was probably prejudice among the parents on both sides. But on the whole, I thought the relations were good.

Evelyn Jackson, African American principal of Douglass Elementary School (interview with Darlene Eakin, 1973).

One thing that I think that helped me was the fact that I had such a wonderful faculty. I had an unusual group of women who were dedicated teachers. With everything that was coming in, they went out of their way at every opportunity that they had to make it work smoothly and it did. For instance, we had a Christmas celebration and the parents came and they mostly were whites. We had the story of Jesus in pantomime. I had a crippled children's class and we had the pantomime and the little girl named Mary was in a wheelchair and the boy, who played Joseph, was a very tall, very dark little boy, and it didn't affect the parents or the children. It worked very well. These teachers were very professional teachers and knew how to see things and do them well and get the results that they wanted.

The only incident I did have—right at Preston and Warnock there was a Standard Oil gasoline station in the northeast corner. You went around the side, way back in there behind this station there was a white couple who lived there and this fellow was one of those motorcycle riders. He spent his money, you could see, instead of putting it on the children, he'd spent it on his boots and belts and caps and everything. He sent one of the little girls to school one morning, with frost on the ground, and he sent her to school barefooted. Well, even though it was a poverty neighborhood, the teachers insisted that the children wear socks. They didn't come to school without socks and shoes. This child had none. So up on Preston Street where all the shoe stores are there was a girl who ran a store that I knew. Years ago we lived next door to one another, and her name was Mrs. Shugerman. We went around there and bought the child some shoes and a pair of socks. White child. When we sent the child home, he came the next morning. He got bad with me and I got bad with him and he said, "She better not wear them home," and I said, "Well, I'll take them off when I send her home but every day when she comes in here she's going to wear shoes and socks." Well, when I left [Douglass], he was my best friend. He admitted that he'd taken his money and bought all these belts and things. He told me that he was wrong and we became good friends and that was the only incident I ever had.

Now I did have a trouble with a fella in Miss Overall's room, in the sixth grade. Miss Overall was a friend of mine, we had been friends since we were kids. She said, "You know Evelyn, I have a boy in there. When I am teaching reading he gets into the chair and he rears back." You know how you put a chair back? "He won't read and he won't do anything." She said, "I don't want it said that I started anything. Could you come up here." So I went up there, there he was, reared back. So I went on in, I didn't look at him, I sat down, they were reading, and I looked over. I said, "Aren't you taking part in the reading?" "No." I said, "Well, what's the matter with you?" "Don't want to be in no nigger school." I said, "You don't know what it's all about, do you?" I play the piano, and I went around and I played something with all the black keys. And I played a tune with all white keys. I said, "How does that sound?" "Sounds crazy." I said, "Yes, it does." Then I played a song that I knew, with white and black keys. I said, "How does that sound?" He said, "That sounded right." I said, "See, if you put the black and white together, we will make it."

The remaining narratives come from black students, most focusing on high school. These interviews reflect the extent to which black students who attended a desegregated school did so by choice. While some of the students had happy memories, most recall their time in formerly white schools with ambivalence at best or even hostility because of their encounters with prejudiced faculty and the lack of access to activities.

Deanna Tinsley, African American student (interview with David Cline, 2005). Tinsley mentions the Portland neighborhood, which lies along the Ohio River west of downtown. Historically, it was majority white, working class, and largely Catholic. It stood close to the expanding black neighborhoods of the west end. Other interviewees have less positive memories of the welcome offered blacks in Portland.

I went to James Bond Elementary School, which was a neighborhood school and it was segregated. I recall those teachers trying to prepare us to go to Western Junior High School, which was only four or five blocks from my house. That was the year that we would integrate that school. To prepare us the teachers wanted us to be ideal little model people. There wasn't a lot of talk in terms of coping with racism, because really people didn't talk much about racism directly like that. It was kind of indirect; you had to get that at home. When I grew up, it was always "you've got to do better, you've got to act better, you've got to be better," in order to make it. That was the mantra and that was from school and from home. So our job was to get over there and not show off and not get into trouble and do our best work and that's what we were told.

I had a good time those years at Western Junior High. That's where I met my husband because he came from another elementary school, Western Elementary School, which no longer exists. I found people to be wary but accepting. I think it had to do with that Portland neighborhood having always been rather mixed. We had people who did act really nice, like little ladies and gentlemen, and those who acted crazy, just like they do now, on both sides, white and black. But we did not have any classroom disruptions. There wasn't that atmosphere. You went into the classroom and folk acted the way they were supposed to act and, pretty much, the teachers were in charge. I found that we had some teachers who were curious but not unkind. I had a really good experience. I guess an overwhelming feeling after all these years is that Western was fine, it was OK. We didn't have difficulty getting to know people, there were friendly kids and not-friendly kids, just like there are now.

There were some teachers that I was leery of, but there are teachers today that you would be leery of. But I never felt any particular racism that I can remember. The one example, though, that I do have is this one teacher asked me one day to come to her house. I thought that was a compliment. I didn't know what that meant, so I told my mother and said, "Well, can I go to her house?" And she said, "Well, you know what she wants, don't you?" And I said, "Uh uh. I don't know what she wants." I just thought it was a friendly thing, especially since in elementary school, some of the teachers did have you to come to their homes. They had little reading groups and whatnot, or they taught piano. But what she wanted was a housekeeper. So somehow my mother knew that and she said, "You can go if you want to, but she wants somebody to clean; she wants a housekeeper." I said, "A housekeeper?"

Now I must have been thirteen, maybe, or something like that. But anyway, I did go to the house. She wanted me to fold towels and do other kinds of housekeeping work. Well, my father didn't like it. I mean, I didn't mind it. It's just that it surprises me even now to think that a teacher would ask a student to come to the house and the student, of course, how would you know? Now, I was naive but mother wasn't. She let me experience it. It really wasn't bad. I mean, I think she may have paid five dollars or something like that to do stuff, which was OK. But because my father didn't want me to go back, I didn't. I think he probably was right in that. For me to have work, that was not an issue, but that it was a teacher just didn't sit right with him, having her asking the student. But that's the only thing, and I just remembered that just this minute ago.

All of us liked the PE [physical education] teacher Mrs. Claxton. She was a little wiry teacher who expected everybody to do what they were supposed to do. Black girls had kind of hard time at first because no black girl wanted to shower and wash hair because hair, for black girls, is an issue. It's just too much work and you can't just brush it back and make a ponytail. I mean, you've got major work to do. So I think Claxton eventually had enough empathy to understand that that's just not going to be something that they are going to want to do without a whole lot of argument. So she worked that out with the girls.

Another thing I remember is a teacher who let everybody bring their music, which I thought was really smart because it's a culture-building thing. So I can remember we had some very heavy music, you know compared to—it wasn't light at all. In those days, you had Ray Charles and you had, oh, Curtis Mayfield and people like that who sang very deep, heavy music. I can remember him wondering why in the world these young people would be listening to that music, but that was the music of the day and it was bebop and rhythm and blues and it was morphing at that time from the old R&B, the old bluesy-bluesy R&B, into the R&B rock 'n' roll. It was just about that time when that was happening and it was not the happy jump-around music that the white kids would bring, altogether different.

See, I have good memories basically of those three years.

Louis Mudd, African American student (interview with Tracy E. K'Meyer, 2000). When desegregation began, Mudd availed himself of the transfer option to stay at the formerly all-black Madison Junior High. But at high school he elected Male High, the most prestigious formerly white school in the system. He explains both choices and the atmosphere at Male.

Between my seventh- and eighth-grade year was the year that Superintendent Carmichael put together what was known as the Louisville Plan, which received a lot of publicity. He was on the *Today Show* and so forth. It actually extended an option to kids, to African American kids, to either go to the closest school or remain where they were. I was at Madison Junior High. A lot of my friends left and went to Western Junior High School. I chose to stay at Madison. Mom and dad and I sat down and we talked about it. I actually think mom and dad were a little bit afraid for my safety at Western. Western sat right at the corner of Twenty-Second and Main right on the southern fringe of Portland. I think they were a little bit afraid as to what could happen. They asked me if I wanted to stay at Madison, which is what I wanted to do anyway. I stayed at Madison but my best friend went to Western. I was one of the few people that stayed at a segregated junior high school by choice. There was a feeling that by going to Western we would get more current materials, see a new book for a change. The opportunities would be greater. My dad was in the school system and he didn't buy it. He and mom chose to allow me to stay at Madison.

By high school I had started playing the trumpet. Male's band was considered to be, at that time, the best in the state. A typical trip for the Male High School band was the Orange Bowl Parade, where a typical trip for the average high school band in the state was, if you made it as far as Cincinnati you were lucky. Male was a well-touted program and a much publicized program. I wanted to be in the band at Male, which I ended up doing. That was a major portion of my decision. Having college aspirations, I certainly didn't think Male would hurt me in that regard. Certainly, Central could have prepared me for college as well as Male, but Male was considered to be a very strong academic environment, one of the strongest in the state. But it was primarily the decision to play in the band which led me to Male.

At Male, the opportunity was there, but you never forgot that you were black. The educational exposure was there, but you got no breaks. There was no compassion. Our principal was the president of the board of aldermen, but he was a racist. We went to class and we observed the rules and we played by the rules. But every chance that the faculty got to step on us they did, with very few exceptions. There were some good teachers at Male. There were some teachers that went out of their way to be fair to black kids, and they were ostracized by some of the other faculty members because of it. There was a racist football coach that used black kids for his personal gain. You had an athletic program that at that time, as was the case all over the city, realized it needed the black athlete in order to continue to excel. Some of the personnel in the athletic department were slower to migrate to that position than others. You had an absolute refusal to have a black cheerleader. You got this lily-white cheerleading squad and if you had a basketball game, when you looked out on the court, you'd have four black basketball players and one white. You always had the one white, though. No, no, no, don't make the mistake of putting five black players out there. That's how you lose the job. But you can win with four black players out there, or three and two, and you're OK. We will tolerate three being out there or four if that means winning, but we will not tolerate five. You had an office staff with a female counselor and a male counselor that were totally insensitive to black kids. They were intelligent enough to mask it, but they were racist people.

Sterling Neal, African American student (interview with David Cline, 2005).

When I first got to Male, one of the professors, Mr. G——, told me, "Neal,"—
I don't know why he singled me out—" you know we brought your people
here because you don't have a history or a culture." So I said to Mr. G——,
"That can't be true, Mr. G——"—because this is what I'd been taught. I said,
"When whites were in caves, blacks, Africans, were smelting iron." G——
jumped around, "Who told you that? How'd you know?" And from that day
on, we had problems.

All the way through Male, if you look at my transcript, you'd see all these
circles, behavior problems. I was just a normal kid, I thought, but one thing
I didn't do was allow for anybody to abuse me. So finally, when I got to
be a senior, the dean of the school, Dean C——, called me in and said,
"Mr. Neal, look at this." I looked at my grades, and really it was embarrass-
ing. I graduated with a seventy-two average. So then he said, "Look at this."
There's a test you had to take. It turned out that I was in the top 7 percent
of students that took it in the country. They had to recognize me in the assembly hall. I didn't think anything about it. I was trying to figure out why
these grades were so contrary, and I thought that was really what he was
trying to explain to me. Then he looked at me and said, "You cheated." I said,
"Cheated?" He said, "Admit that you cheated, and I'll let you graduate with
your class." I said, "Mr. C——, I cannot tell a lie." [Laughter] I was going after
George Washington. I said, "I didn't cheat." So C—— said, "You're not going
to graduate with your class." I said, "Well, I have more than enough hours."
He showed me where I didn't.

So I went to the Latin II teacher and told him that I needed to take two
classes from him. He had tossed me out of his class as a junior. He looked at
me and said, "Neal, I've been waiting for you. I'm a fair man. If you take one
of my classes, I don't care what grade you make. I'm going to pass you." That
heartened me. Then he said, "But if you take two, I don't care what grade you
make. I'm going to fail you." So I went back to the dean and told him, complaining, and he looked at me in the eye and said, "Mr. Neal, that's academic
freedom." [Laughter] So when I came out of Male High School, I was fairly
alienated to American society.

Henry Owens, African American student (interview with David Cline,
2006). Formerly the industrial school, Manual High had by 1954 merged
with Louisville Girls High and had a full curriculum, with a focus still on industrial engineering. It attracted fewer black students than Male. Owens's
narrative reveals the social consequences of his extreme minority status.

I wanted to go to Manual because I thought I would get some engineering background. I wanted to be a construction engineer. That was what I said. That was the school where I thought I would get those kinds of experiences. I took a lot of subjects that I probably wouldn't have taken if I had been at the black school, like trigonometry, and geometry, and language. We had a lot of language, Latin. Of course we had that at the black school also. Not Latin, but we had French and some other languages, but Manual offered German. I didn't take German, but I took Latin, and two or three years of French. All kinds of stuff, drawing, mechanical drawing. They taught you all the different shops, how to run machines and stuff.

Later on I could kind of see the social aspects of what happened to me. I kind of had a nerdish experience in school. I didn't have a girlfriend or whatever. Didn't go to the dances because I didn't feel like I was supposed to go, maybe. I did have a white friend. He had one of those Edsels that had just come out, and we rode to some of the games, basketball, football games, he and a couple of guys. But I really didn't know the whites in terms of where they lived, or who they were, or who their mother was. Now this guy had been to my home, and I'd been to his house, but not other than that. I never went back to the reunions. Socially I think it was a negative for me and the other kids because we were there, but we really didn't have the full experience of going to school and having girlfriends, or relationships with women and stuff like that. I was very fearful of that because this guy Emmett Till had just gotten killed around that time, and my parents did speak to me about mingling with white women and stuff like that because you might get hurt, or killed, or whatever. "Get in trouble" is what they would always say.

Nobody ever called me a nigger, or threatened me. I didn't have that kind of problem. But I never was socially connected. Although they treated me with respect, I guess, I never had any real social connections. I think too what may have helped my experience was we had a singing group, two whites and two blacks. We were the Dew Drops. We got kind of popular around the school. We did assemblies and the school prom. So I think that may have helped me, too. I guess I was an acceptable black because I was quiet. I didn't raise any real serious questions about race or nothing like that. I guess I was a team player, maybe, in their minds. I don't know.

My academic part slipped. I went from being an A student to a D. I had never gotten a D or C, probably. I think my parents had a part in that. I think they believed that the white student was smarter, so when my grades went down they just looked at it as I was doing good, really, because I was competing against these other kids, and I was probably doing better than most would have done with a C. They had never been in a white situation like that, so they didn't know what to tell me, or advise me, or nothing like that. I had one teacher one time that did make a—I guess it was like a racial remark. I asked him about my grade. I think he gave me a D or something like that. He used to walk the kids out. He'd open the door, and he'd go out first. When the kids would leave then he'd close the door and go back in the room. So it was about at that time when the kids were coming out, and I said, "Mr. B——"—he's the only teacher I remember the name, too. "Mr. B——, why did I get a D?" And he said, "What did you expect?," and closed the door. It could have meant anything, but I took that as being a racial remark.

Gerald White, African American student (interview with Tracy E. K'Meyer, 2000). Shawnee Junior and Senior High was in a section of the west end that underwent a rapid racial transformation in the 1960s. Although it was all white before 1956, after desegregation, African Americans began attending. After the neighborhood's racial makeup shifted, the school became majority black, but at the time White attended it was still almost all white.

The first day of integration I went to Shawnee Junior High School. I stayed there three years. I really didn't want to go to Shawnee High School but my parents were saying, "You're always running your mouth about integration and all this kind of stuff. Now here it is and you've got to go." When I got there I had to share a locker, I will never forget. Stood up in class and the teacher says, "Well, who wants to share a locker with him?" There was this young lady, she said, "I'll share a locker with him." A white girl. Now, I was tall and she was short, so she took the bottom of the locker and I took the top. That went on all year. Then the last day of school of the first year, I was cleaning out the top of the locker and she was cleaning up the bottom of the locker, and the principal came by and saw it. He thought I was stealing something from her and he slapped me. I've never been slapped by another man. So that altercation ended up with my parents and the police and everybody coming to school. He asked me, "What is it you want to do, Gerald?" I said, "I want to get out of here and I want to go to Central." His name was Mr. F——, and he said, "Well, you've got it done." He signed my transfer and I went to Central High School. The irony of it is now I run the magnet program at Shawnee High School, and his office is now my office.

Louisville Male High School yearbook, 1959. Members of the senior class. Raoul Cunningham is pictured second row, fourth from left. (Courtesy of the Jefferson County Public School Archives)

Raoul Cunningham, African American student (interview with Tracy E. K'Meyer, 1999). Cunningham refers to his role as a student leader of the spring 1961 mass sit-in campaign for an open accommodations law in Louisville.

Brown came out in what, '54? That would have made me eleven. Louisville desegregated '56. I was in the eighth grade and going to DuValle Junior High School. I was on the line between DuValle Junior High School and Parkland Junior High School. I had a choice. I made the decision with my mother to stay at DuValle. Parkland was all white. DuValle was all black. But I chose to go to DuValle.

Then, when I went to high school, I went to Male. It was a horrible experience. David Hawpe, the former editor of the *Courier Journal*, and I graduated together and we argue now. He did a column on a teacher at Male named Mr. [deleted] and talked about what a great teacher he was and I called him and raised hell. The man was a good teacher—I took him for two courses—but he was a racist. When I was arrested for sit-ins, he tried to flunk me. He gave me Ds, but he didn't flunk me. The first grading period I had gotten As in both of his classes. He was an out-and-out racist. My point to David was, how could the man have been a good teacher when he was a racist?

There had never been a black senior class officer or even a black on the prom committee or anything. So we said, "OK." Some black students got together and decided I would be the one that would run. All the blacks signed my petition. The day of the deadline there were ten petitions in, they extended the deadline, took names from my petition to put on a white kid's petition, and the election organizers shut us out again. You had to get X number of signatures. Well, with one-fifth of the class, I had more than enough. So they just took them from mine to allow another kid to run and, in effect, to make sure that it was lily white.

Blacks were one-fifth of the class out of 207 graduated. Of all of us that went to college, only two went to an integrated school. We had had such a bad experience. My mother and I just argued profusely: "I'm not going to an integrated college, that's all there is to it; I've had it."

■ The contrast between Cunningham's rejection of an integrated college because of his experience at Male and Evelyn Jackson's reminiscences of the harmony in her newly mixed-race classrooms highlights a central tension in the memory of the local response to *Brown*.[19] Oral histories reveal two divergent ways of remembering desegregation: teachers and administrators remembered with pride the relatively peaceful and early transition in the public schools in Louisville, while black students offered a striking critique of the difficulties they faced. Most narrators who were adults in 1956 shaped their stories implicitly or explicitly to explain why desegregation in the city went so well. The tone of these accounts reflects a public dialogue that at the time emphasized Louisville's leadership in race relations. Many of these interviews were conducted in 1973, when the celebratory rhetoric and praise for the people who led the process of school desegregation in 1956 remained relatively fresh and thus influenced the memories of events. In contrast, the young black students who entered the newly mixed schools in the early years share memories of disillusionment, even bitterness, with the realities of the educational experience after *Brown*. Nearly every one of the young people quoted here became an activist in the civil rights or black power movement. *Brown* and the resources promised to them by desegregation had raised their hopes. The interviews reveal their disappointment when that promise was not met. All these interviews offer accurate expressions of the narrators' individual experiences and perspectives. Together they demonstrate the difficulties of assessing the initial wave of school desegregation in Louisville.

The public memory of massive resistance, reflected most dramatically in iconic images of school integration at Little Rock, along with the scholarship and public dialogue that emphasize the failure of desegregation, make it surprising to encounter the more upbeat appraisal of the process in Louisville. The stories of the men and women, both black and white, who worked within the system in 1956 affirm the relative success of local desegregation. Narrators recall how strong leadership from the top and in-school programs helped prepare teachers, parents, and students for change. Though they share stories of individual conflicts, principals Higgins and Jackson insist that, as Higgins put it, "There was a rather nice acceptance of the idea" of desegregation and that neither school faced significant problems. The transfer option was controversial at the time, but in retrospect both teachers and administrators credit it with helping Louisville avoid serious trouble and enabling people to feel they integrated "because we wanted to, rather than integrating because we had to."[20] Few narrators mention any opposition; those who do dismiss it as not serious, led by unimportant people who quickly gave up or went away, and easily neutralized. The portrait of well-intentioned leaders, an intelligent and liberal process, and an accepting community may seem tinted by rose-colored glasses. An element of nostalgia often shapes oral history interviews. But these positive memories cannot simply be dismissed as such.[21] Instead, they should be read both for what they reveal of the events they describe and for how intervening influences shape the public memory of the past.

Evidence from Louisville's first wave of desegregation provides partial support for the narrators' assertions that school integration was successful and accepted without major confrontation. In the first years, the local papers regularly carried news about the number of students attending mixed facilities—defined as having at least one member of each race. In 1956, when Carmichael boasted that 73.6 percent of students attended integrated schools, only 19 percent of blacks and 13 percent of whites went to single-race institutions. One year later, the *Courier Journal* reported more progress; at that time only 11 percent of students went to all-white or all-black facilities. By the end of the decade, transfers had decreased, so that less than one in ten students attended schools outside their residential district and 80 percent of students were in mixed-race schools. And, though the picture was worse in the rest of the state, in the Louisville schools no black teacher had lost his or her job due to desegregation.[22] These numbers gave local officials reason to brag about Louisville's achievement, particularly compared to the near total lack of desegregation throughout the South.[23]

Polls and news reports of the time also substantiate the narrators' memories of the public embrace, or at least tolerance, of desegregation. In January 1957, Kemper and Associates conducted a poll of white and African American opinion about Louisville's desegregation plan. Among blacks, 86 percent affirmed their support for school desegregation and for the local plan. This number reflects the high level of consensus on the issue in the black community in the 1950s and the history of black leaders pushing to overturn the Day Law. Whites were less enthusiastic, with only 38.7 percent indicating approval of desegregation. Yet among those opposed to it, half accepted the change as the law of the land that could not be reversed, and only 28 percent of all whites polled called for a return to segregated schools. These numbers indicate that even if the majority of whites in the community disliked school desegregation, they acknowledged that it could not be avoided. Even when most whites did not endorse the change, as one historian of school desegregation asserted, the "main determinant to successful desegregation was the quality of local leadership."[24] In Louisville white civic leaders, from the mayor to school officials, voiced their intent to uphold the law, largely to prove the city's progressiveness. Less well known by name but as important on the ground were the white and black parents, PTA leaders, teachers, ministers, and members of community groups who hosted forums, held social exchanges, gave sermons, and in other ways smoothed the way for desegregation.

Likewise, in the fall of 1956 the press contained few reports of resistance. On the contrary, news coverage throughout the first year emphasized normalcy in the classrooms, and reporters, like Walker and Owsley, downplayed the significance of the opposition. The *Defender* gave more attention to outspoken segregationists like Millard Grubbs and his fledgling Citizens' Council, but both it and the *Courier Journal* noted the small turnout at opposition events and the failure of efforts to spark more defiance. The *Defender* chronicled the case of one white woman who kept her children out of school in protest, but that coverage only highlighted the failure of the effort to initiate a widespread boycott.[25] Meanwhile reporters—both local and national, black and white—who went into the schools told stories of students shyly getting along and teachers adjusting.[26] In short, the press reported no significant disturbances in the schools, which helped shape the narrators' memories of minimal conflict.

That peace also helped to forge Louisville's image as a progressive leader in southern race relations, which became a source of pride for those who participated in the process. In the days and months after the opening of the schools the city garnered national attention and praise, beginning with Benjamin Fine's reporting for the *New York Times*. The media coverage included a news documentary that focused on the Morris and Douglass schools, as well as notices that reached audiences abroad. Perhaps the highest-profile compliment came when President Eisenhower called Carmichael a "wise man" and invited him to the White House to discuss how he had accomplished peaceful integration. Capitalizing on this congratulatory wave, black leaders added school desegregation to their litany of successes in the postwar era and used that record to agitate for progress in other arenas.[27] But white civic leaders also took pride in this record, as the Owsley and Walker narratives, among others, reveal. Later events might tarnish the city's reputation, but the story of Louisville's successful school desegregation became a powerful public narrative in the 1950s and 1960s, and helped shape individual memories of events.

Finally, the nature and timing of the interviews conducted in 1973 reinforced the tendency toward nostalgia. Many of those interviewed in that project had held positions of authority and were responsible for some part of the process of school desegregation, including a city official, a Board of Education president, principals, PTA leaders, and teachers. They had firsthand knowledge of the decision making and preparation for desegregation, especially at individual schools, and their narratives provide information often unavailable in other sources. But their position also gave them reason to feel some ownership of the process, to have a stake in the outcome, and to seek some share of the credit for it. The narrators' role in the events introduced a positive bias in their telling of the story. The interviewer's questions reinforced this tendency by eliciting comments about the reasons for Louisville's success and the planning and preparation that went into it. Finally, the timing of the interviews also shaped the content. In 1973 controversy over the prospect of "forced busing" was stirring nationally, with the possibility that it might happen in Louisville and Jefferson County. Several of the narrators pointedly praised the voluntary nature of the Louisville transfer plan and attributed the lack of conflict to the element of choice. Thus praise for Louisville's peaceful and successful school desegregation of 1956 served to critique the turmoil elsewhere while warning against systems of "forced" integration.

Still, the influences shaping the 1973 interviews do not undermine the historical significance or usefulness of the resulting narratives. Contemporary evidence corroborates the broader picture painted by these interviews, including the African American embrace of and white acquiescence to desegregation, and the lack of significant opposition or conflict in the schools. More important, all oral history is the memory of past events filtered through present circumstances. Taken together, the 1973 interviews provide a snapshot of the memory of school desegregation produced by the circumstances of the early 1970s. Scholars must weigh and juxtapose this particular memory against others to understand the richness and complexity of the story.

Indeed, the narratives with young African Americans who were part of the first generation to integrate the schools in Louisville convey a strikingly different memory. Tinsley recalls some fond memories of her years at a desegregated middle school and Owens found limited acceptance through his singing, but most of the narrators tell stories of confrontations with hostile teachers and administrators, accusations of cheating and theft, and a lack of equal access to extracurricular activities. Cunningham conveys their collective judgment when he notes that by the end of high school he'd "had it" with integrated schools. Together these stories conjure an anti-nostalgic memory. Like the rosy tale of desegregation's success, however, such memories should be taken neither at face value nor rejected as distortions of the "truth." Daily life inside schools often went underrecorded in other sources. Interviews with those who were young at the time provide perhaps the best and only evidence of the impact of desegregation on student life. But as is the case in the interviews with teachers and administrators, their perspectives reflect the time and circumstances that produced them, as well as intervening events and attitudes.

The interviews with young people arose from two projects conducted in a context different from that of the 1973 recordings. Half of the narrators were recorded as part of a study of the civil rights movement in Louisville because of their roles as teenage participants in the sit-ins. Their memories of school desegregation were elicited in response to questions about what led the young men and women to activism, pushing them to discuss moments of racial conflict. The others were interviewed as part of an extensive study of the community crisis sparked by the beginning of school busing in 1975. By the time of the interviews, the promise of school integration had diminished as policy makers, black leaders, and some scholars declared it a failure and abandoned it. The public and scholarly dialogue about that failure included pointed critiques about what African Americans had lost in the process of desegregation.[28] The former students' memories of their struggles in the new school environments reflect key elements of that critique. Thus these stories—and the way they diverge from the consensus of success in the earlier interviews—reveal that the memory of school desegregation depends not only on the narrator's position and perspective in the past but also on the resonance such stories hold in contemporary public dialogues.

Little extant evidence documents the troubles black students faced in the schools. The interpersonal relations between students and teachers do not often make it into the public record. Moreover, the contemporary newspapers, sympathetic to desegregation and eager to showcase its success, rarely dwelled on problems within the schools. Still, intimations of some of the attitudes attributed by the narrators to their teachers and principals exist. In Carmichael's 1957 memoir, he cites teachers' anonymous complaints about having to teach black students. The memoir also includes excerpts from principals' reports about the first year, which despite mostly favorable reviews contain stories of violence between students and worries about the lack of discipline among African Americans. The tone of these reports hints at the atmosphere black students encountered in the schools, and corroborates students' negative memories of desegregation.[29]

Louisville residents' divergent memories about school desegregation in the 1950s and early 1960s raise questions about how to assess its success. Louisville did more than cities elsewhere in the South, but "it wasn't sufficient to accomplish the thing," as Ruth Higgins put it. School integration in the community met little overt opposition, but parents both black and white demonstrated passive resistance by choosing the transfer option. White officials, parents, and activists worked to smooth desegregation, but they could not see or did not acknowledge the structural impediments, especially housing segregation, that limited it from the start. The Louisville desegregation plan opened up access to resources for young black students, but it also exposed them to a racist learning environment. For some African Americans, the promise of the progress achieved dissipated and left a profound sense of disillusionment. Thus, like a cup half full or half empty, the extent or success of school desegregation in Louisville after *Brown* depends on the perspective of the observer.

More important, these different viewpoints offer insight into both the success and limitations of early school desegregation. Interested in maintaining the city's progressive image and drawing on the piecemeal reforms of previous years, Louisville school officials developed and implemented a desegregation plan that fulfilled the letter of *Brown* and went further in meeting its spirit than most of the South, measured by the number of students attending at least minimally integrated schools. Community groups, civic leaders, and school staff cooperated to prepare students, teachers, and parents for the change and to make it happen with minimal conflict.

As a result, school desegregation was not a drain on the energy of civil rights activists but became a spark for further action. But the much praised peace of the transition rested at least in part on factors that limited the number of families affected: housing segregation that ensured most children were assigned to schools attended by a majority of their own race and the transfer option that allowed students to escape more fully integrated ones. Moreover, all the careful preparation for desegregation could not erase engrained racial prejudices that shaped white responses to black children. The pro-desegregation efforts of leaders and community people laid the foundation for a long Louisville tradition of support for the idea of integrated schools; the experience of young black students demonstrated the work still needed to make them truly equal.

In the long run, the low numbers of students affected by school desegregation—noted at the time and getting worse throughout the succeeding decade—most challenged the memory of Louisville's success. Indeed, in later interviews many local people remembered the schools in the 1960s as still segregated, largely forgetting the events of 1956. By the late 1950s indications of the limits of school desegregation had become apparent. The *Defender* regularly critiqued the school system's glowing reports by pointing out the continued existence of single-race schools and the lack of teacher integration. Other critics emphasized that even in schools identified as successfully mixed, the number of black students often remained small. While some elementary schools reached near racial parity, more often black pupils represented a tiny percentage of the student body. The narrators' memories of their experience in high school reveal the problems faced by such a minority. Finally, black leaders continued to challenge the Board of Education for "fostering continued segregation" by changing school district lines, among other practices, to accommodate white transfers back to formerly all-white schools.[30]

The shortcomings of desegregation became clearer during the following decade. Although transfer requests declined over time, the number of students in even minimally mixed schools began to decline drastically by mid-decade as resegregation took hold in the system. On the surface, desegregation persisted for a time, with the proportion of students attending school with members of another race fluctuating between 82 and 86 percent and the number in all-white or all-black institutions remaining under 10 percent between 1961 and 1965. During the same years, the number of black teachers in the Louisville system grew, as did the number serving on integrated faculties. But by the turn of the new decade those trends had reversed, mirroring a similar phenomenon in other border cities—St. Louis and Baltimore—that like Louisville in the mid-1950s had gotten ahead of the rest of the South by integrating with residence and choice-based plans. In 1971 the Kentucky Commission on Human Rights (KCHR) examined schools for "racial polarization," defined as a situation in which more than 90 percent of a student body consisted of one race. Its investigation revealed that fifty-one out of sixty-seven public schools in Louisville suffered from racial polarization, the highest number since desegregation began. The KCHR report also showed a decline in the extent of teacher integration. In short, much of the progress in school desegregation heralded in the 1950s had evaporated. Or as journalist Jack Lyne put it more colorfully, "The 1956 success story was now nothing more than a cherished, cloudy memory."[31]

The root cause of this retreat in the public schools in Louisville and along the North/South border was the worsening of housing segregation caused by white movement to the suburbs and urban renewal. In Louisville, after *Brown*, school officials acknowledged that some school segregation would continue because of housing patterns, and thereafter they blamed residential segregation for the existence of some all-white schools. In the 1950s many whites moved out of the west end of Louisville, pushed by growing pollution from the industries on the edge of the neighborhood and attracted by the easy credit offered for new housing construction in the surrounding Jefferson County suburbs. A second wave of whites left the west end after the neighborhood's elementary schools enrolled large numbers of black students. As a result, the percentage of African American students in the city increased steadily from 26 to 46 percent between 1956 and 1969. In addition, the concentration of blacks within certain city neighborhoods contributed to the growing polarization of the schools. Local urban renewal displaced African Americans from the central and near east areas of the city, while housing discrimination excluded them from new residential developments and funneled them into the increasingly black and overcrowded west end. The stark result was that while in 1960 only 28 percent of Louisville's black population lived in the west end, by 1969 85 percent of African Americans did. The concentration of blacks into a small geographic area, combined with white movement to the suburbs, drastically increased residential segregation in the city. Indeed, the KCHR reported in 1969 that the city was more racially separated than ever in its history. The school system struggled to stay integrated in this increasingly polarized community.[32]

Meanwhile, the whites who flooded into Jefferson County landed in a school system in which integration already lagged behind that in the city.

County Superintendent Richard Van Hoose had promised to follow Carmichael's lead and integrate in the fall of 1956 with a plan that moved a small number of black elementary students into white schools. But no white students shifted to previously black schools. Prior to 1956, the county lacked black junior or high schools—those students had gone to Central High or to the nearby private Lincoln Institute—so Van Hoose proposed that those students could now transfer to white schools. In the first years after implementation, the rate of integration remained low compared to the city, with only 47 percent of students attending mixed facilities in the first year. Meanwhile, Van Hoose made no effort to integrate teachers until 1963. In the mid-1960s Jefferson County inched toward more desegregation at the elementary level, closing all but one formerly black school and sending the students to white facilities. That one school, Newburg Elementary, remained all black throughout the decade. In 1965, federal Health, Education, and Welfare (HEW) officials investigated the county and declared its schools segregated. With federal funds at risk, Van Hoose partially relented, assigning white teachers to Newburg for the first time.[33]

In the late 1960s evidence mounted that whatever progress Louisville had made in desegregation was eroding, even while the bar for declaring success was rising. In 1964 the Civil Rights Act threatened to cut off federal funds for school districts not in compliance with *Brown*. By the end of the decade federal agencies and the courts insisted that districts demonstrate the actual mixing of students in significant numbers, rather than merely token change. The Supreme Court signaled this shift in *Green v. County School Board*, which called on school districts to demonstrate that their procedures had eliminated racially identifiable schools. This new thinking would dominate the court's approach to school integration into the 1970s, when it paid increasing attention to outcomes and forced the next wave of change not only in the South but throughout the country.[34] But if the absence of racially identifiable schools represented the measure of successful desegregation, and if school systems were evaluated according to the racial balance in their classrooms, Louisville and Jefferson County had a problem. In 1971, a legal challenge to the all-black Newburg Elementary set the wheels in motion to force school officials to solve it.

CHAPTER TWO

The Beginning of Busing, 1971–1980

In 1995 and again in 2005, the *Courier Journal* printed articles marking the twentieth and thirtieth anniversaries of the beginning of busing for desegregation in Louisville and Jefferson County. On these occasions the paper invited readers to submit their stories, providing a platform for them to remember the events of 1975 and their impact on the community. Many of the stories recount harrowing trips on buses through mobs of antibusing demonstrators, conflicts in the schools, and a sense of an education interrupted. Although few of those who wrote letters or were interviewed by reporters talked explicitly about the reasons for the opposition to busing, the bitterness over it and the conflict it caused remain palpable in both years. These anniversary reminiscences reveal the extent to which the negative reaction to busing, which included mass rallies by opponents, a white student boycott of the schools, and riots in the south end of the county, came to dominate the public memory of desegregation in the community. Many of the narratives that follow likewise tell the story of the turmoil that accompanied busing both inside and outside the schools. By the time of these anniversaries and interviews, the 1956 integration process and its relative success had been overshadowed; the public dialogue about school desegregation was hereafter filtered through memories of the community trauma of busing in 1975.

Yet the *Courier Journal* anniversary forums also hinted at another story. The reminiscences included scattered stories of participants' positive experiences, assertions of lessons learned, or expressions of pride in contributing to the effort to overcome discrimination. The interviews in this chapter shed further light on this less publicized, less dramatic story.

Indeed, these oral history interviews recover the story of people who, like their predecessors in 1956, endeavored to make integration work and to maintain peace in the community. Some strove to protect children on the buses, others focused on calming parents' fears, and a few raised their voices against the racism of the antibusing forces. Thus, while oral histories about the early years of busing document the conflict and the extent of opposition, they also uncover the persistent efforts of people from diverse backgrounds to carry out desegregation.

The use of busing to desegregate schools in Louisville and Jefferson County, as in other districts around the country, resulted from growing federal government insistence that schools implement *Brown*. By the late 1960s the Supreme Court had ordered schools to eliminate dual systems, and officials from the federal department of Health, Education, and Welfare (HEW) were investigating districts and citing them for continued segregation. In a 1971 decision, *Swann v. Charlotte-Mecklenburg Board of Education*, the court ordered that district to achieve racial balance in its schools and gave the green light for the use of mass busing to do so. Resistance to what many opponents called "forced busing" arose immediately as conservatives critiqued the court for going too far. White parents objected both to the influx of African Americans into their neighborhood schools and to the requirement that they send their own children into what they saw as inferior black institutions. Black communities, meanwhile, showed a mixed reaction. While parents expressed anxiety about the change, most civil rights leaders acknowledged that busing was the only way to ensure equality. In 1972, just as the idea of merging and desegregating the Louisville and Jefferson County schools was first raised, busing became a hot political topic nationally. In 1974, when busing looked likely in the local district, Boston revealed how ugly antibusing confrontations could become.[1]

The road to busing in Louisville and Jefferson County began in 1971 when HEW officials ordered the Jefferson County Board of Education to address the lack of integration in the elementary schools. In response, the county school board announced its intention to close the still all-black Newburg Elementary and send those children to different white schools. This proposal put the complete burden of desegregation on African American families and spared the white community from any busing at all. Nevertheless, white parents reacted with ire, and a group of mothers organized the first antibusing group in the area. At the same time, some black parents objected to the loss of a community institution. In the end the school board reversed its decision, citing opposition from both sides as justification for rejecting federal demands. By voting not to meet the HEW deadline for achieving integration the board seemed to invite a lawsuit.[2]

The Kentucky Civil Liberties Union (KCLU) and the Legal Aid Society obliged less than a month later by filing a suit in federal court asking that the county school system be integrated through redistricting. The KCLU then turned its attention to the city and met with black community and civil rights groups to gauge their preferred approach to desegregation and interest in a lawsuit. Despite some signs of black ambivalence—based on concerns about losing both special programs and African American authority in the city schools—in June 1972 the KCLU and the NAACP jointly filed a suit. They asked that the court order the desegregation of the city schools through the annexation of unincorporated suburbs to bring young people in to help balance the student body and to raise extra tax revenue to help the financially ailing system. The Kentucky Commission on Human Rights, prompted by its extensive research on housing patterns and school segregation, intervened in the suit, asking the court to bring about comprehensive desegregation through the merger of the city, county, and Anchorage—a wealthy white independent district on Louisville's northeast border.[3]

In December 1972, Judge James F. Gordon of the federal western district of Kentucky combined all the county and city suits and heard arguments on them together. He quickly decided that he could not order a merger of schools across district lines. He further declared that the systems in question had done all they could to comply with federal law on desegregation and praised school officials for acting promptly in the wake of *Brown*. His decision pleased school officials, but civil rights leaders appealed. Late in 1973, the Sixth Circuit Court of Appeals in Cincinnati overturned Gordon's decision, declaring that the vestiges of segregation had not been eliminated in either Louisville or Jefferson County. The appeals court ordered officials of both systems and Anchorage to develop a joint plan for remedying the situation and suggested that district lines should not stand in the way of successful integration. The Louisville Board of Education agreed that any real integration would require a merger of the systems. The county board filed an appeal, but the court ordered it to begin making plans for integration while the case was pending.[4]

In the midst of the negotiations for a desegregation plan, however, a July 1974 Supreme Court decision threatened to disrupt the prospect of a metrowide solution in the schools. In *Milliken v. Bradley*, a case challenging a desegregation plan for Detroit and its suburbs, the Supreme Court rejected the busing of students across city and county district lines. As a result, the Sixth Circuit Court had to reconsider the Louisville and Jefferson County suits, eliminating the possibility that schools would be integrated by fall 1974. In the retrial, civil rights attorneys argued that *Milliken* left the door open to exceptions in cases where both districts had been found out of compliance and where students had been sent across district lines in the past for the purpose of segregation. Both conditions applied in Louisville. In December 1974, the Sixth Circuit Court upheld its decision of the year before, opening the door once again for countywide busing.[5]

In the spring of 1975, a merger of the Louisville and Jefferson County school systems made *Milliken* moot by erasing the local city-county boundary. With the financial stability of the Louisville school system deteriorating, the city school board pressed to bring the two systems together. Although the city had debated merger before and African Americans had opposed it, the serious financial crisis facing city schools now softened that resistance. The county board of education continued to object—as the wealthier partner they had more to lose—and unsuccessfully challenged the state law allowing merger in court. After the law was upheld the process went forward, and in April 1975 Jefferson County absorbed the Louisville city system. Prolonged negotiations to work out the details of the size of the merged school board, the status of former city staff, and other points of contention went on simultaneously with those about a desegregation plan. The merger brought together two very different systems—one urban, minority, and poor, the other wealthy, white, and suburban—as well as divergent cultures and approaches to education. Tensions sparked by these differences and the perceived inequalities of the merger process shaped the way people inside and outside the schools viewed and experienced integration in the newly combined district.[6]

Once the systems merged, the new board began to tackle the problem of how to desegregate. Judge Gordon did not seem in a hurry to pressure school leaders for a workable busing program even as late as June 1975. But in July the Circuit Court of Appeals grew impatient and ordered Gordon to impose a plan. He did so in August, giving parents one month's notice about where their children would go to school and how they would get there. Gordon's edict mandated that the student body of every school consist of between 12 and 35 percent African Americans—a ratio that civil rights advocates criticized for requiring a white majority in every institution. To ensure this, both black and white students would be bused; African Americans would travel to formerly white schools in the county, and suburban whites would be transported to formerly black schools in the inner city and west end. Yet black and white students did not share an equal burden. African Americans would be bused for eight or nine years of their school career while whites would be bused for only one or two years. The first letter of a student's last name determined the school assignment and busing years under what came to be known as the "alphabet plan." First-grade and senior-year students were exempt for the first year.[7]

The African American community had a mixed response to these developments. Concerns about busing and what it would mean for black children surfaced early. In the 1971 discussions about how to integrate the county elementary schools, some parents objected to the busing of black children out of Newburg and to the closing of the school. While the lawsuits were before the courts, black leaders began to weigh in, stressing the importance of equality within any busing program. In particular, they argued for the protection of black teachers, administrators, and coaches and for some guarantee of black input into decision making. Black parents expressed more concern about the proposal to create a white majority in every school and its potential impact on their children's experience. To counteract negative effects, a coalition headed by the Black Panthers rallied for the inclusion of black history in every school's curriculum, and a west end community group pledged to host classes in African American history and culture as an afterschool program to help children get what they would miss in white-dominated institutions. As the opening days of school and busing approached, parents began to worry about the potential danger to their children. After the first week of school, when the threat to black students on the buses became real, these worries led a group of African American women to form United Black Protective Parents to protect their children and to ensure they received equal treatment in the busing process.[8]

As the debate over busing heated up, however, local black leaders, parents, and students also voiced their support for it as a strategy for achieving equal education. The *Defender* ardently championed busing as the best way to achieve integration and equality in the schools. Frank Stanley, the publisher, argued that blacks had long been bused to poor schools for segregation; now it was time to transport them to good ones for integration. In addition, the paper regularly carried stories of various African American leaders, including congressional candidate and businessman Marvin Drane, civil rights leader Lyman Johnson, and Reverend G. K. Offutt, who called busing the great equalizer and the price blacks would willingly pay for a quality education. Even black power advocate Morris Jeff, who asserted that he did not favor integrated education in principle, conceded that under the present dual system blacks never got equal resources. On the eve of the fall semester in 1975 black parents and students echoed these sentiments. To promote support for busing and peaceful desegregation, a group of black high schools students published a "10 Commandments for Parents," calling on them to obey the law, get their children to the bus stops, and support them in their education. Meanwhile, black pro-busing organizations held forums to educate the community about the need for the plan, and the *Defender* ran a series of ads featuring black teachers and civic leaders who called on people to remain calm and to stand up against fear and for equality.[9]

In 1956 the national media had hailed Louisville as a city that accomplished school desegregation without strife. Twenty years later, the outbreak of violence that greeted the beginning of busing in the newly merged city and county school system earned Louisville a place alongside Boston as the poster children for massive white resistance to court-ordered school desegregation. Instead of a dismissible band of picketers in front of the Board of Education offices, this time angry mobs, bonfires, and barricades greeted the busloads of black young people sent to integrate the white schools in the south and southwestern corners of the county. Not every school saw outbreaks of violence, but the disorder, combined with the mass rallies, demonstrations, and flood of letters to the editor by white opponents of busing, created a community crisis in race relations like none Louisville had seen in the modern era. The nature of the crisis, its roots, and the responses it provoked reflect the way the context for school desegregation in Louisville had changed since the 1950s.

By 1975 the Louisville community had experienced a decade of racial change that led to rising tension and white resistance. The wave of sit-in demonstrations that had rocked the South in the early 1960s came to Louisville in the spring of 1961. The Louisville campaign saw mass arrests but relatively little violence or outspoken opposition compared to other southern communities. It led to the passage of the first city open accommodations law in the region and seemed to confirm Louisville's reputation for racial progressiveness. In 1966–67 the open housing movement called for a similar local law against housing discrimination. Whites had responded quietly to the opening of restaurants and theaters to black patrons, but they balked at the prospect of residential integration. Mobs of angry whites armed with two-by-fours, rocks, and cherry bombs attacked protesters, and city officials used increasingly aggressive legal tactics to silence civil rights leaders. In letters to the editor and public meetings, opponents invoked the rhetoric of "forced housing" common to white homeowners' movements throughout the country. These efforts represented one component of a more assertive white backlash against federal intervention on behalf of racial equality and helped fuel the rise of the conservative movement. Race relations worsened in 1968 when a civil disorder in the west end gave city officials an excuse to target and prosecute a group of six black leaders—the "Black Six"—for conspiracy. The riot reinforced many suburban whites' views of the city and of blacks as disorderly and dangerous, while the prosecution gave African Americans reason to distrust the authorities. Thus, by the start of the new decade, as efforts to promote school desegregation and educational equality revived, racial tensions and starkly divergent ideas about what still needed to be done created an unwelcoming climate for further change.[10]

The most obvious local manifestation of the white backlash against civil rights advances was the antibusing movement. White parent opposition to busing first appeared in 1971 in response to plans for moving black children to white county elementary schools, and led to the founding of the earliest and longest-lived antibusing group, Save Our Community Schools. After it became clear that the courts would order countywide busing, white opposition spread. By the summer of 1975 the Ku Klux Klan and other extremist groups had begun recruiting and holding rallies. A spate of other antibusing groups also formed, including Concerned Parents Inc. and Union Labor Against Busing, which coordinated opposition among the white labor union members who worked and lived in relatively new suburbs in the county. The rising tension exploded into violence at the end of the first week of school. On Friday night, crowds of up to ten thousand antibusing demonstrators gathered outside Pleasure Ridge Park, Valley, and Southern High Schools in the south end of the county and fought with county and state police. Throughout the next month other demonstrations downtown led to injuries and vandalism. Mobs vented their anger by attacking buses as they entered white neighborhoods, prompting officials to assign armed national guardsmen to ride on them. Tension spilled into the schools, bursting out in conflicts between students and infecting the relationship between faculty and young African Americans. Meanwhile, many white students boycotted the desegregated schools. The worst of the violence had passed by the end of spring in 1976, but in each of the following few years, die-hard busing opponents launched smaller demonstrations at the start of the fall semester.[11]

A less tumultuous story, and one certainly less noted in the news media of the time, also had roots in the civil rights campaigns of the 1960s. While sparking furor among opponents, the open housing movement had also forged an alliance of black civil rights activists and white liberals.

Antibusing demonstration, 1975. (Courtesy of the Louisville Defender
Collection, Special Collections, University of Louisville)

Organizations such as the National Council of Jewish Women and the League of Women Voters, interfaith committees, and more activist inter-racial groups had petitioned, demonstrated, and held forums on behalf of open housing. The persecution of the Black Six rallied many of these same groups to fund-raise for their defense. As opposition to countywide school desegregation grew, many of these organizations and individuals took a stand for integration and busing as the best means to achieve it. In 1972 the Ad Hoc Committee for School Integration started an educational campaign about the need for busing. After the Circuit Court of Appeals cleared the way for busing, the National Council of Jewish Women sponsored forums to prepare the public. Meanwhile, the local Human Relations Commission organized teams in the schools to promote good relations, and individual ministers arranged dialogues between black and white churches. Perhaps best known at the time was Progress in Education (PIE), an advocacy group organized by white and black activists that denounced the open racism of the antibusing movement. This unheralded pro-integration movement also included individual parents, especially mothers, who volunteered through the PTA or on their own to work in the schools and promote community calm. The pro-desegregation campaign climaxed in the spring of 1976 with a petition against bigotry signed by more than three thousand people and ninety-five organizations. Disparaged by some civil rights advocates as mere words, the "Declaration of Independence Against Bigotry" gave people a concrete way to voice their opposition to the ugliest aspects of the antibusing movement. As the worst of the crisis passed, many of the individuals who had worked for desegregation quietly continued to monitor racism in the schools and labored to improve the busing plan.[12]

The narratives in this chapter, arranged in three sections, tell the story of the beginning of busing and its impact inside the schools. They document the sources of white opposition to busing and the community crisis that resulted from it, and thus corroborate the public memory of, and the bulk of historical scholarship about, the busing crisis of the mid-1970s. They also, however, reveal a largely forgotten alternative story of how people supported busing to achieve desegregation. The white backlash against busing has obscured this alternative from the shared community memory and scholars have largely ignored it in their histories of school desegregation. Finally, these interviews provide a view of the lived experience within the schools, with reflections about anxiety in the face of the unknown, tensions between teachers, and hardships suffered by black students, but also about budding friendships, more equitable resources, and personal growth. Thus oral history both adds support for desegregation and the often behind-the-scenes efforts to ensure it to the story of what happened outside the schools and enriches our understanding of what went on within them in the early years of busing.

The Opposition to Busing

The narratives in this first section explain some of the sources of the antagonism against busing and the actions it led to. People give their own reasons, comment on those of their family, or convey what they understand as the motivations for the antibusing movement more generally. A number of the narratives include the often repeated assertion that opponents objected to the federal usurpation of parents' rights to make decisions about their children's school, and not to desegregation per se. Contemporary evidence belies such statements, but they illustrate the common arguments of 1975. The interviews go on to describe some of the tactics used by opponents, including lobbying, boycotting, and demonstrating. The depictions of the latter—and the violence that resulted—convey the atmosphere outside the schools in the first weeks of busing and reflect the community memory of the trauma of the time.

Harvey Sloane, white mayor of Louisville (interview with Ethel White, 1988). Sloane, a liberal Democrat with support in the west end, places the blame for much of the turmoil on the lack of time to prepare for busing.

When the order was handed down I said, "This is something we're going to have to do. I don't happen to agree with it, but it is the law and we're going to see that the law is enforced and obeyed and it's going to be done peacefully."

The city school officials had been working on alternative patterns and magnet schools and various ways to desegregate the schools, and preparing the police for what might occur. None of the people in authority really thought it was going to occur until next year when we would have had a much longer time to work with the schools, the parents, the citizens. In hindsight I think it was a great mistake on the part of the court to give this community only six weeks to prepare for a massive desegregation effort. We didn't have enough buses. We didn't have the preparation of the teachers, bus drivers, students, and there was pure chaos the way it started. I was shocked that they would only give us this kind of time to prepare for it. You needed a strong presence of federal law enforcement people, federal marshals. You needed a strong federal judge who was going to be very specific about what could be done and could not be done. You needed to work with the consensus of the community as much as possible. Obviously we needed to prepare the police, and we had been working with our police force in terms of riot training on a regular basis at Churchill Downs. But there was no way to prepare for the chaos that ensued.

Jean Ruffra, white mother (interview with Ethel White, 1988). Ruffra, whose children attended a white elementary school in Jefferson County, tells the story of the founding of Save Our Community Schools and explicates her view of the ideology of the antibusing movement.

In 1971 the Department of Health, Education, and Welfare issued an order that there were three schools in Jefferson County that were out of desegregation guidelines: Newburg Elementary, Cane Run Elementary, and Schaffner Elementary. Because I had a child in [Schaffner] this was of utmost interest to me because it knocked on my door! So I became interested in the issue and so did other parents and several of us met in my home and decided that we should ask some questions. At that time the school board said that they would have to rearrange the school districts and "bus" some of these children from Cane Run to Schaffner to Newburg, etc. We didn't like that idea so we became more interested in the busing issue.

In early 1971, Joyce Spond, Rita Roundtree, and myself formed our own organization, Save Our Community Schools Inc. We did not agree with the HEW order or [later] the court order and we believed the way to disagree was to change it and to change the laws. We lobbied in Frankfort. We lobbied in Washington to have laws passed to prevent the courts from ordering busing. Many influential people in Jefferson County and in the state of Kentucky belonged to Save Our Community Schools because we were not the marching, banner-waving type of protestor. We protested but we did it in a way that we felt would be more constructive than destructive. We never lost sight of what our organization stood for in that we were a pro-education, antibusing organization. We believed in education and we were not really opposed to blacks and whites going to school together; that was not the issue. We were not opposed to children riding a bus to school. We wanted to be certain that when those children stepped off of that bus that what they were going to receive at the end of that bus ride was a quality education.

I think the reason these people became so frustrated and so violent was the fact—and this is where I agreed with them a thousand percent—that a federal judge sat there and ordered someone in the school system to draw up a map and tell the parents in Jefferson County you will send your child to this school. You will send your child to that school. You're black so you have to go to this school. You're white so you have to go this school. We had to have x number of blacks, x number of whites and during this whole preparation not one word was mentioned about quality of education or what kind of education these children were going to receive.

Todd Hollenbach, white judge executive of Jefferson County (interview with Ethel White, 1988). In Kentucky, the county government is headed by a judge executive, an elected position roughly the equivalent to a mayor. Hollenbach uses his narrative to defend the actions of his administration and to explain the motives of the opposition.

The plan was to have the county keep order in the county and let the city handle the city. The city did not have jurisdiction in the county unless called upon. Then if there were problems in either area the state police would be the backup. I was criticized for the way we handled the riots. The county police handled them; I'll defend them to the day I die. The county police force is and was then recognized as one of the tops in the country. We were modern, we were proud, we were well trained. They said we weren't well equipped because we didn't go around looking like Hitler's Third Reich. I told these men, "You're going to be dealing with your neighbors. You're going to be dealing with people who had never so much as gotten a traffic ticket, but the federal courts are fooling with their kids! This is the way they perceive it. These are not criminal people out there, these are your neighbors!" Well, my county officers were being scorned, spit at, abused, and I didn't want another police force coming out there beating people, thrashing people, teargassing people, another force that didn't have to deal with these people and but for being called upon had no jurisdiction to. So I know there was some criticism at the time when the riots started in the county.

I don't know that anybody could have ever anticipated the magnitude of it, the scores of thousands of people who turned to the streets rioting. I think the socioeconomic background of the rioters is one where they resent being told what to do by the federal courts. They are very proud people, they're hardworking people. They're the element of society that rightly or wrongly feels that historically they've been put upon. I think that that became very obvious to the people of the southwest [part of the county], the burden that was being placed on their children. The working class of white people in the southwest where the majority of the riots were has a proud, fierce, independent history. They're conservative and they weren't going to have any federal court tell them and they weren't going to have any county judge and they weren't going to have anybody tell them what they were going to do with their children.

They weren't rioting against blacks or against whites, they were rioting against the federal courts and against this onerous ruling! But lo and behold it all happened. They rioted, far excessively over what I or anyone anticipated might have happened. I know we were criticized on many fronts for not exerting more force. One of my young troopers lost his eye, which was just absolutely tragic, but considering the magnitude of those riots it was almost miraculous that that was the only major injury with thousands, scores of thousands of people rioting, looting, burning.

Michael Gritton, white student (interview with David Cline, 2004). Gritton lived in the southwest county suburbs and attended Pleasure Ridge

Park High School. In his narrative he explains how his family reacted to the beginning of busing, emphasizing his own support and his father's opposition. His story indicates how some white families avoided participating in busing.

I have never argued with my mother and father about anything substantial in my whole life before or since the way we argued about that. I would have been about thirteen or fourteen—probably right at the age where you think you've got it all figured out—and I thought busing was completely and utterly right and just. The justice argument made a lot of sense to me. My father then and even now I think would say, "This was somebody telling me where to send my kids to school. I moved into this neighborhood. I knew where the school was. There's absolutely no reason for you to take my kid and make them go somewhere other than the neighborhood school." He claimed that it had nothing to do with race and I'm not sure that I believed him. I actually do believe him more now than I did then because I think his argument has held up a little better about that—that there was something that was going to be fundamentally lost in the undoing of the community school idea that I didn't acknowledge or understand when I was an eighth-grade brat.

My dad felt very, very strongly that he was defending a principle and he did not like that principle being violated by anything. My dad attended protests. He graduated from Valley High School, which is a little farther out toward the south on Dixie Highway. There were protests in front of Valley. My neighbor Ernie borrowed a baseball bat to take with him to one of those protests. I think we still have the bat somewhere with bumper stickers on it, just because later on we thought that was sort of an interesting thing to hold on to. So the way my dad experienced it, it was the government imposing a solution on him to solve someone else's problem and he couldn't figure out why that made sense. I think his argument was if the schools in the west end are bad, let's fix the west end schools. Let's not ruin our school. This is the only thing I can remember ever really disagreeing with my parents about on an important public policy issue that affected our life and decisions we were going to make. I can't ever remember before or since that we disagreed about anything with that much vehemence, with that much firmness, where we both were utterly convinced that we were right. It was very traumatic.

Here's what happened with my family: My sister and my cousin Dana, who lived right down the street, were in the seventh grade. The way Louisville bused white kids was by the alphabet of your last name, Gs would get bused in the second and seventh grade. So the very first year that busing was going to begin, my sister and my cousin Dana were slated to be bused. My mom and dad and my Uncle Danny and Aunt Suzie decided that Dana and Shelly would go to school down at this cabin we have on Rough River Lake, which is about an hour and twenty minutes from Louisville in Breckinridge County. They essentially attended school in Breckinridge County for their whole seventh-grade year.

They tried to get me to go down there. There was a boycott, so lots of white parents refused to send their kids. We held me out for a couple of days and then they talked me into going down to this place, so I went for a couple of days. I'd already missed a week of school and I remember being in this country school called Ben Johnson Elementary. In the classroom they had the sixth graders and the eighth graders in the same room. Again in a bratty eighth-grade way, I thought to myself, this is like being in Abe Lincoln's. I don't want to be in a one-room schoolhouse. So to my parents' credit, it was only after they sent me for a couple of days and I protested vehemently that this is going to ruin my life and ruin my education, that they cobbled together a solution instead where I stayed in Louisville. Two of the best teachers of my whole life I happened to have in my eighth grade year at PRP, so it was a fundamental break for me that I got to go there.

Bonita Emerick, white student (interview with Elizabeth Gritter, 2005). Emerick's parents opposed busing and kept her out of school as part of the antibusing boycott. Emerick's family had lived in the west end and in 1975 had only recently moved to a white neighborhood in the county. Here she tries to explain her parents' perspective and actions.

My cousin tried to get my parents to join with the KKK and play [music at] some rallies and for some reason my parents didn't want to be involved in that. This was actually a Bullitt County rally, which was going to be the KKK. They were going to garner all this support and make a plan to come into town and do something. Whenever they'd talk about such violence as blowing up buses and things like that, my parents didn't see that that would solve anything because some innocent children could be on those buses. My dad would stand up and say that he believed in everything the KKK stood for, but I think it was the fear of the violence or possibly the fear of being put in jail. I don't think he would be one to physically go up there, even though he would think it was neat that somebody had burned a cross in somebody's yard.

Once school started, my parents did ask me did I want to go to school, and of course if you ask a fourteen-year-old child if they want to go to school,

Antibusing rally with Klansmen, 1975. (Courtesy of the Louisville Defender *Collection, Special Collections, University of Louisville)*

your answer is no. So, they just didn't send me. My dad called it communism. They were moving in and trying to tell him what to do with his children. I think he saw it as much just fighting the system as fighting the blacks. Of course we thought that the blacks wanted this, wanted to come in and take over. My dad was angry. Judge James Gordon was the federal judge who ordered busing. My dad would call him a communist, and I think he would make comments that he wished somebody would kill him, as much or more than he talked about black people.

There was the one incident where the truant officer came to our house. My mom says to the officer, "I've been seeing on the news and in the paper that all the people that you've asked about sending their children to school, if it was for fear of the violence or if it was for fear of the black people, because you didn't want your children going to school with black people"— and excuse my language that I'm about to say—but my mom told the truant officer that day, I can still remember this, my mother says, "I'm here to tell you that I'm not sending my children to school because of damn niggers, monkeys, and apes." "We just moved out of that mess and I don't want my child to go back to that." So she says, "You can go tell Judge James Gordon and whoever else has sent you down here to all go screw yourselves." Except she didn't even say it that nicely.

My parents thought if enough people stuck together and held their kids out of school then they would have no choice but to see, well, this isn't working and there's not enough jails to hold everybody who's not sending their kids to school. My mom and dad became angry at her own brother, who chose to send his children. She got mad. She even told him—he was a World War II veteran—she said, "I always thought you were a brave man." She says, "But now I realize you only went to war because they told you you had to. You're not really brave at all." She was angry at him because he went ahead and sent his children to school.

Marcella Robinson, white school bus driver (interview with Ethel White, 1990). Robinson refers to her neighborhood of Fern Creek, a middle-class, primarily white suburb on the eastern fringe of Louisville in Jefferson County. She gives a dramatic account of the scene on the streets outside the schools in the south end of the county during the first days of busing, and makes some observations about community attitudes toward the court order.

The first day, as we went into the bus compounds, people were already gathering at the entrances. Protesters, for the most part protesters. They were loud. They were angry. There had been protestors for a few days in other areas already. They had put barricades up at the rear entrance to the compound where the buses left. We were given that morning a national guardsman to ride with us. The young gentleman that was with me was very, very young. I would guess he was twenty-one perhaps. Very, very nervous. These were his friends and neighbors. One of his first questions was what my route was going to be, and he was relieved because it wasn't anywhere near his home. I understood his feelings. I didn't want to be driving near my home either, because I was afraid I'd be facing angry neighbors.

As we started leaving the compound, one of the drivers had come back and said there was a blockade and she wouldn't go through it. We talked about it. One of the supervisors said we need to go on through if we can, try it. When we got up to the entrance, they had wooden sawhorses set up across the entrance. There were probably fifteen people, not any large group. They were angry. Some of them I recognized. They had very strong opinions. They felt like if we did not run the buses that busing wouldn't happen. As we came up, they banged on the sides of the buses with sticks and broomsticks, and some of them had bats, and they banged on the sides of buses and shouted at us. One lady in particular stood right in front of the bus behind the barricade. We drove probably two to three miles an hour until we just drove up over the barricades, and the lady kept backing away and backing away until she was out into the traffic. The barricades just went crunch, crunch, crunch. [Laughter] Those buses are large and heavy. It wouldn't do them any damage. More damage was being done by the bats and things on the side. They didn't break any of our windows, and actually, they didn't hit the bus with enough force to do any real denting or any damage. I think they were unsure themselves. They wanted us not to get out. They wanted to block us, but once they saw we were going to come on and that they really couldn't stand in front of that bus as long as it kept moving, they weren't willing to be run over. It was a bluff, and we called it, and we won.

After we got out of the compounds, our major concerns were parents that were at the bus stop. They wanted to know, "What are you seeing? What's happening?" We got that a lot. "Anybody bothering the bus? Anybody coming up to the bus?" The parents would be at the bus stops with their children, with strong holds on them, holding on, not real sure if they wanted to put them on but at the same time willing to give it a try. When I think back, I really admire the number of people who were willing to give it a try.

When we arrived at the schools, there were guards outside, and we took the children in. That afternoon was about the same. We had protesters along the way. I can't remember how many days there. It seemed like we went to school a couple days and had a weekend and then started up again. The first day we had problems, we had a lull, and we felt like, "Wow, this is good," and then it flared up again. Here in Fern Creek, there was opposition. More of it was downtown. They were in the mayor's office and in front of the schools. Over in the Okolona area, it lasted longer, and it was larger. Our buses, many of them were blocked in that area and couldn't get through. We had to turn around and go back, because it would be one thing to push aside one person in front of your bus, but twenty people—you can't do it. You can't be sure you might not get someone under your wheels. The buses would have to stop. So, there was a lot more problem on Preston Highway and around Southern High School. I talked with drivers to those schools who had come through it, and they were shaken. They were afraid. Many of them quit the first day. Many, many of our drivers quit those first days.

I don't think any of us felt real good about Judge Gordon. That's very frank. We didn't feel like that he was concerned about us as a community. We felt like he was going to make us be in compliance, whether or not our community needed it. You have to remember those of us in the east end really didn't have an idea of what was going on in some of the city schools, and we didn't feel like there was a need, educationally, to do this. I don't think we ever perceived ourselves as being a racially biased city. Here, at least in the east end, we've always had blacks that lived in our community and had no problems if they moved into our subdivisions. Usually, if they could afford to buy, because we're a little more expensive in this end of town, they probably were teachers or businessmen, professional people that we were happy to have. Maybe I should back up, I didn't believe then that the problem wasn't racial bias. I felt like that was a good deal of what we saw. Many of us that were involved in the school buses, we dealt with the black children, the black community more than a lot of people did. I think we lost perspective because of that. I think because we were losing some of our racial bias, we thought everyone was. That's why I think we had our heads stuck in the sand somewhat.

We woke up to that quickly. I was ashamed of my community. I will be honest with you. I think actually the protests did it for me more than everything as far as waking me up, because as I said, I was ashamed of the actions of the white community. I felt like, "What are you afraid of? What are these people going to hurt?" They were not protesting sending their children to the west end. They were protesting the blacks coming out here. A lot of them did have problems with their children being bused, and yes, I do too. I did then, and I do now. I think that it's a major problem for children to get up at the hour they get up and spend an hour on a bus to go across town when there's a school right here in the neighborhood. But, at the same time, I have to be honest enough to tell you that there's an awful lot of this community that chooses to do that, because they want a special program across town. They don't mind when it's something they want. So, it kind of makes their complaint invalid when they say, "I don't want my child on a bus for an hour." If they want a special program, they put them on there for an hour.

Ken Miller, white national guardsman (interview with Elizabeth Gritter and Timothy P. McCarthy, 2004). Because of the violence against the buses, local officials requested that national guardsmen ride on them as protection. Miller describes the atmosphere on one of those buses as it carried black students from the west end to a formerly white middle school in the south end of the county, in an area of some of the largest antibusing demonstrations.

As I got in the bus one morning in western Louisville—just typical kids in a school bus, and maybe a little more noise than normal because of the nervous energy. But then as we got closer to Jesse Stuart School it got dead quiet in that bus. It was like we had gone into Vietnam or something. I thought, "What in the world?" The kids on this bus are American citizens and this is their America too. We weren't wanted there. It was just an awkward feeling. I never thought I would feel something like that. I felt because of the green uniform and because I represented authority that for just a second green was black. I had maybe just a sliver of what it feels to be black in America. I mean I could go home and take the uniform off, and I could blend into that crowd and probably nobody would know who I was. But for a while I couldn't blend into that crowd and I sensed my empathy with the kids in the bus. They didn't want any of us here.

Of course, I had a loaded pistol. The parents were counting on us. You know, if my time rolled around, I think I could chamber a round in [and be ready to fire] that pistol. "What do you do if somebody comes out of the woodwork and challenges the driver?" We gassed up one day. We pulled into a gas station, and this bus driver lady always got her gasoline at that particular station. The man came up to the door, she pulled the thing, and the doors opened up. He said, "I can't help you today. You're going to have to leave." This is where she always fueled up. What was the problem? He said, "I'm being watched." She said, "Watched by who?" He had received a letter that day from the Ku Klux Klan and that they would not be real happy if he was providing gas for Jefferson County school buses. He said, "I'm being watched and you'll just have to go on." Do I chamber a round? Do I faint? I felt kind of like Barney [Fife] with one bullet in my pocket. I just looked at him and looked at her and nothing happened.[13] We got gas some place and the storm blew over.

Charles Summers, white principal at Fairdale High School (interview with Elizabeth Gritter, 2005). Fairdale High School, a formerly white school in the south end of the county, experienced some of the most volatile antibusing demonstrations. Summers describes the turmoil inside the schools and conflict over suspensions, for which he blamed the black students who were bused in from the west end. Summers mentions Charles Elliott, who was a prominent African American minister and civil rights leader in the community.

We had many meetings that summer with specialists telling us what to expect. They all kept telling me that Fairdale was going to be a hotbed and I believed them. It got pretty nasty in my area. Most of the people are blue-collar workers in Fairdale, very few professional people. A lot of them had moved out of the west end of Louisville to Fairdale to get away from blacks and then here they send them out there. The service station close to school, where I did business, they wouldn't sell me gas. They wouldn't service my car. I had to go someplace else, just like I had caused it. Some of my best friends turned against me. They wouldn't go to ball games. They wouldn't do anything with the school. They just quit. Thank God it's better now. But the first two or three years, well, that's one reason I got out when I did. I was only fifty-four when I retired. I would have stayed on to at least sixty, but after I got my thirty years in I left. It wasn't like running a school. It was like being a cop, breaking up fights and taking knives off of people, and it wasn't worth it. So I got out when I could. It was pretty ugly. I used to get up in the morning and my stomach would just start turning. I said, "This isn't good. I keep on, I'll have an ulcer." So I had to have three years of it before I could retire. I was in it three years.

We had a call one morning, one of the buses was having a problem coming from the west end down here. Something had riled them up on that bus, and they came in the building just tearing up jack. I got the assistant principal. We went down there and got them back on the bus, and I said, "Get in here and get every one of their names. We're going to suspend every one of them." Well, they were giving us John Doe and Mickey Mouse and everything else. We wrote up what suspensions we could, but it didn't do any good. The next day I had Charles Elliott, he was a reverend, down here. He came out there and said, "If we didn't reinstate those students . . ." and all. I had somebody from the board come out and meet with me and we tried to explain to him why we had to have some order. You couldn't let them just take over the school. Then, we had a big meeting on that. The parents came out there and we talked, and we finally got it settled and I let them come on back to school.

I'd say even the second year it got better. You know the juniors, they became seniors, and they'd been there a year, and they were beginning to settle in. The ones that didn't want to go to school were sort of weeded out; they quit. The second year wasn't bad at all, and of course the third year, the last year I was there, we had very few problems. We could have pep rallies and you could have somebody come in as a speaker and not be embarrassed. So it took three years to get better. It gradually got better, a lot better. But the first year, a nightmare. It drove me out early.

John Whiting, African American principal at Shawnee High School (interview with Tracy E. K'Meyer, 2011). Whiting describes the busing of students from Shawnee to Fairdale and Valley High, another formerly white south county school and the site of antibusing demonstrations. Students from the west end neighborhood near Shawnee met at that school to get on buses that drove south together to the county schools.

I didn't go to Vietnam, but my Vietnam was busing. I remember the first day getting thirty-three busloads of black children together in the gym and telling them how much we thought of them and they had a lot to live up to and trying to pump them up. Then at the end of the school day I had the National Guard there with me. I remember it was such a beautiful day. As I listened to the walkie-talkies they were catching hell at these other places, Valley and Fairdale. So when I counted the buses coming in, I think about twenty-three of them got out of the county neighborhoods without any problems. Then the National Guard people were in there with me with their walkie-talkies and six buses were caught behind the lines at Fairdale. So we kept waiting. Then three behind the lines at Valley. To have those buses come in with windows broken out, kids screaming and hollering, that was really, really devastating to see the kids coming in like that. I had talked to the deputy superintendent, I got him to ride the bus with the kids. He was so angry with me. He got off the bus and said, "I don't blame these kids for arming themselves," was what his words were. That's how much of a shock it was.

Support for Busing and Desegregation

In the following narratives speakers tell about the steps they took to promote integration or to help implement it smoothly and safely, from joining the lawsuits to working in the community and in the schools. In their comments some of the narrators indicate the reasons they supported busing or why they worked so hard to see it succeed. They also list some of the measures taken to try to prepare parents, to keep calm and promote understanding, and to stand up for the students. Most of this activity went unheralded at the time; the quiet, behind-the-scenes efforts were overshadowed by the more dramatic and attention-getting violence of the opposition. Thus these oral histories excavate an almost forgotten story that contrasts to the scholarly and public consensus of overwhelming white opposition to busing.

Suzy Post, white mother and civil rights activist (interview with Timothy P. McCarthy, 2004). Post was a leader in the Kentucky Civil Liberties

Union and one of the plaintiffs in the case that led to desegregating the city and county schools. Here she explains her reasons for joining the suit.

It's unusual to find white plaintiffs. It was just like mother's milk to me. We needed white people who had children in school and I had four in school at that time. So, I didn't think twice about it. I didn't think it was brave. I didn't think anything other than it was an extension of my belief system. There were two reasons for me to attempt to integrate the schools racially. One was it would be a much more positive experience for our children to learn to interact with different cultures from a young age than it was going to be when they got out there in the real world and didn't know how to do that. So that, for me, would be a real plus. The other thing was that segregated schools had, generally speaking, fewer resources available to them than white schools, and that was I think a big piece of it for some of the black parents at the time. For example, Central High School was the center for the black educational scene in Louisville. At the time we filed the lawsuit Central High School had windows out. The playground was a wreck. This is a high school. The auditorium had seats missing. As soon as Judge Gordon announced that the schools were going to integrate via busing in September '75, all of a sudden Central High School was transformed. They put in trees. All the windows were fixed. They had new seats in the auditorium, magic. So those were the two reasons. Then there's the other moral thing, which you can't quantify, about continuing to live as a divided society, which I think is inherently destructive to whites and blacks and Asians and homosexuals and anybody. It's sick.

Sherry Jelsma, white parent (interview with Ethel White, 1988). Jelsma started as a PTA volunteer in her child's school. She attended a workshop about the merger and then became a human relations volunteer in the schools. She describes some of the organizing aimed at making busing and desegregation work peacefully. Kammerer was a formerly white school in the county; Coleridge-Taylor was a formerly majority-black school in the west end.

In summer 1975 there was a workshop downtown that leaders in the various schools attended to work on thinking about the merger and desegregation, because we knew that eventually we would be having a desegregation plan.

That was in a department called human relations which had been fairly recently set up. We worked all day at that workshop. As we were in the workshop we found we would have six weeks for the order to be put into place.
So from that time all of us that were there became heavily involved. Human
relations chairmen is what most of us became.

We did all these things. We tried to get PTA volunteers at every school to
meet the buses. Of course, when school actually opened in September we
had to have the National Guard on the buses with guns and we had helicop-
ters following the buses downtown. It was not cookies and milk. It was a little worse than that. We set up a lot of workshops. We did a lot of talking, and
there was a core developed of people that worked this thing right through.
We involved groups; I think that was a good thing. It was interesting to see
which groups would come forward and which groups chose to remain in the
background and didn't want to get involved with a very messy and volatile
situation. The Junior League came forward as a very stabilizing group with
volunteers that were intelligent and caring. The League of Women Voters
got involved and was helpful but was more on a legal end of it, prepping
for more reform, a lobbying type of situation. The Council of Jewish Women
helped. Those are the three women's groups that were very involved. The
city and county government became involved more in terms of providing a
base or a setting for a discussion, calling in what they would call key community leaders and listening to them or giving them a plan, getting reaction
to it. But those people who were really in the trenches were the PTA and the
women's groups around town.

My son was assigned to Kammerer Middle School and I had planned to
be a human relations chairman there. But when the busing plan came out
he was to be bused to Coleridge-Taylor School in downtown Louisville. So I
made a switch and went there. The first thing I noticed was that there were
no books in the library; there was nothing. There were empty shelves. My
love was the library, so that was the first thing I did was get some books.
That involved literally taking a car and going around to people's houses
and getting books and magazines, National Geographic, loading them up in
the car and taking them back to Coleridge-Taylor and getting the librarian
to catalog them. It was that kind of basic stuff that had to be done as well
as the organizing and the reaching out and identifying the people, the parents that went to the school. We wanted to have a meeting at Kammerer of
all the people who were going to Coleridge-Taylor and we wanted to have
the principal of Coleridge-Taylor come to Kammerer and talk. The principal happened to be black. There was resistance to having that occur, a lot
of resistance! We finally were able to achieve that. But to get the white

people to go downtown to these schools was an enormous effort. And the black people didn't want to come out here! Everybody was terrified!

Georgia Eugene, African American mother, PTA volunteer, and community activist (interview with David Cline, 2005). At the time of the desegregation court case she worked as a staff person in the city schools. Before the lawsuits she was not in favor of merging or desegregating the city and county schools, but after the court order she became part of a team of women running a rumor-control hotline.

Now in the city school system where I was working, we knew that the thing was in court, so we were making plans. I'm sure they were making plans in the county too, but we were making plans based on what if you have to do this. Sarah Joe Hooper, who was over multicultural education in the city, had written a plan for Operation Hotline and talked about opening up a rumor-control network. We had just completed the document when the writ of mandamus came in. On that day I was on my way down the hall, and ran into June Key, who was also on her way down the hall because we had heard the same information. I told June, I think we needed to open the hotline that day because the rumors were going to start the moment the decision got out. So that night, Louis Williams and I stayed and operated the hotline.

I coordinated the hotline, June and I together. Our role together was to keep the volunteers flowing because we stayed open all kinds of hours. It was crazy. I remember, [laughs] and I forget which one of the white ladies was on there, and she got off the phone and she said, "I know who the niggers are, but who are the yaps?" I said, "You." [Laughter] She said, "Who are the honkies?" I said, "You." [Laughter] She said, "I have never heard those terms in my life!" I had to commend her because she stayed on the phone. A lot of the calls really were trying to get the accurate information. "I really want to know what's going on!" But we got a lot of bomb threats, I mean everything, you name it; it was just open season.

June Key, white mother and PTA volunteer (interview with Ethel White, 1988). Key became a member of the Community Consensus Committee, dedicated to bringing about peaceful compliance with desegregation and busing. She shares an insider's view of those efforts and expresses her pride in the people who participated.

Prior to the merger we worked with a lot of people in our city schools and with a joint committee of county parents. This group of parents, PTA leaders from the county and a group of leaders from the city, began to work together on how can we, as the responsible parent organization, help bring about a smooth merger and, especially with a desegregation plan, smooth opening and continuous school in the best interest of the children? That's really what that group was all about. They just wanted things the best and safest for the children.

The city-county government had a committee called the Community Consensus Committee. If I remember correctly, there were twenty-one citizens from Louisville and Jefferson County along with the county judge and the mayor. I happened to be chosen to be a member of that group. The committee was established to help bring businesses, school people, ministers, representatives from different target groups together to see what role they could play in helping for a smooth transition. We had many, many workshops. We'd issue invitations to certain community leaders who seemed to be those that others perceived as knowing what was going on. We wanted those people to come in so we could tell them facts rather than fiction. So a lot of it was first based on community leaders, then it was parents who we knew were going to cause problems. They were telling everybody at school they were going to. We didn't bring just the nice people who wanted to work with us. We brought the people who didn't feel like they could cooperate. We had to work with the whole spectrum from the person who thought they were going to lie down in front of the bus and not let it roll to the person that said we should have done this ten years ago. You had to get people talking to each other! That's the only way to solve problems.

We had to try to get people to understand that the bottom line was, one, we were going to be under a court order. So it wasn't a choice of whether we want to do this or not; whether it's right or wrong we were going to be under a court order. Number two, we had to open school by state law. Number three, we had to open it as safely as possible first and then hope that learning and teaching could go on as soon as the atmosphere was calm. And we were going to be one school system; that was not going to be reversible. So we had to work toward answers. Thank God an awful lot of people put their shoulder to that and worked on answers.

Anne Braden, white civil rights activist (interview with Tracy E. K'Meyer, 2001). In 1975, Braden was a leader of the Kentucky Alliance, a relatively new civil rights organization. During the busing crisis she helped organize Progress in Education (PIE) to rally a pro-integrationist and antiracist response to the antibusing movement.

You began having all this opposition and you were literally having antibusing rallies of ten thousand people. We had over a weekend to work on getting people together for the first meeting we had that formed PIE. Not all the antibusing rallies were Klan rallies, but it was having big rallies for the first time in years! We hadn't heard of them in a long time around here, but they were very visible. There were these other people that were just antibusing, including so many of the unions, the GE [General Electric] local, and all that. I think there hadn't been violence until the buses started rolling, so it must have been Thursday or Friday that school started. They were throwing rocks at the buses, they turned over some buses. There was a violent attack.

We had over a weekend to work and we figured that somebody needed to get people together, white people especially, to support busing and to oppose the hysteria that was building up, because it was getting very hysterical. They were putting pressure on merchants to put up no busing signs in their window and threatening them if they didn't, and people were scared not to. It was that kind of hysteria all over town and certainly out in the county. The Kentucky Alliance was a pretty viable organization in a way because we had lists of people to call. There were about three or four of us, as I recall, got on the phone that weekend and just called everybody we could think of. It was mostly Alliance people. We called people to come to a meeting at the [First] Unitarian Church to talk about what we could do to counter the hysteria. There must have been about a hundred people. It was mostly white. They decided to form an organization that night and set up committees to get public expression supporting busing to oppose the violence, a letter-writing committee to get letters in the paper to organize support for the merchants that may not want to put up an antibusing sign. They decided to call this Progress in Education because they wanted to deal with education and not have the schools torn apart. It wasn't that many people, when you think about the ten thousand people opposed. But at least it was a little dissenting voice.

In the meantime, the United Black Protective Parents formed and we began to meet those people. Both of the organizations went on really pretty much to the end of the seventies, because after things quieted down we were trying to deal with racism in the schools and the suspensions and all the stuff that was happening. We were constantly out at the school board raising [deleted from transcript] with them about something. That first fall, I

Pro-busing demonstration, 1975. (Courtesy of the Louisville Defender *Collection, Special Collections, University of Louisville)*

don't know how much influence it had, but at least a lot of people knew we were there. Somebody's got to raise a voice so other people have a place to go, and I think PIE played that role.

Benetha Ellis, African American mother, leader of United Black Protective Parents (interview with David Cline, 2004). United Black Protective Parents visited the schools in the county to monitor the treatment of black students, meet with principals, and make a counterdemonstration to the antibusers.

We started organizing because the kids that were going to high school, they were the ones that was getting the things thrown at the bus, the buses were being rocked, kids were called all kinds of names, fighting in the halls, suspensions, expulsions; everything just skyrocketed in high school. So us parents got together and said, "Now, wait a minute, something has to be done." Because there wasn't anyone doing anything, anybody in authority, no organization. I mean, no NAACP, no Urban League, no one was doing anything. The NAACP president told me he wasn't going to fight no Klan. We had told him we weren't asking him to fight no Klan. We just asked him what was he going to do about the kids being mistreated. So they didn't do anything. They weren't going to do anything and that's when we said, "Well, we'll just have to do it ourselves."

The school system called a meeting, I think, over at Park DuValle. We had about two hundred parents at that meeting. After the meeting, you know how you hang around? We decided there was nothing going to happen in the school system. That's when we knew we had to do something. That's when we formed the United Black Protective Parents. That's when we started going to the schools. Any school that a parent wanted us to go to we would go. That's when we really saw actually what was going on. They were suspending our kids daily. The teachers, the principals, they didn't know how to deal with our kids, so they would just throw them out of school. We would go in with the parents and talk to the principals and the administrators and let them know, "Look, you're not doing this right. You're not dealing with that kid. Our kids are not the type of kids that are going to stand up and be called all kinds of names and not fight back." Right or wrong is indifferent, that's just the way they are. I remember a group of us parents going to Pleasure Ridge Park and there was this horde of people around the buses. They were throwing everything on the buses. My kids had no one to protect them. So we started going out there and confronting those white parents, children, and teachers to make sure that our kids had some support out there. Then we started attending all school board meetings. Whether it was out there, or wherever it was, we would go.

We have actually come face to face with the Klan. They were demonstrating at the school board. They would be out Dixie. We would just go and we'd confront them. It wasn't very nice, but we confronted them. We didn't ask for it, we didn't know anything about it. But our kids were out there and we had to deal with it. They looked just like the typical parent, but the language and the things that they said to us—of course, we weren't polite either. So it was just verbal attacks back and forth, back and forth. I remember one time we went and it was the ladies that went, and we were surrounded by the Klan. We had to call in Reverend [Charles] Elliott and all of them to help us get out of there. It may have been about twenty of us and about fifty of them. But they had men and women as well and most of ours at that time were women.

We were fighting for our children to be the best they could be. That was our main objective. We were angry because we didn't ask for it. It was unfair to our children. We had to protect our children any way we could, and that's what we did. Somebody had to do it and it had to be us.

Busing's Impact inside the Schools

This final section contains narratives from teachers and students describing the situation inside the schools. Their accounts present a nuanced picture of the impact of busing on students and teachers. They remember the ways they experienced the opposition and its results, including teaching to empty classrooms and confronting violence and hostility. But they also talk about access to resources and the ways people changed and grew. Most interestingly, these narratives demonstrate that people do not see their own lives in starkly dichotomous terms; rather, they see both the good and the bad in their own experience. These observations thus provide a basis for a more balanced long-term assessment of the consequences of desegregation.

Laura Kirchner, white elementary teacher (interview with Elizabeth Gritter, 2004). Kirchner was a teacher in a low-income black school in the inner city before the merger. She describes the difficulties caused by the white student boycott of that school during the first year of busing, as well as the tensions sparked by the transfer of white county teachers into city schools.

When we started school in fall 1975, we had very few white kids that showed up. It was Christmas and we were still having things like where the year before I had forty-five kids in my room, I might have eight. By this time they were going after the families and bringing judgments against them to force them to put their kids in school. When that started happening, we started picking up more white kids. Then you were constantly catching a kid up. You would pick them up one at a time or two would show up, so you were constantly backpedaling. You're going to be held accountable for a year's worth of learning. Those parents didn't want to hear their kid's going to be held back because they missed three-fourths of a year of school. I had a white mother that was just mean as a snake and she didn't want us ever to correct her child. I had a couple of mothers come in and tell me, "If you try to retain my child, I'm going to get even with you," and this type of stuff. They expected their child to pass even though they didn't come in till January, and we did. We pretty much moved kids on.

Before merger, when I was in a former black school, we had nothing. With the poverty of the city school system, there was nothing and we were forty-five kids to a room. We had no PE, music, art teachers. Nothing existed. Your music was when you sang a song. They brought these white teachers in [from the county], well, they thought we were holding out on them on supplies and things and we only had one little box of chalk among us and didn't have a lot of textbooks, didn't have basic necessities. We didn't have new maps. So all of that had to be equalized between the city and county because now we're one system. Things started getting better, but that first year was bumpy. We had a lot of complaints. The county teachers stayed together and they were sure that we white teachers that had been in the city schools before gave them the worst kids and this kind of stuff. I mean nobody trusted anybody. They were sure we were holding out because we had to have more than this.

The white parents were being so nasty. You had to protect those little white kids so carefully because if anything happened that would have been blown up ten miles. So I was watching them, but I didn't want my black kids getting abused. It was a hard year. You were constantly playing Solomon and trying to keep everybody watched and everybody safe. I'll never forget I had one little boy, he was a little white boy. He got sick. We had taken his temperature and it was like a 104. We didn't have a sick room. I'd found a cot to put him down on, called his mother. She said, "He's your responsibility." There was many a time they'd miss their buses and things. The parents wouldn't come and we'd have to take them home, and things like this. PTA was hard to come by. They didn't want to do anything, not in the city schools. The white kids were bused two years, so the parents weren't going to do anything in these black schools. They're just going to put in their time and then they'll go and work at their home schools. It took a while to win that over. First year was rough.

Clint Lovely, African American teacher and football coach at Central High School (interview with Elizabeth Gritter, 2005). With busing, Central changed from an almost completely black student body to a majority-white student body. At the same time, many of the black teachers were transferred to the county to integrate those faculties. Lovely expresses how the merger and busing affected him and hints at his approach to teaching in the newly integrated environment.

When I heard we would be undergoing desegregation I had a lot of anxiety, believe me. A lot of anxiety because everything I had done had been with black people; I had not really done a lot with white people. I did take classes with white people at Kentucky State, but they were in the minority. [Laughs] To be scrutinized as a teacher teaching whites—I said, "Do I teach them the same way that I do black students?" So there was a lot of anxiety, on both sides, I would think. Because they didn't know what to expect and we didn't know what to expect. Let me back up: the first anxiety was merger. That was the first stressful moment that we had, because we were going to be taken over by the county. The county didn't have a lot of black people in it, all the black people were here. There were a few schools in the county—Thomas Jefferson, Seneca—that had some brothers, but the vast majority of the blacks, 90 percent were in Louisville public schools. We just didn't know what to think, we were really apprehensive. There was some fear that we would lose jobs, we just didn't know.

When we did merge it came out OK. We actually got a little salary increase. They did move us around to different schools. Where Central was 70 percent black teaching wise, it all of a sudden became 80 percent white teachers and 20 percent black teachers. It happened over night—just boom, there it was. The teachers at Central had to integrate the staffs at other public high schools because there were not enough black teachers at those schools at that time. So they had to move them around with the kids. Now, none of the teachers lost jobs. None of them actually lost jobs; we were just moved from school to school. In fact we got a raise. We liked that; that helped a lot. That helped cushion that blow, but we kind of lost empowerment. We didn't have the power that we once had when we were with the city system. It was almost like a new set of rules—their rules—and we had to play by them.

I was a PE teacher and I just decided I was going to teach PE the way I teach PE. Quite frankly, I got along very well with my classes. In health class while we were talking about life skills, we got to talking about integration and some of my white kids were very bigoted. Some said they wouldn't want to live in a black neighborhood, "But Coach Lovely, you are different. You can live in my neighborhood because you are different." That struck me as being odd. Why am I different? I said, "No, I am not different. What has happened is that you have learned about me. Since you have been around me you realized that I am OK." I don't know whether it was because I was a professional and they saw me in a different light. But we talked about that extensively. In fact, the rest of my lesson was on that that day.

Ken Rosenbaum, white teacher, curriculum coordinator, and president of the newly merged teachers' union (interview with Elizabeth Gritter, 2004). Rosenbaum worked at Highland Middle School, a primarily white school in the city. Because of his position he had to respond to incidents of resistance by white teachers.

I remember we had black teachers in the city who went to the county and had to face their colleagues saying, "Oh, here's one of these black teachers who probably doesn't even have a degree and they're just here because they're black." We had that. We had white teachers who came from the county into the city system who'd never seen a black child. At that point in my career I was no longer a classroom teacher, I was what was called curriculum coordinator. And let me describe a funny situation. A white county teacher had been on medical leave during the whole busing desegregation thing. She came back and came to my school. She has extreme discipline problems. So I call her to my office and say to her, "Marge, what's going on?" And she said, "Well, it's not my fault. You see, they don't know how to read and they use foul language and they sit in the back of the room in a group and they don't listen to what I have to say." And I said to her, "I'm really confused. Who's they?" And she says, "Oh, you know." I said, "No, I don't know. You have to tell me." She says, "Well, I can't." "What do you mean?" "You know." I said, "No, I do not know. You must tell me." Big tears in her eyes and she said, "Well, it's the black kids. They don't know how to read. They act like fools. They don't bring their books. They sit in the back of the room." And I responded, "Well, that's because you let them. And you know what, this is a middle school and if you let any middle school kid do this they will." Her response to that is that she went to the library and said, "How well do you know that Ken Rosenbaum?" She said, "I think he has black blood." [Laughter] See, she could not comprehend that anyone, unless I was a black person or had black blood, could think these black kids could perform. Isn't that sad? I wonder how many Marges we have out there.

Dan Withers, African American teacher (interview with David Cline, 2004). At the start of busing, Withers was transferred to Pleasure Ridge Park (PRP), a white school in the south end of the county, to integrate that staff. He tells of the reception he encountered there.

There's a lot of war stories at several different high schools, especially out in the county. The PRP transition, it was pretty good, it was pretty smooth. There were a few problems. I think the one that struck me the most is when I first drove through the entrance at PRP. Like in many other high schools, there was a lot of adults standing there, white men and women. They were holding bats and bricks and I said, "Oh, my goodness. What's going on here?" I was driving an MG Midget at the time, a convertible, and I said, "This doesn't look good." But I drove through and nothing ever happened to me. At that particular site, PRP, the buses were not rocked. Our buses were not hit by bats. They were just standing there, but it was rather intimidating to drive through, initially. Then after a while, they stopped coming.

Inside the building, it was pretty cordial. The transition again was good. I don't know of any black student who got harassed. I was one of the few black male teachers. I know there were several parents who said, "Mr. Withers is the one that you go to if you need help." So I would have kids who came to me. But there was never anything they came to me about that was really, really serious, like being stalked or intimidated or something like that. It was just the parents advised them that Mr. Withers is a person that you need to go to. So it gave me the opportunity to form a lot of relationships with the young black kids. I enjoyed that part of it. Basically, I was telling them it's a challenge: "Your mother and father didn't raise quitters. You find out what this teacher's expectations are and then you meet those expectations. You don't have to like him or her. He doesn't have to like you. It's a matter of you doing what's required, just like everybody else." This is the way I would counsel students. There were teachers who obviously didn't agree with busing, didn't agree with having the larger number of black students in their building. But there were other teachers who were quite inviting, accepting of the diversity.

There was this one situation with white students who were going to walk out in protest because of busing, and the principal was out of the building at a meeting when it initially was supposed to happen. The assistant principal got on the speakers and in a rather weak tone said that he understood their feelings and why they felt this way about busing. His announcement was more or less in support: if you walk out, it's OK. We're not condoning it, but it's OK. What I really respected about the principal when he came back, he got on the intercom and he was very strong and in a strong voice: "If you walk out of this building, there will be a suspension and I will schedule appointments to get back into this school in such a way that it will be ten days before you get back. You can walk out if you want to, but you will be suspended." That nipped it in the bud and stopped it right there, so there wasn't a walkout. So I appreciated the principal for taking a strong stand. I don't know what his views on busing were—didn't matter. He said, "The law is systems will be desegregated and the busing is the way we're doing it. If you walk out, then this is the consequence."

I felt welcomed by the principal. There wasn't any big transition where I was introduced to the faculty. Basically, we formed relationships on a one-by-one basis. There were some teachers who you'd speak to in the hallway and they would turn their nose up. So you just learned those individuals and I would stop speaking to those folks. But there were other people who would come to me and be quite open and quite friendly and quite inviting. So I developed relationships at PRP, but it was done on an individual basis, not the whole staff.

There were parents that would resist. I had a parent who called me one morning and was complaining because I assigned his daughter a seat adjacent to a black boy. So he called complaining and I said, "I sat her in the front because she was talking. I wanted her to be away from the crowd." "But she's next to a black kid." I said, "What difference does that make? First place, I'm in the room with her, so I don't think anything is going to happen." I had to tell him, "I'm black too, so what difference does it make if she's sitting next to a black kid? I don't understand what the problem is." Well, then he ended up calling me a racist. I said, "I don't understand. I don't have a problem with her sitting next to a black kid, but apparently you do. So I'm not sure who's a racist here."

Frances Bloom, white teacher (interview with Elizabeth Gritter, 2005). Bloom was transferred from a black elementary school in the west end to a formerly white county school in the south end. Bloom refers to the Cotter and DuValle neighborhoods. Cotter Homes was a large public housing complex in the Park DuValle section of the west end.

I was a white teacher leaving a black school and going out to a white community, but it wasn't my choice. We were pretty much sent by the board, and we were told where to go. I didn't have enough seniority to make any choices. I was a little concerned about going out to Valley Station area simply from the reputation, and I wasn't familiar with the area. I can remember conversations with some of the white county teachers when I just thought, "You've been teaching twenty years, and you're asking a question like this?" I was sitting at lunch and this teacher was talking about one of the black kids having taken off their shoes and wanted to know how she should handle that, because she'd never taught black kids. I said, "What would you tell a white kid?" "Well, I'd tell them, but she's a—." "Tell the black kid to put the shoes on. Same thing." I remember thinking, what an idiotic question. That you would think you'd have to treat a black child differently from a white child just because the skin color's different. I don't think that's what parents wanted.

There were questions about, "Well, how do you talk to the parents?" I said, "The same way you talk to any other parent." There was a couple times when we would either send a school bus down to the neighborhood where the black kids were bused from, or go down there if we needed conferences with parents, or we'd go down in a car after school. But a lot of teachers, especially the older white teachers that were out there, were very unwilling to go to the Cotter and DuValle neighborhoods to conference with a parent. They found ways to get out of it. I went a few times. A lot of times they would handle it over the phone. I think that's kind of different; I think face to face really works. Parents want to meet the teachers and get the sense of the classroom and the atmosphere in the room, and what's going on, and how you're going to treat their child. I think most parents—I don't think it's a racial thing at all—want you to treat their child with respect, teach their child at their level, and move them on, give them a little progress.

I think most of the faculties, there was some resistance to the change, but I think everybody recognized that we were there to do a job and our job was to teach kids, and that it didn't really matter which kids you were teaching. One principal said, "You get what you get. These are the kids you're going to work with and you give them your best." I think that was an attitude that most teachers had. I think there were some older white women, who were nearing retirement who just really had a difficult time and I think that might have helped them to move on into retirement. But I think they just couldn't make that change. I think most teachers are in it because they enjoy teaching, and after a while, you don't really look at the color of somebody's skin. Once that first year of busing was over, basically it took a few months initially for teachers to get over the fears and the changes and like and realize that kids are kids. They're going to do the dumb things that kids do. You don't treat children differently based on race. I think that came pretty quickly for most people.

Sandra Wainwright, African American teacher (interview with Tracy E. K'Meyer, 2000). Wainright taught at King Elementary in the west end. When busing started she was transferred to Great House Elementary School in the east end of the county. She tells how she got the news and her reaction to the transfer.

1975. That's when they decided they were going to do busing. I thought, "Well, I hope they don't call me [to be transferred]." They were sending letters home with our new teaching assignment. I told the babysitter who was watching my children that day, "Don't open it but accept it and I'll call you." Lunchtime came and I called home and said, "Is my letter there?" My babysitter said yes. She opened up and said, "You have been assigned to Great

House Elementary School." I said, "Where is that?" Way out in St. Matthews. I started crying. Several teachers had called home and found out what they had. They transferred almost everybody out of King School. I went home and I told my son, "I don't even know where this school is. I don't want to leave." I mean, I was screwed up. I looked at that big old school and I said, "I don't even like that school. I don't want to go." But something on the inside said, "Yes, you do. You have to go."

Many a morning when they were saying, "I pledge allegiance to the flag of the United States of America, and to the republic for which it stands, one nation, under God, indivisible, with liberty and justice for all"—I wouldn't say those words. It took a long time. Some little boy went up to me and said, "You look like my momma's maid." I said, "Let me tell you, son, I might look like your momma's maid but I'm your teacher. You give me respect and I'll give me respect. But don't you forget who I am." I never had trouble out of that little fella anymore. You look like my maid!

Dawne Gee, African American student (interview with Elizabeth Gritter, 2004). Gee's family lived in a white neighborhood of the county and she would have attended Pleasure Ridge Park High even without the court order. Thus, although she took a bus to get to school, she distinguishes herself from the students bused in from the west end. She refers to TARC buses, which were the city's public transportation buses.

One day I missed my bus, and there were still some other African American students out there too. I don't know if they missed their bus or what happened. We were all standing out there just kind of talking and goofing off. There was a group of white students out there, and they had sticks and chains and they were screaming, "Niggers go home." I thought, "I am home. Hey, wait a minute." So they start chasing us. Well, we ran for the TARC [Transit Authority of River City] bus. They caught a couple of kids and they beat them. Just beat them. So we ran until we could stop the TARC bus. We were beating on the side of the TARC bus screaming, "Hey stop!," because he wasn't at a stop. This guy was kind enough to stop. We jumped on the TARC bus, and I had never ridden a TARC bus before. So I rode the TARC bus home, and when I got home, I called my mom. I was crying so hard she had no idea what I was talking about. Probably thought I was severely harmed, but I wasn't. Mentally maybe. It was just traumatic, traumatic.

We had KKK in our school. For Halloween, they wore their KKK outfits. It's the first time I ever realized they're not sheets. They're uniforms. They're tailored. They have zippers in them. They have hems. I thought they were sheets with little holes cut out, and they are tailored uniforms. One of the guys called one of the football players "nigger," and he hit this guy. The black player hit the guy in the KKK uniform in the nose. That sheet just bled. You could see red all through that sheet. That was on Halloween. They shouldn't have worn those uniforms, though. That was not good.

Violent incidents that first year were continuous; they were daily, the first year. You didn't know when they were going to happen. Any time of day. After school you were really very careful. Get on your bus and get out quick. They happened all the time. The second year it was a little better, but not by much. The third year it was better and you saw people trying to make an effort to make it better. I decided to go out for cheerleading. They hadn't had any black cheerleaders. So I thought, "Well, let's shake the tree a little bit." Well, it wasn't so bad. I did it. I made the team. One of the football players spit on me, though. I thought, "Wait a minute. You're on my team." He spit on me, but I made it.

I felt bad for a lot of the African American students because there were so many neat things to do at Pleasure Ridge Park. Now I got to do them because I didn't live that far. I ran track. I was in drama. I did choir. I did Spanish club. I did all these different things. A lot of the other students they can't do that. How are they going to get home? They didn't always have buses for them to get home. TARC in that area at the time did not always run right or did not always get them to where they needed to go. So here you wanted to become part of something. Number one, a lot of the people don't want you there anyway because you're black. So that's one strike against you. Number two, how are you going to do it because it's twenty miles away from where you live? So that's another strike against you. You feel uncomfortable anyway because you don't know what these things—because it was never at your school anyway. Heck, you didn't even have books at your old school. So that's another strike against you. There were so many strikes against a lot of the African American students. It just wasn't good.

I think I had it mild and that other students are a lot more bitter than I. I think they probably had it a lot worse than I did. My school bus ride was not very far. I was already in a white neighborhood, so I didn't have to go that far. Other black kids would have to get up at ridiculous times of the morning in order to get out there and get their bus. I think that was hard for them. I don't know if any of them ever had trouble with teachers or anything like that. I would say no at PRP. I think the teachers were wonderful there at PRP. But they didn't feel part of the school. How could they? They couldn't do any extracurricular activities. They're afraid of being beaten. They know

Pleasure Ridge Park High School yearbook, 1980. Dawne Gee, then Smith, is pictured as the first African American cheerleader. (Courtesy of the Jefferson County Public Schools Archives)

the KKK is there. So they're fearful of what's going to happen to them. We had several times where the school was, well, I don't know if I want to call it lockdown, but nobody could come out of their rooms because there were riots. There were literally riots where they had a hundred or more students that were fighting, and they were trying to break these fights up. I mean they had sticks and all kind of things that they were fighting with. So, I mean there were crazy things that these people went through. Their buses would be pulling out of the school lot and people would be throwing rocks at them screaming, "Nigger, go home." I don't think I'd like that at forty-two. Could you imagine that at thirteen or fourteen years old?

Darnell Farris, African American student (interview with David Cline, 2004). Farris was bused to Southern High School in the county, a hotbed of antibusing activity during the first year of busing, and then switched to Atherton, a city high school that before 1975 had been primarily white.

School started on like a Wednesday or a Thursday. The flashpoint really happened that first weekend. I remember being really scared, and a lot of people said they weren't going to school. There were threats about what was going to happen to kids that went to school. The road that leads to the school, you come off the interstate and you're on a two-lane road and there's cars honking. They would have diesel trucks outside the school blowing their horns all day. There's nothing that has a sound that's that loud and it would go on all day long, but especially first period. That weekend there was so much rioting and looting, we made national news. That was not a proud moment one bit.

I remember that Sunday the pastor of our church being really concerned about the students. He told us all to come up front and he prayed for us. I remember that next Monday morning the bus was only half full. When we got up that morning, got on the bus, there was a man from the National Guard. He had a forty-five. It was cocked and ready to go. He had an M-16 and this was not in a case, this was ready to go. When you see stuff like that, you're trying to get on a bus, and you try to be brave. It took probably about forty minutes because we're talking about narrow roads and everything. So you're wondering what's going to go on. You look out front and you've picked up a state trooper escorting you. That's the first thing before you even get off the interstate. Then you pick up another one and then you look up in the sky and there's a police helicopter and we're being escorted in. It was very scary. When we pulled into that lot where most of the teachers and the students would park, there had to be no less than about fifty to sixty state troopers and just whatever else that it took to keep some quiet. On the other side of the street were protesters blowing the horns. It was just really hard to concentrate.

Sometimes we would have good weeks where nothing would happen and there would be a day just out of nowhere, no rhyme or reason, where it would be really, really bad. They would tell all black students to report to the cafeteria. This is ten or fifteen minutes before we got on the bus. They would tell us how bad it was outside and to keep your books up beside your head in front of the bus window glass in case it gets broken and to not taunt anybody. We would leave in convoys of thirty buses. They would hold up the street and the buses would come out and they would be *rolling*. I mean like fifty miles an hour taking a curve. Not until we got on the interstate did we feel any kind of safety. There were a couple of areas where there are overpasses and there were some kids from some other schools that used to come and taunt us. We got shot at a couple of times. That's the first time where I've ever said that anything that I've ever done in my life actually came with a cost. When you think about the history of this country, people actually paid a price so we can have an education.

At home, we would always talk about it at the dinner table. My dad only got through sixth grade. He came here from Richmond, Kentucky, which is a much smaller town. When he left World War II he came home and married my mother who came from a large family and she had only gotten through twelfth grade. They wanted to put their three kids through college, which I think is amazing considering he was just a common laborer. But we only had one choice, you were either going to school or you were going to Porter's, which is the local funeral home. [Laughter] All during that year where my grades plummeted there was like a little war going on at my house because this was like, "Don't let them get to you. You're supposed to keep your head in a book." I'm like, "You don't understand. I'm being shot at. It's impossible to concentrate."

My grades plummeted. I was on my way to be a scholar. I was an A, B all the way through. That's the first place I've ever had an F, first place I've ever had Ds. I had no control over it. What you don't understand is you also have teachers that have biases too. There's one in particular that used to be real good at that kind of stuff, saying just little things and you just know that you weren't going to get a favorable grade. [Big sigh] So I sat and took my F and waited for the next semester and took it again. Keep on taking it till I got something favorable. I took advanced everything just to get my GPA up to a 3.0, a respectable amount to get in an architecture school. I graduated from Atherton with a 3.0, which I thought was respectable enough but it would have been a lot better. I feel sometimes kind of angry that I missed out on the scholarships and stuff like that, which I was truly destined for. To a certain extent I had to learn to like school again. It was really hard to try to concentrate on something with all this swirling around.

Now looking back over it I think it's probably one of the best things that ever could happen to me. You know how you say sometimes you go through a bad situation and it makes you stronger. It really does. It made me end up being a fighter because I can sit in a room, listen to conversations going on, and I can debate the issue without getting upset about it. But at the same time, I'm just not going to sit there and let people impose their will on me.

Michael Gritton, white student (interview with David Cline, 2004). In this excerpt Gritton describes his relationship with the black students who were bused into Pleasure Ridge Park from the west end, and the positive impact their friendship had on him.

At PRP, the main part that I remember is the black kids being bused in. Your homeroom was suddenly diverse. Your classrooms were diverse. The advanced program classes were less diverse than the others, I think, because there were fewer kids that could meet the test to demonstrate that they could be there. I started playing organized basketball at PRP starting in the eighth grade. We had an integrated team from the beginning, which was great. We had a fantastic basketball coach named Joe Burkes. There were good friends of mine from that eighth-grade class like a black guy named Gary Griffith who ended up being the vice president of the senior class and I was his campaign manager, along with being the campaign manager of the white class president. By the time you get to be seniors, class officers are being selected, one is white, one is black, they're friends. There's a true sense of us being a class together. It wasn't obvious that that was the way the story was going to work out when it started.

There were other friends of mine from that team who were black kids, and just by meeting them and learning a little bit about their life you learned about a part of Louisville that you'd never experienced before. When you grow up in PRP the idea of the west end was almost as foreign as New York City. I don't remember even setting foot in the west end before I came back to Louisville as a grownup. There was no reason to go. You couldn't imagine why anybody white would ever be there. I mean, that may be stating it a little too boldly, but that's the basic idea. So all of a sudden there are guys on your team who need a ride home. There's a reason for you to go and all of a sudden you're seeing things with your own eyes in your own town that you'd never seen before because you didn't have any reason to go there before. I remember the self-conscious feeling of bringing a black kid home to my house for the first time—and again, that sense of eyes maybe watching you or a sense that this is just a little bit odd. I haven't done this before, we're sort of breaking new ground here. There must have been lots of white kids at PRP who had that same experience over the course of the three or four or five years that they would have been there.

Diane Robertson, white student (interview with Joe Mosnier, 2005). Robertson lived in the east end of the county and was bused in elementary school from Dunn, her suburban neighborhood school, to Coleridge-Taylor, a formerly black inner-city school. Robertson uses the term "open-classroom," which refers to school architecture in which multiple classes shared large open spaces. Her story illustrates the different atmospheres in the various levels of schools.

Coleridge-Taylor itself was relatively new, just like Dunn was, to be honest. It was fairly new, but it was still that open-classroom concept. So I went from a brand-new elementary school into a fairly new, but one where it was just one large room. When you're thinking in terms of security, it was even more daunting because I didn't even have my own classroom. I was in this huge space which my parents, being traditional-type parents, didn't understand at all. I was so overwhelmed with the idea of this long bus ride and all the things that went with it, that it was just the icing on the cake. I mean it was traumatic.

At the beginning, I just remember being terrified. I guess that's the only word I could say, just terrified going in. But then toward the middle of the year, there was such a sense of community within that school. I had never seen children guard one another and take care of one another like that before in my life. The one thing that stands out in my mind is that I had forgotten my lunch money one day. I had nothing to eat. The little children that lived in the area all banded together and I had like six free lunch tickets by the time lunch rolled around. I could have gotten six lunches. I thought, oh, my gosh. At Dunn, it would have been like, "Whatever." It was just those little acts of kindness, that sense of sharing. Whatever the little children that lived in the neighborhood brought, it belonged to everyone. There was no, "This is mine and that is yours and what I have is better than yours." It was truly a sense of community, something that to me was so foreign. My mom loved it. They took care of one another, and when I joined their school, even though I looked different, I became a member of their community. They just took me in with open arms, and not just me, but I mean all of us.

If you ask me my perspective, I would have said it was a success. This is exactly what needed to be done, because when I went to Dunn I was very quiet, and because I was so quiet I got lost in the mix. But when I went to Coleridge-Taylor it was just a whole different view of the students. Suddenly my grades shot up. I just gained a self-confidence that I don't think I ever would have mastered had I'd stayed at Dunn in the east end school.

[For middle school] I went back to my home school. There was a little bit more resentment on the part of the black children that were brought out to the east end, but it was probably because of the long rides and things. The animosity was there and it was prevalent. I guess the fears that we had going into Coleridge-Taylor were really more founded going into middle school, as opposed to an elementary school. There were definite tensions. I remember an African American boy, the first year I went back, getting into a verbal fight with a teacher, and basically I remember him screaming, "You made me come here"—you know, basically you deal with me. I remember the teacher screaming back, "I didn't invite you here." It was that type of an attitude.

In high school there was underlying animosity, just the disrespect, things that weren't quite as prevalent in elementary school. In my sophomore year I was standing outside a class getting ready to walk in, talking to a friend. There were groups of children that would kind of roam through the hallway and they came running by and they, just random, stuck a kilt pin right into my hip. It went so far down that we couldn't get it out. So I went down to the principal's office and, of course, they called my mother. [Laughter] She came in and saw the pin; she was the one that pulled it out. It wasn't pretty. So that's when I changed schools for my junior year. Now, I don't remember it being like a war zone or anything like that, but there were definitely children who were there that didn't want to be there.

Edith Yarborough, African American student (interview with David Cline, 2009). Yarborough was a student at Shawnee, but when busing started she was transferred to Fairdale, where she was denied admission to the advanced program. She also illustrates problems for black students in the formerly black but now majority-white schools.

I was involved with the first class that was bused. I was bused from Shawnee High School to Fairdale High School. Fairdale High School was one of the two high schools that had a huge amount of turmoil. We're talking about the rocks, the bricks, the fires, white parents protesting because they didn't want us to watch a Dr. Martin Luther King film, parents screaming at you, and the faces, the anger. You're wondering, "Man, what is going on?" Then your parents, that fear that they had every morning, all the things they told you what to do, how to protect yourself, and then walking you to the bus stop. You knew that that creates tension. It creates tension among adults, among children, among faculty members. Faculty members also were dispersed into different schools because they wanted to not only integrate their students but also integrate the faculty and the staff there.

All the different work and achievements I had strove for at my school at Shawnee were dismissed. I was in the advanced program, that is the gifted and talented program, but we're in the city schools, and the county schools had a different measurement. So, when you try to go in to the culture of the county schools, you were told you'd have to take the advanced program test because probably your scores were not strong enough to qualify for their program. Well, my scores were strong enough, but I'm sure there were two different measurements and two different bars, as we now know. So I was denied access into Fairdale's advanced gifted program. They said, "Well, Edith, we're going to let you go back to Shawnee." "OK, I can go back to Shawnee." Honestly, Fairdale was a better school as far as their books, the materials. They had real lab equipment. We didn't have that at Shawnee. It was amazing. The books are up to date. Our books weren't like that, so it was amazing as far as equities—not equitable!

But I wanted "Miss Shawnee." [Laughter] Basically, you represent that school. You're a model for that school. To be known as Miss Shawnee was almost like you were the queen bee. It was somebody who the faculty looked up to, the students looked up to. You were a leader. But when I got there they had already chosen Miss Shawnee for the year, the junior year where I was bused to Fairdale. I was disturbed by that. My bubble was busted. And it was a white female chosen. She was a white female who didn't have the history. I was like, "What? I've been at this school for almost three years. I went to the Shawnee Junior High School; I went to Shawnee Elementary, and I'm not going to be Miss Shawnee?" [Laughter] My tiara I did not get. So what can I say? [Laughter] So I'm like, "What? What happened?" Students voted, but then you had more white students.

■ The tumult, both inside the schools and out in Louisville and Jefferson County, replicated scenes in cities throughout the country as diverse as

Boston, Charlotte, Nashville, and Detroit. Indeed, the story of the busing crisis in Louisville and Jefferson County encompasses many key themes of a larger regional and national narrative. The roots of the crisis lay in resegregation caused by both housing discrimination and the decisions of school policy makers. Prompted by local individuals and organizations, HEW and ultimately the federal courts pushed for a remedy. The initiation of mass busing sparked widespread demonstrations and a boycott of the schools by whites. Although couching their opposition in terms of resistance against intrusive government authority over parental and community decisions, the antibusing forces launched often violent protests against buses bringing black students into their neighborhood schools. Meanwhile, blacks greeted busing with some ambivalence, fearing for the safety of their children and regretting the loss of black-majority institutions. Although in Louisville most African Americans nevertheless rallied around the busing plan for the promise of access to better resources, persistent inequality in treatment led to disappointment, disillusionment, and for some the belief that integration did not work. The combination of white hostility and black disillusionment led conservative pundits and segments of the public to conclude that busing was an illegitimate program opposed by local communities, and that school desegregation ultimately failed because of this extreme measure.[14]

Historians who have told this story have focused much of their attention on the origins, motivations, and actions of the white opposition, linking it to the rise of the modern conservative movement that rejected an activist federal government.[15] The memories shared by people in Louisville and Jefferson County back up these scholars' findings, documenting the sources of the antibusing movement and the crisis it sparked in the community, as well as the tribulations suffered by black students. But this narrative obscures much of what happened at the time and why. Other oral histories presented in this chapter complicate the understanding of the ideology of the antibusers, and contribute to a counternarrative about a community coming together for integration. These stories establish the reasons people worked for busing and desegregation, and the conclusions narrators draw about the positive results for themselves and their schools. Both fill gaps in community studies of the history of school desegregation. Moreover, locally, the pride in the achievements of busing despite the rancor against it, and recognition of its benefits, laid a foundation for the defense of desegregation in the community thereafter.

When remembering the beginning of countywide desegregation in 1975 and the turmoil sparked by the antibusing movement, these narrators echo what scholars of white resistance have found in other communities, namely, that the roots of the movement lay in fears of federal government interference in individual rights, parental decision making, and neighborhood schools. In particular, the narrators with the closest ties to the antibusing forces use their interviews to defend and normalize the opposition by playing down the violence and emphasizing people's fears for their children. As Todd Hollenbach insisted, the antibusers were not troublemakers or criminals, but only parents worried that the government was "fooling with" their children's lives. Moreover, in retrospect, busing opponents are adamant that they did not object to desegregation per se or harbor racist motivations. Even Bonita Emerick, who quite frankly describes her parents' prejudices and quotes her mother asserting her racist views, explains that her father believed he was fighting a communist system more than fighting blacks. Looking back as an adult, Michael Gritton accepts his father's assertion that at the time "it had nothing to do with race." These narrators reflect a racial innocence that was claimed by the opposition and has been underscored by some of the scholarship on the antibusing movement since.[16]

Yet other interviews and contemporary evidence reveal that antiblack hostility animated some of the opponents of desegregation. Marcella Robinson, for example, admits that prejudice was a factor and that some white protesters simply did not want blacks coming into their schools. Some white teachers resisted integration and displayed hostility to or at least discomfort with black students and parents. African American teacher Dan Withers recalls confronting white parents who complained about their children mixing with African Americans in the classroom. And according to both Anne Braden and Benitha Ellis, the Klan and other extremist groups sponsored many of the demonstrations against busing. In these interviews, contemporary observers thus acknowledge that at least on a grassroots level race and racism influenced the opposition to integration, something that most antibusing activists immersed in the crisis at the time were unwilling or unable to do, at least in public settings.

A closer look at contemporary evidence further highlights the roles attitudes about race played during the busing crisis. The most overt expressions of racism came on the streets during spontaneous eruptions of anger. On the first days of the semester, mobs of whites gathered outside the main high schools in the south end of the county and attacked the buses carrying the black students with bats and bricks. At Pleasure Ridge Park two men carrying signs with Nazi symbols led the crowd in a chant of "White Power," while other demonstrators shouted "Niggers go home." At Fairdale, a group of teenage girls led a singsong chorus of "You ain't bad. You ain't cool. Keep the Niggers out of our school." In the evening of the first Friday, the crowds grew, set bonfires, and by the end of the night engaged in violent confrontations with police and state guardsmen. Thus, in an unorganized setting, faced with the reality of black students coming into schools they felt were theirs, some south end whites displayed racial animosity in a more public, open way.[17]

Then, as the fall progressed, antibusing rallies and publications began to emphasize the danger in the newly desegregated schools, focusing on the criminality and brutality of black students. In September, organizers tried to whip up enthusiasm for a school boycott by featuring stories of black violence against white students. In one rally three mothers testified about incidents involving their own children, with each greeted by roars and standing ovations from the crowd. In October the newsletter of the National Association to Restore and Preserve Our Freedom (NARPF), a local right-wing organization that focused on busing as one of its many targets, solicited similar stories and began printing them regularly in its issues through the spring. Each story involved blacks unaccountably accosting, robbing, or harassing an innocent white victim while teachers looked the other way. In such settings, there was no mention of the victimization of African Americans, such as Dawne Gee's harrowing escape from a group of white students, or of the numerous other incidents reported in the mainstream press. Rather, the antibusing forces developed a narrative of disorder in the schools based on assumptions about the flaws in black students' characters.[18] This narrative is reflected in the memories of Charles Summer, who emphasized the problems with the behavior of the newcomer black students and the objections when he suspended them. The assumption of black guilt for the disorder in the schools reveals that at least some opponents of busing could not see beyond their notions of racial difference and black character.

A similar blindness prevented many whites from recognizing the structural racism in the housing market that necessitated busing. Some busing opponents at the time, and a few of the oral history interviews, expressed the idea that blacks were welcome in suburban neighborhoods, and that if they wanted access to those schools for their children they should simply move there. Marcella Robinson, for example, recalled her area in the east end as open to blacks, as long as they were of the same economic bracket. Sue Connor, the leader of Concerned Parents Inc., testified before the U.S. Commission on Civil Rights that in Jefferson County blacks and whites simply lived where they wanted to and since blacks from the west end would "obviously" move to new subdivisions eventually, there was no need for busing. Several letters to the editor of the *Courier Journal* echoed this point. As one writer from the northeast suburb of Anchorage, which was exclusively white and among the wealthiest sections of the metro area, asserted, "If parents are dissatisfied with the school in their neighborhood, there are homes for sale or rent all over Jefferson County." Another boasted, like Robinson, that blacks were "welcome in my neighborhood."[19]

African Americans at the time might well have been surprised to hear of this welcome. These comments betray at minimum a naïveté or willful forgetting about the obstacles that until recently had kept the suburbs of Jefferson County nearly all white. In 1973 and 1974, the Kentucky Commission on Human Rights had documented persistent and worsening housing segregation in the metro area. Only in the years immediately preceding the advent of busing had a small number of black families, like Gee's, begun to move to previously all-white neighborhoods in the county, and when they did they encountered hostility, for sale signs, and cross burnings. Indeed, during the first fall of busing a black family in the southwest county neighborhood of Okolona was subject to repeated vandalism and violence against its home, including attempted bombings reminiscent of the 1956 Wade house case.[20] The insistence that place of residence is a free choice that anyone can make in the face of this evidence to the contrary reflects the white community's unwillingness to grapple with the historic and continuing barriers to housing for African Americans. Over time, courts and policy makers, with assent from much of the white public, would use this reasoning to determine that since residential segregation was a result of personal choice, busing could not legitimately be used to overcome it.

As much as the motivations and actions of the opposition take center stage in scholarship and public memory, the opposite is the case for the story of those who supported desegregation by busing. Community studies of court-ordered desegregation too often minimize the role of individuals— whites and blacks—who actively sought school integration and believed busing was the best way to achieve it. Although black plaintiffs and organizations were the instigators of the legal battles that led to desegregation, their later disillusionment has come to overshadow their determination at the time to get the best education for their children regardless of the sacrifice. Meanwhile, their white partners in those battles, who supported integration in principle or because it was the law of the land, remain almost invisible. As Jeanne Theoharis argues, this renders the "anti" position as normative and tilts the balance of scholarship toward a negative account of why whites objected and why integration failed.[21] In contrast to contemporary conclusions about African Americans' disappointment with school desegregation, in 1975 the black community in Louisville rallied around busing, largely for access to better educational resources. As one African American speaker at a rally just before the start of school in 1975 put it, "Quality education is where the white kid is because there's where the white man puts his resources. That's where I want my kids."[22] Edith Yarborough remembers that when classes started, parents were justifiably frightened, but they stoically walked their children to the stop and put them on the bus. Going further, United Black Protective Parents, a group of African American mothers, went to the schools not only to confront the opposition and to protect their children physically but also to press teachers and principals for fair treatment. Meanwhile, as several observers noted, there were no demonstrations or disturbances in the west end. As Mattie Mathis, a cofounder of United Black Protective Parents put it, in contrast to the attacks on black children in the county, "The children that came in the west end, the white children, we never did that to them. We always tried to make them feel at least comfortable."[23]

Alongside African Americans were a small number of white citizens who worked with them for school desegregation, for busing as the best means to accomplish it, and for community peace. According to June Key, many white volunteers wanted to make busing work as peacefully as possible to create a safe environment for their children's education. Others were more explicitly pro-integration, such as Suzy Post, who sought to overcome the sickness of separation in society. As several narrators recall, people tried to smooth the way for integration through parent exchanges, a rumor hotline, human relations groups within the schools, and dialogues between pro- and anti-forces. As the opposition to busing heated up, it inspired other white Louisvillians to stand up against the overt racism they saw in the antibusing movement. Progress in Education, the most prominent pro-integration group during the crisis, organized explicitly to give people a vehicle for opposing the violence and extremism of the antibusers. The actions of these individuals and groups, and others given credit in the interviews such as the League of Women Voters and the National Council for Jewish Women, parallel the efforts that paved the way for desegregation in the city schools in 1956. Moreover, many of the same organizations and individuals had participated in the campaign for open housing in 1967. These activists, whether working behind the scenes or on the front lines, were part of a continuous, though often overlooked, cooperation between whites and blacks in the long struggle for equal rights and equal education in Louisville.

A more detailed, nuanced account of the support for desegregation and busing by both blacks and whites forces a rethinking of the busing crisis in Louisville, and elsewhere, that can lead to a new more balanced narrative of the time. Rather than project the disillusionment many blacks felt later back onto this period, we need to see that at the time, many African American leaders and parents saw school integration and busing as necessary for securing equality in education. And at least some whites were willing to work with them to achieve that goal. Finally, the pro-integration, probusing response of both blacks and whites in this period was the basis for action in the coming decades in an ongoing struggle for equality in the schools. Many of the individuals who took a stand in 1975 remained committed to defending and improving the desegregation plan when it was challenged in the coming years. The United Black Protective Parents and PIE took the lead in the 1970s, monitoring school board meetings and keeping pressure on issues of disproportionate suspensions and funding in inner-city schools. Key continued to work on school integration issues, even traveling to other communities to share the Louisville experience. As will be seen in the next chapter, Jelsma played a pivotal role negotiating a compromise to make the busing burden more equitable in the early 1980s. In short, the experience in 1975 of navigating the turmoil of the busing crisis, trying to ensure a safe and equal educational environment for children, and fighting back against the vocal and violent opposition gave people an investment in the school desegregation plan and determination to protect and improve it.

As battles over busing raged in the community, teachers and students struggled with its consequences inside the schools. Ever since the onset of mass busing for desegregation, social scientists have studied and debated its results, especially for black students and to a lesser extent for black teachers and administrators. Observers at the time and scholars since have noted uneven discipline, tracking, and the displacement of black faculty. These problems, along with the resegregation that occurred in many urban districts in the 1980s and 1990s, inform the verdict that integration failed.[24] The oral histories contain abundant evidence of this negative effect on black students. The bus ride to school could be frightening, akin to going into battle. Tension and sporadic violence filled the hallways of the schools. In class, young African Americans faced unwelcoming faculty and tracking. Those students in the advanced program recall very few black faces, and Edith Yarborough represents the black students who were locked out of the higher-level classes at their new schools. African American students who were bused into the suburban schools had difficulty enjoying extra-curricular activities because it was hard to join a club or team if you had no way to get home afterward. Black teachers were transferred, and in their new county schools faced bigoted students, hostile parents, and suspicion from white faculty. Thus oral history documents in a more personal way many of the elements of the negative portrait of the black experience in the desegregated schools. Experiences like these likely contributed to the sharp decline in black support of the busing plan in Louisville, which went from 63 percent in 1976 to 49 percent in 1977, although these numbers would rebound in the following decade.[25]

But oral histories also shed light on positive experiences within the schools and on the benefits experienced by individuals. By telling stories about their personal experiences, the narrators paint a picture of better resources for inner-city and formerly majority-black schools, a lessening of racial tensions, and individual perseverance and growth. As Laura Kirchner recalls, after merger and desegregation the city and county schools had to be equalized, which greatly benefited the inner-city institutions and, as Clint Lovely pointed out, resulted in a raise for city teachers. Less tangibly, Withers recalls a welcoming environment in the county schools, particu-larly from the principal whom he praises for standing up to white students, indicating the importance of school leadership in setting a tone. He also savored his role as a support for black students, though he recalls relatively less harassment and violence than Gee, perhaps reflecting the difference in perspective between students and teachers. Withers and other teach-ers concur that while there were ill feelings between white and black staff and some hostility from whites about the process, with time those tensions lessened. Perhaps with an urge to defend their profession, all the teach-ers assert that white faculty either got over their racism and learned to see students as just children, or quit, so that the situation improved relatively quickly.

As much as the student narratives detail the disturbance the young-sters endured in the transition to desegregation, they also convey the very personal and often positive influence of the experience. Over time, black students were more able to participate in activities, especially sports, but also student government. In those activities, students formed friendships across race, although they were limited by residential segregation that kept blacks and whites far apart and almost completely alienated out-side of school. Nevertheless, Gritton illustrates, extracurricular activities opened up opportunities for young people to learn how the others lived, giving them a perspective they likely had not had before. Finally, the students who went though busing often conclude that despite the hardship and turmoil, the experience in some way benefited them. As a white child terrified of being bused to an inner-city black school, Diane Robertson found warmth and a sense of community that not only dispelled her fears but also gave her confidence and a spark of enthusiasm for learning that she had lacked before. Perhaps Darnell Farris put it most clearly and succinctly when he concluded his narrative with, "It's probably one of the best things that ever could happen to me. You know how you say sometimes you go through a bad situation and it makes you stronger? It really does."[26]

When the *Courier Journal* published twentieth and thirtieth anniversary articles about the memory of busing, the tragedy and turmoil of the first year and the damage to the educational process for both blacks and whites came across in students' recollections of being bullied and intimidated and in parents' assertions that their children did not benefit at all. On these public occasions of remembering, however, other voices leaven the stories of violence and harm to the community. "It was horrible," concluded one bus driver, but another said, "I am happy to have played a part in implementing a plan that . . . helped to bring down some of the barriers that separated our community."[27] Reflections such as the latter represent a different memory of busing. The stories they hint at, together with the oral histories in this chapter, comprise a counternarrative to the popular and historiographic tale of black disenchantment, racism, violence, and unremitting white opposition to school desegregation. Moreover, understanding this alternative memory of busing helps explain the subsequent pockets of determined support for maintaining some form of the busing plan in the face of a national rejection of active policies to ensure integration.

The recurring urge to reflect collectively on the onset of busing highlights how important the crisis over it was for the community. The narratives here were in many cases the stories people wanted to tell, even when being interviewed about something else. And they tell them with powerful detail and drama. This reflects the magnitude of the crisis itself. The controversy over busing constituted the most violent and divisive civil rights struggle in the modern history of Louisville. Moreover, it resonated with a prolonged and politically important national debate. Finally, the busing plan and fight over it are still invoked in, and are still pivotal to how people understand, ongoing debates about school desegregation and student assignment in the community. Indeed, contemporary Louisvillians are more likely to call up memories of this chapter in the long history of school de-segregation than of events that followed, so that the public dialogue about that history has a large silence in the middle. That silence covers the complex story of the following two decades, which saw repeated efforts to re-form and defend desegregation in the face of challenges that in many cities led to its demise.

CHAPTER THREE

The Continuing Struggle over Desegregation, 1981–2007

In the spring of 2007, as Louisvillians reacted to the possibility that the Supreme Court would invalidate their school desegregation plan, the former NAACP president Maurice Sweeney wondered why, "As we discuss and debate the state and purpose of desegregated schools in Jefferson County, there seems to be a bit of history missing. For some reason we jump from 1974 to 2007 and forget about April 4, 1984."[1] On that date, a series of hard-fought negotiations between school officials and representatives of the NAACP and other civil rights groups produced an agreement to reform the busing plan. Sweeney might have added that the community amnesia applied likewise to a second major reform in 1991 and to a series of pivotal court challenges to the desegregation plan beginning in 1998. At each of these moments the community confronted the question of how to make the plan more equitable or—once federal courts began giving the green light for doing so—whether to scrap it in favor of neighborhood schools. Whites who opposed court-ordered desegregation from the beginning used each debate as an opportunity to push for the reduction or elimination of busing. Some African American leaders, out of disillusionment with the inequity of the desegregation plan, likewise called for its end. In the midst of each round of debate, however, a coalition of blacks and whites stood up for preserving integration and diversity in the schools. As a result, the school board over time altered but did not end the busing plan. First, it created magnet programs to encourage voluntary white enrollment in inner-city schools. Later it assigned students to facilities based on their residence instead of their name, and eventually gave parents a choice among a "cluster" of schools. Thus, during a time when the national political mood was becoming inhospitable to school desegregation plans, indeed when the legal tide was turning against even voluntary efforts to maintain mixed facilities, in Louisville and Jefferson County a biracial integrationist coalition and eventually the school board itself fought to protect diversity in the local schools.

Nationally, the erosion of support for school desegregation began at the top, with presidents and federal judges setting the tone. Richard Nixon had never approved of court orders for desegregation and campaigned against busing. By appointing William Rehnquist, a consistent opponent of school desegregation plans, to the Supreme Court he began the process of packing much of the federal judiciary with conservative judges.[2] Ronald Reagan favored ending mandatory desegregation plans and replacing them with parental choice, reflecting his goal of reducing the role of the federal government in local affairs. During his administration, the Justice Department acted on the assumption that school desegregation had failed and that communities should be allowed to "return" to neighborhood schools.[3] Although neither President Bush made opposition to busing a part of his respective campaign rhetoric, both appointed justices who would prove pivotal in decisions undercutting desegregation plans, and George W. Bush's administration filed a friend-of-the-court brief in the case that would in 2007 force the Jefferson County Public Schools (JCPS) to alter their student assignment program. These presidents and judges helped create a climate that made affirmatively pursuing desegregation increasingly difficult.[4]

The Supreme Court wrote that climate into law, circumscribing what local districts could or were required to accomplish. Almost at the dawn of the court-ordered busing era, the *Milliken* (1974) decision made desegregation more difficult in northern and western cities by forbidding transportation across school system boundaries, thus separating urban and suburban districts. Because of white flight to the suburbs, this strict demarcation left city schools struggling to maintain mixed student bodies with fewer and fewer whites, a process that was almost doomed to fail. *Milliken* had less impact on large southern districts, such as those in Louisville and Charlotte, however, because they merged their city and suburbs into combined school systems. In the following decade, such southern school districts worked out busing plans with the support of black communities and lower court judges, making the region more desegregated than any other in the country by the mid-1980s.[5]

A series of Supreme Court decisions during the next ten years reversed this history of successful desegregation. The process began in 1986 when black parents in Norfolk, Virginia, challenged a school board plan to end busing and create segregated neighborhood elementary schools. The Supreme Court upheld the school board, concluding that once a system had been declared desegregated—or "unitary" in the language of the court—as Norfolk had been a decade before, it no longer needed to continue efforts to keep it that way.[6] Then, in three succeeding decisions, the Supreme Court consistently sent the message that it was time to release local districts from mandatory desegregation. In 1991, in *Board of Education of Oklahoma v. Dowell*, the court affirmed that unitary status released the district from its obligations, a decision then used as a guidepost for future cases. In *Freeman v. Pitts* (1991) the justices declared that when a district was found to be desegregated in one area, such as students, it did not need to have a program to desegregate in another area, such as faculty. Finally, in *Missouri v. Jenkins* in 1995 the justices terminated Kansas City's court order and made it harder for urban systems to integrate schools by attracting whites from the suburbs to attend them voluntarily. In doing so, the court hinted that it would not look favorably on even voluntary desegregation efforts. The lower courts took the signal and began overturning plans in Rockford, Illinois; Charlotte; and Jacksonville, Florida.[7] Thus by the late 1990s school desegregation was being rolled back throughout the nation.

The history of the past thirty years of school desegregation and resegregation has been told to date primarily by education, policy, and legal scholars. Using social science methods, these scholars have amassed a statistical and aggregate body of knowledge about the impact on education, particularly for black and Latino students. Others meanwhile have traced the development of lawsuits and the court opinions in the cases that were the key stepping-stones away from desegregation.[8] These studies paint a picture of the larger context affecting local struggles concerning Louisville's and Jefferson County's desegregation efforts. Yet what are often missing are the values, experience, and assessments of the men and women who were parties to the ongoing debates over the schools in this era. Historians, who put such actors at the center of the stage, have not yet developed a narrative of this period, perhaps because it is so recent and thus there has not yet been the time for critical distance and interpretation. The struggles of these years are still part of the lived experience of the community, and thus the history of them bumps up against the memory of the people who engaged in them. This chapter harnesses those memories to counter the amnesia decried by Sweeney, to recall the history of the reforms in and challenges to school desegregation in Louisville and Jefferson County.

To tell that story, this chapter is divided into three sections representing the three phases of the battle over school desegregation between 1984 and 2007. The first section covers reforms in 1984 that led to a change from assigning students to schools based on their last name—the alphabet plan— to a residence-based system and the concurrent debate over how to make busing more equitable for black children. In the oral histories, people who participated in formulating and negotiating the reform explain the issues involved and what they saw as their accomplishments. The second section focuses on the 1991 controversy over school superintendent Don Ingwerson's proposal to end desegregation at the elementary level and assign those students to neighborhood schools. In this section, representatives of the two sides of the ensuing conflict share their views of the proposal and the factors that brought about the compromise outcome. Finally, the third section conveys the story of the three court cases that whittled away and then overturned the Jefferson County desegregation plan. In this section activists who launched the cases, school system staff, and citizens who participated in the debate outside the court explain their positions, assess the cases, and describe their reactions to the result. Because of the complex twists and turns in desegregation policies and in debates during these years, each phase of the story will begin with an introduction to the key events.

1984: Reforming the Busing Plan

By the time Jefferson County Public Schools hired new superintendent Don Ingwerson in 1981, there had been almost continual tinkering with the busing plan to make it more efficient and popular while keeping schools within the prescribed student-body racial balance. The school board redrew boundaries for individual school districts to try to keep up with residential shifts as whites moved out of the county, though that white flight slowed after 1978. System officials added first graders to the busing plan in 1979 and a year later ensured that white students would be bused in consecutive years to reduce dislocation. Then, when Ingwerson arrived, he began to expand the magnet and other optional programs to encourage voluntary white enrollment in inner-city schools.[9] These alterations meant that the first generation of students under the busing program often went to multiple schools in their careers. By 1983 Ingwerson had decided that he needed to give students more continuity. He also pledged to reduce the overall amount of busing. At this point, school officials believed they were no longer under court order, because in June 1978 Judge Gordon had declared the schools desegregated and ended his direct oversight of the case. This was later contested and the schools not formally released from full court supervision until 2000. But in the early 1980s officials acted on the assumption that they could make changes to the plan and that they were continuing to desegregate voluntarily rather than under court order.[10]

In April 1983, to begin the process of reforming the system, Ingwerson appointed a citizens' advisory committee made up of parents and representatives of concerned organizations, and a staff committee to meet with them. In their discussions the citizens' committee, led by its black members but with strong support from some of the whites, insisted that any reform should aim to create a more balanced burden of busing between whites and blacks, in particular at the elementary level, and that no student should be bused for eleven years. In early 1984, however, the school staff insisted that demographically it would be impossible to accomplish those goals. Because there were so many more white than black students in the system, the latter had to be bused more often to maintain the racial balance ratio in each school.[11]

Superintendent Ingwerson broke the impasse in February with his own proposal, which caused an explosion of opposition. Ingwerson's plan exempted elementary schools from reform, keeping them on the alphabet assignment plan at least for the time being. He proposed creating a magnet school at Manual High, located just south of downtown near the University of Louisville, instead of at Central High, as the citizens' committee wanted. Moreover, he suggested moving low-income whites from central city neighborhoods out of Manual, to make room for the magnet students, and assigning them to Central. Most controversially, to achieve racial balance in the middle and high schools, Ingwerson wanted to cut the west end into small satellite zones from which blacks would be bused out to schools in the suburbs. This would nearly eliminate busing for older white students and amount to what blacks quickly derided as "one-way busing." Blacks and their white integrationist allies regarded this as an attempt to undermine Central by loading it with low-income students, and to worsen the already uneven burden of busing born by black families. To fight these changes, and to call for a more equitable system of school desegregation, black ministers began to host mass rallies at their churches, while the Kentucky Alliance ferried protestors to public hearings on the proposals. Meanwhile some white parents and citizens' committee members called the inequality of the plan immoral and urged the superintendent to bus more white students for more years to even the balance. As the Board of Education vote on the plan approached, community pressure built for a delay in the decision.[12]

At the last minute Ingwerson intervened and asked the board to delay the vote to allow negotiations between school officials and representatives of civil rights groups, led by the NAACP's president Sweeney, to develop a compromise. After intense discussions, the negotiators came forward with a plan that satisfied most of the groups opposed to Ingwerson's proposal. The compromise created an attendance zone for Central that reached into the wealthy, white, east end of the city, with the intent of guaranteeing the school a stable white student body and extending the burden of busing to those neighborhoods. The negotiators also agreed to keep the proportion of blacks in each school to within 10 percent of the overall population to prevent drastic resegregation. Finally, the new version of the busing plan established an assistant superintendent to monitor the progress of both desegregation and minority employment in the system. The school board adopted the plan on April 4, 1984.[13] Civil rights and community groups had rallied not only to defend the principle of equity within desegregation but also to put a system in place to ensure it. In the narratives that follow members of the citizens' and staff committees and negotiating teams describe the issues in the conflict and the process for resolving it.

June Hampe, white mother and citizens' committee member (interview with David Cline, 2005). In 1975 Hampe's child was assigned to Meyzeek Middle School, a formerly majority-black school in the Smoketown neighborhood in central Louisville. Because she and her husband believed in integration, she decided to throw herself into supporting it and became an active volunteer at the school. Her volunteerism led to her being appointed to the citizens' advisory committee. Later Hampe served as staff to the school board, helping prepare for the lawsuits that challenged the assignment plan. In her two interviews (2005 and 2009) she defends the ideal of desegregation and the school board's means for achieving it.

I feel very, very fortunate to be on the citizen committee that redesigned the deseg plan in 1984. You ever want to smell a political process, that was— [whistles]. Our school board is composed of seven elected board members. Each board member named two people from the portion of the county that they served and these were parents or people like that, and that's how I was put on. Then there were some people representing organizations like the NAACP and the Urban League and League of Women Voters and things like that, some religious groups. They told us we would meet two or three times; we might have a weekend retreat but that would be all that would be asked of us. Well, horsefeathers! We wound up meeting night after night after night, and this went on for weeks and months. It was chaired by the now deceased Ray Nystrand, who at that time was head of the College of Education in the University of Louisville. So there were a lot of well-known, recognized people in the community, black and white, and then there were some folk that were just kind of interested parents on it as well.

What we did was examine the deseg plan as it had been approved by Judge Gordon in '75, look at our shifting needs, and try to say there has to be a better way to do this, how will we do it? One of the things that we were most interested in looking at was the discontinuity in the busing years. Wouldn't there be a way to smooth that out? Wouldn't there be a way to do that for black and white students? So we wound up then keeping the basic concept but rearranging the mechanism. That was a major step toward stanching the white flight we were still having and some black flight too. That began to turn the tide. That really began to help a whole lot and created a lot more stability.

Geoffrey Ellis, African American minister (interview with Tracy E. K'Meyer, 2011). In 1984 Ellis worked for the Kentucky Commission on Human Rights and was also the chair of the education committee for the NAACP. He was appointed to the citizens' advisory committee, where he became a leading voice against Ingwerson's proposals.

This controversy came because some of the African American community felt that we were bearing the burden of the busing in terms of the amount of kids that were bused. One particular thing we said was, "Don't bus our babies!" We didn't think the younger children should be bused at all; course, that wasn't going to be possible. We quickly come upon the fact that because of the housing patterns we were going to bear the burden, because a lot of the African Americans lived in the west end. We wanted an equal share of the load to be shared. We felt that white folk just did not want to have their kids come to the west end. We said if it's the schools physically then you need to put money in the schools physically. If it's the schools academically then you need to shore up the schools, because we are going to have two-way busing—we were pretty emphatic about that—and we're going to have a greater load sharing by the white community. We were going to have that happen and we stuck with that and it came out pretty good, we think.

Sherry Jelsma, white chair of the Board of Education (interview with Ethel White, 1988). In 1975 Jelsma was a human relations volunteer at Coleridge-Taylor Elementary School, where her son Franklin was bused. In 1984 she was the chair of the school board. She often defended Ingwerson and his proposals, but she was given much of the credit for bringing the school board around to compromise with the NAACP and other civil rights leaders.

In 1984 the school board got out from under the court order and we had to decide what we were going to do about desegregation. The schools had been ruled desegregated and so we were under no obligation to do anything technically, but we wanted to continue desegregation. Of course the local NAACP wanted us to continue and the other groups did too. So the year I was chairman of the board of education we were to adopt a new desegregation plan and that is when we changed from the alphabet plan to the geographic plan. The plan that we proposed had all children in the same high school for four years, all children in the same middle school for three years. The only alphabet busing was in the elementary school. So it was a huge difference.

Some of the black groups felt that it was one-way busing because we set up geographic areas called satellites in the inner city which would belong to a certain suburban high school or middle school and the students would go to that school. Not that many white satellites existed; in fact, I don't think any existed. There were only black satellites. The white people were going to inner-city schools, however, because of the boundaries that we drew for the inner-city schools. We also created magnet schools, all in the inner city, which would draw white students to the inner city so those schools would not resegregate. It became a very heated issue. There were rallies against the plan by various groups. What finally happened is we had a negotiating team of black community leaders and white community leaders. The white ones were the school board attorney and the school board. That was one side. Then the black community sent its leaders forward to negotiate with us and that was very, very visible, it was in the paper every day. We negotiated very hard on the attendance zone of the inner-city schools because that was in lieu of white satellites.

There were hearings before the negotiations began at Central High School and various other high schools. The worst was at Central High School. I was taken to the car by armed security. The Klan was there trying to cause trouble. There were signs. There were people shouting and singing "We Shall Overcome" and there was just a lot of vocal activity against the geographic

Jefferson County School Board, 1984. Seated left to right: John Heyburn,
C. Mackey Daniels, Sherry Jelsma, Rick Johnston, Jim Hearn. Standing left to right:
Bob Schmidt, Mike Wooden. (Courtesy of Sherry Jelsma)

plan. The shout was "one-way busing," however, if you really looked at it, it wasn't one-way busing, and it was academically far superior to the alphabet plan. The black leadership understood that and they were able to communicate that to their people who were scared. It was fear of the unknown and I understand that! I think it's very understandable. The feeling that something was being done to them instead of for them or with them, and the black leadership was able to communicate the fact that we were doing it together for the children and that's what we were doing.

Maurice Sweeney, African American president of the NAACP (interview with Tracy E. K'Meyer, 2011). Sweeney, like Ellis, worked for the Kentucky Commission on Human Rights. In 1984 he was also president of the NAACP.

When we got word that the school board was reconsidering the school desegregation plan nobody really knew what it meant. Like many institutions the trust factor was not there with low- to moderate-income neighborhoods or the black community or even the more liberal community. Because the

NAACP was still the oldest civil rights organization in the state, I was asked to take a leadership role. We started to ask questions and insist that we be part of the discussions and that there was no reason for the school superintendent to think that he was just going to tell us what was going to happen and not ask us for our input. We had people in the ministerial community such as Reverend Elliott and some other ministers who were solidly behind us and were prepared to go back to the streets. They let the powers that be know that you can either talk with Maurice and level-minded people or we will just go back to the street. The word that we got was that the business community—because of what had happened in '75 and the image that Louisville had gotten, which was second only to Boston, I believe, as far as the notoriety on the six o'clock news—wanted to make sure there was every opportunity to discuss and to find remedies to the situation.

There were many concerns in the community at the time. There was a lack of trust. Black children were bearing an undue burden. White folks really preferred integration as long as it wasn't inconveniencing their children, so the burden was put on the black community. Most of the people being bused for the most years were black students. What few schools were in the black community would be 100 percent segregated if you just let the black folks in the neighborhood go to those schools. Now what had happened was some of the better schools, they put magnets on them. They put a magnet on Male, because white folks wanted to keep that institution white. They put a magnet on Manual, because it was going to be a school for the arts and it was close to the University of Louisville. So now suddenly the only schools left in the black community per se were Shawnee and Central. If there was going to be busing on a high school level black kids were the ones that were going to have to bear that burden. Even when we said lessen the burden we knew that the black community, regardless of the plan, just because of the numbers, would have to be bused for the most years. But we had to find some sense of balance and the only way we could find that sense of balance was in the elementary level, because there were more elementary schools than there were anything else. The big issue was that you were changing from an alphabet plan to a geographic plan and that geographic plan meant that everybody in a given neighborhood would go to the same school, so it was just a matter of where a designated school was going to be. Finally, the fate of Central High School was always a concern.

During the community discussions about all this, a group of us had a lunch meeting at Vincenzo's. We were all together just trying to really understand the statistics—because we were talking about ninety-two thousand students—to understand the magnitude of what we could and could not do. It was more of a continuing strategy meeting. We did have the law-yer, Michael Sussman from New York for the NAACP Legal Defense Fund at that meeting. Dr. Gary Orfield, who was a consultant to the school system, came to us. He said, "I just left Don Ingwerson's office"—who was the school superintendent at the time—"and he asked me to tell you that if you will choose a negotiating team then he will negotiate a settlement." So that's how it was started. The negotiating team ended up being Laken Cosby and Galen Martin, both with the Commission on Human Rights, myself repre-senting the NAACP, then Reverend Goins was president of NAACP ministerial coalition. For the school system there was a legal team from Wyatt, Tarrant, and Combs. I don't recall the superintendent actually sitting in on nego-tiations. We were able to create some great relationships with the school board. We had some school board members like Sherry Jelsma and John Heyburn who were very much hands-on, and they really wanted to make themselves available to us.[14]

I can't remember exactly the length of the negotiations. I remember we would go up on the twenty-eighth floor of PNC Tower Bank to their offices and we would be there till seven, eight, nine o'clock at night, start in the mornings. Sometimes they were pretty intense because we were trying to figure out what schools, what neighborhoods, and the effect. And the media was in our face every day. I mean they were waiting to hear what was going on and I think they had a tendency of making things even bigger or seem even bigger, to the point where people saw me on TV practically every day.

The compromise included several things. One was that we were able to lessen busing for black children on an elementary level, we were able to make sure there were more black administrators, we were able to put a mag-net on Central High school. We put a business magnet on it so that the busi-ness community would embrace it. The community in its attendance zone was Mockingbird Valley, which was a more affluent neighborhood, and if people thought that children of such affluent neighborhoods were going to Central then that would ensure that Central would have the resources to be a viable school. We had the promise of building a new elementary school in the west end, to help the burden, and that school was built. At one time we were the only major city in America where they were building new schools in old neighborhoods. We created a coordinator to monitor, and we also had a citizens group to work with the school system to do some monitoring and be responsible for making suggestions.

I remember when we came to an agreement it was probably about 7:00 at night. I can remember going in my office and closing the door and just crying like a little kid. Because I didn't have any children, I didn't have the same stake as some of the parents had or the kids had, and again it was ninety-two thousand kids. I remember saying, "God, God please allow me to be able to make the right decisions and good decisions." It really wasn't about me, it was about how it was going to affect people that would be here long after I was gone. It was affecting so many kids, and not just ninety-two thousand kids, but you multiply that by however many years. So I felt the awesome responsibility.

1991: Preserving Desegregation

In 1991, Superintendent Ingwerson rolled out another revision of the Jefferson County school desegregation plan that aroused community opposition. By this time the Supreme Court had begun to indicate in the Norfolk case that systems that had been declared unitary—as Jefferson County believed it had been—no longer were under court mandate to maintain desegregation. Ingwerson's action was triggered, however, by the passage of the Kentucky Education Reform Act (KERA), which required testing of all students in fourth grade. Ingwerson argued that KERA required students to attend one school with the same classmates through their elementary years, so that the testing measured the school's performance accurately. At the time civil rights advocates questioned that logic and suggested Ingwerson was using it as a cover to attack busing. Whatever the reason, in September 1991 Ingwerson proposed ending elementary school desegregation. His plan would assign young children to neighborhood schools and then encourage black parents to send their child to white schools voluntarily in exchange for money for a college savings account in the student's name. His goal was to keep black enrollment in any school to a maximum of 60 percent, but because there was no minimum percent set, some schools could become all white. Early analyses indicated that more than forty elementary schools would immediately resegregate under the plan.[15]

Divisions in the community over the plan surfaced almost immediately. A number of black leaders quickly endorsed the change and embraced the notion of black children attending neighborhood schools, reflecting sentiments expressed in other urban areas by this time. Nationally, this position had roots in the black power movement's embrace of separate institutions, including schools, in the 1960s and 1970s. By the 1980s and 1990s more mainstream intellectual and political leaders began to share that position, as black mayors and even civil rights leaders called for ending mandatory desegregation plans and for experimenting with other means for bridging the achievement gap.[16] In Louisville, the Black Think Tank formed in

Don Ingwerson and school staff, circa late 1980s. Don Ingwerson is seated second row center (#25). Laken Cosby is seated to the right of Ingwerson. Row three second from left is Deanna Tinsley. Row four first on left is John Whiting. (Courtesy of Jefferson County Public School Archives)

January 1991 to promote Afrocentric approaches to problems, including housing and schools. The members believed that desegregation was not working for black children. Soon after Ingwerson made his proposal public, the only black member of the Board of Education, Laken Cosby, declared that he saw no problem with majority-black neighborhood schools. A coalition of fifteen black leaders eventually endorsed the plan.[17]

Civil rights advocates, both black and white, soon launched an offensive against the proposal, however, defending the importance of integration in the schools. Leading the way were Lyman Johnson, who had forced the University of Kentucky to admit blacks in 1949 and had thereafter been a leader of the local civil rights movement, and Georgia Powers, the first black state senator in Kentucky. At age eighty-five Johnson brought particular moral weight to the issue when he charged that the plan would take the community back behind the "iron curtain of segregation." Powers meanwhile organized the first rally against the plan at the West Chestnut Baptist Church, whose minister, Reverend C. Mackey Daniels, was known as a defender of equality in desegregation during his term on the school board in the 1980s. Three hundred people attended and heard a parade of opponents of Ingwerson's proposal pledge not to let the community go backward and praise integration as good for both white and black children. At the end of the meeting a group organized Quality Education for All Students (known as QUEST), led by an African American dentist named Madeline Hicks and by Stephen Porter, a white lawyer.[18]

For the following month Jefferson County was once again wracked with turmoil over desegregation. The school board began a series of public hearings on the proposal and leaders of both sides sponsored their own, more boisterous rallies. As October wore on, tempers flared, with anger aimed at the school board's attempts to limit debate and the seeming inevitability that it would support the superintendent. By the middle of the month opponents called for a delay in the vote to allow people to calm down and thoroughly study the likely impact of the changes. Meanwhile, the *Courier Journal* reported polls that documented the split in public opinion. While 85 percent of all respondents said it was good for children to attend mixed schools, 64 percent of whites endorsed ending desegregation at the elementary level. Belying the impression that the black community was evenly split, however, 70 percent of African Americans fully endorsed desegregation and keeping the current system for achieving it. This local result paralleled the pattern in national polls, which showed that the majority of black parents, regardless of statements by some African American leaders, upheld integration as a goal and were willing to send their children to white schools to achieve it.[19]

By November Ingwerson had postponed the vote and promised to appoint a committee to reconsider his proposal. Meanwhile, opponents of his plan reached out to civic leaders and announced that David Jones, the chief executive officer of the local insurance giant Humana Inc., and Hicks would lead discussions between prominent business people and members of QUEST about the proposal. The pressure from QUEST and the business community ultimately forced Ingwerson to modify his plan, the new version of which, called Project Renaissance, was adopted by the school board in December. Instead of ending busing at the elementary level, the new plan created a series of "residential clusters," which were small groups of schools. Students were assigned to a particular school by their residence, but they could request to be transferred to another within their cluster, giving parents some choice. Schools were responsible for developing special programs to attract such voluntary transfers. All schools would have to be within the range of 15 to 50 percent African American, a wider range than allowed under the old system, but narrower than the 0 to 60 percent advocated by Ingwerson. If voluntary transfers did not produce this ratio, mandatory assignments would be made to make sure schools remained racially diverse. With this change Ingwerson and his supporters could claim they shifted to voluntary desegregation in a neighborhood-based system, while QUEST and others could be relieved that racial balance was preserved. Integrationists claimed victory, although many were bruised by the process and continued to criticize the superintendent and the board for rushing the process, stifling debate, and causing community division.[20] In the following narratives, participants in this debate recall their reasoning during the conflict.

Reverend Kevin Cosby, African American minister and community leader (interview with Tracy E. K'Meyer, 2011). In 1991 Reverend Cosby, son of school board member Laken Cosby, was a minister in the west end. He was influenced by Afrocentrism and by the black nationalism of Professor Joseph McMillan of the University of Louisville, and he was a member of the Black Think Tank.

You have to understand the context of the late eighties, early nineties. There was a reemergence or reawakening or reemphasis on Afrocentrism during this time. So you had Public Enemy who were rapping about black nationalism, black consciousness. You had a reemergence of Malcolm X, people were wearing Malcolm X caps. You had Spike Lee. So this was the context of the time. I think it was the black community attempting to define itself, what direction are we going, especially for poor urban blacks who did not benefit from integration, who were left behind. One of the tenets of black nationalism is the establishment of black institutions. Part of the whole nationalist agenda dating back to Booker T. Washington, Marcus Garvey, Martin Delany, Elijah Mohammed, Malcolm X, was re-institutionalizing poor black communities with institutions owned by African Americans. Institution building was vital for those with a black nationalist agenda—that's so loaded—for those with an empowerment agenda for the community. So one of the institutions that was important to us was the schools. There is a saying that goes that the black community went from segregation to desegregation to integration to disintegration. What integration did was co-opt the best, the brightest, the professionals within the black community away from the black community, so that their skill sets were no longer in the service of African Americans. So the black nationalist empowerment agenda was to reconstitute institutions that served communities that were socially isolated.

In retrospect, I think the mistake we made was we romanticized to a great degree the glories of segregated neighborhoods. This was where Lyman T.

Johnson in his critique was absolutely correct. We romanticized it. It's what psychologists call the greener pasture illusion. We had a greener pastures illusion about how great segregation or all-black schools were. But you cannot have strong black community schools when the strong black community that we knew in the forties and fifties no longer existed. The west Louisville that I grew up in was a community of professionals. I lived on Westchester Avenue, which was right next to Chickasaw Park, and down the street from me lived the Reverend F. G. Sampson. Reverend Sampson was probably the greatest orator in America. He was idolized by Martin King Jr. Right down the street from me was Martin King Jr.'s brother. I tripped over Dr. King's feet when I was a kid. So this is the neighborhood I grew up in. Muhammad Ali lived on Grand. One of the great pediatricians in Louisville lived right around the corner from me. So you had all these achievers and doctors and lawyers right behind me, literally in the house. My father was a realtor, Cosby Realty, my mother was a piano teacher and educator. So this is the neighborhood I knew in the sixties growing up, and that community vanished during the seventies and eighties. So I was saying, well, since so many of our kids are underachieving, since gangs seem to be proliferating in west Louisville, maybe we can return back to what we had in the sixties. But that was not the answer.

But, at the time I had bought into the whole nationalist agenda. It was not necessarily segregation and it was not the separation that was espoused by Marcus Garvey and the Nation of Islam. The Nation of Islam perspective was we need to separate because whites and blacks can not coexist. That was never my perspective. My perspective was that since we do have de facto separate neighborhoods that we must build institutions within poor separate neighborhoods in order to improve the quality of life of the people in the neighborhoods; that was the perspective. What's so unfortunate was that the media at the time projected me in a way that did not reflect my position. My position ultimately was diversity, but I was dealing with the hand that had been dealt me. Namely, you've got his black community, you've got these black kids being bused out. They're not achieving, they are dropping out, and then they are being bused back to separate, socially isolated black neighborhoods. So maybe the answer is putting more money into schools that empower people in their own neighborhoods and providing teachers that really do care about black kids. That was the thinking at the time.

Madeline Hicks, African American dentist and mother (interview with Tracy E. K'Meyer, 2011). Hicks was the daughter of Milburn Maupin (see chapter 1), who was a deputy superintendent in the Jefferson County Public Schools during the 1975 busing crisis. She attended an integrated public university out of state but by 1991 had returned to the community as a dentist and had a son in the schools. She was one of the founders and leaders of QUEST.

The schools here had been integrated for a long time and I had seen the transition. I had seen what happened in the seventies when my father was having to get on some of the school buses with the kids, the buses that were being rocked or whatever. I was in college but I still was aware of what was going on here. But at the same time I saw the aftermath of that, when people had gotten used to being with one another. Some people would choose to be in certain away schools as they were called at the time because they had one kid there and they found out the education they were getting was a good one, the environment was satisfactory and they might want all of their children to be in the same school for convenience or for whatever reason. That was a far cry from what happened in the seventies. People were working with one another where they had not before. It seemed through the busing we had a mix of people so that we worked and got along and functioned as a society where we were no longer as suspicious of each other and a lot of the stereotypes were broken down.

So, leading up to 1991, KERA had mandated change in what happened in the classroom; it was the edict from the state. Dr. Ingwerson stated that KERA would dictate that the busing plan would need to be done away with. We didn't see where that was the case. Apparently there was some pressure on him to undo the busing plan from somewhere and that was a good excuse. To oppose him there was a public meeting at West Chestnut Baptist church. Whoever wanted to show up showed up, and I remember some of the speakers that night. Senator Georgia Davis Powers was one of the speakers, Steve Porter, who I later worked with on the project, was one of the speakers. There were a number of us, just citizens who care about this community. Some of us got together and formed an organization called QUEST, Quality Education for All Students. I was co-chairman of QUEST. The other chair was Dr. Jim Chatham [minister of the Highland Presbyterian Church]. There were some parents in the group. The people that I worked most closely with on formulating our policy position were: Dr. Chatham, Steve Porter, and Jim Hill who's now an attorney in DC. The four of us were the people who did most of the grunt work. Jim Hill is African American like myself, and Dr. Chatham and Steve Porter were both Caucasian.

We wanted to see the schools integrated, we did not want the busing plans reversed, we believed the notion of neighborhood schools was a farce. We met at several school meetings and expressed our views there, we also went out to the schools to see what was happening there, physically to see what was happening. We also got some experts; Gary Orfield from Harvard came down. We had some little meetings where we had some experts to come out and talk to us and we invited some of the community people to come in. We thought we knew what would happen if busing were taken away, but we studied what was happening in other communities. There is one school system in Virginia where the system had been integrated and when the school busing was taken away and there was no intentional integration, the school system suffered. We looked at some other large school systems in the country where the public school systems had deteriorated and people would send their kid to private school because the public schools were so bad. We don't really have schools that bad here. That's why most of the teachers in Jefferson County don't want to see busing taken away, because they believe it's best for kids, they believe it's best for this community. That's why Jefferson County schools voluntarily said no, we don't want to undo this. We see where we are now, we are happy with it. We're happy where we are with our kids. Every school system has problems but overall ours are less than many other cities this size that have a diverse population. So there was an intentional desire on the part of educators to keep things going. Even though Dr. Ingwerson was against it, we talked to many people within the school system that didn't want it to be undone.

The final plan that came out seemed very thoughtful. That's when the cluster concept was born. That plan seems like it worked fairly well. The schools seemed to be very—prosperous would not be the right word, but there were good things going on and it seemed like a good balance and overall inside the schools there were really innovative things happening and I didn't hear of a lot of negativity. We thought it was a win because if Dr. Ingwerson's original proposition had happened we would have been back where we were in the seventies.

Stephen Porter, white attorney (interview with Tracy E. K'Meyer, 2011). Porter was a native of Louisville who first became active in civil rights as a Duke University student in the 1960s. He returned to Louisville as an attorney. During the busing crisis he had supported desegregation but had not become involved. When Ingwerson sought to reform and then limit desegregation, Porter became interested in preserving it. He was one of the founders and leaders of QUEST and later an attorney for intervening plaintiffs in the Central High School case.

In 1975 I was a parent and I was an attorney and I was in favor of desegregation, in favor of the new busing plan, in favor that the city and the county systems had merged, had good friends on the boards of those systems, and agreed with that decision and wanted my children to go to a desegregated school. So that's background, I guess. Then when there were various proposals for reforms and things that came about during the time from 1975–91, I never had any real need to get real active. But then in 1991 there was the proposal to just get rid of busing totally and get rid of a desegregated system and that's when I said, "Nope, we gotta get back into it."

I'm sure there were some community people that were behind it, that were in favor of it, but the proposal came from Ingwerson. His proposal was basically to go back to neighborhood schools. He announced that at the start of the school year in 1991, sometime in September as I remember. They tried to hide what was actually in the proposal, so a group of us got together to see what they were actually proposing. What it would mean was the only schools that might have any integration at all were schools that were somewhat near a black neighborhood and somewhat near a white neighborhood. Out of the 140 to 150 schools there would have only been about twenty-five of those that would have fallen into that category. The rest were going to become either 95 percent black or 95 percent white or more.

The school system was having these public forums where they would announce, here's what's going to happen. The first one I went to was October 7th at Pleasure Ridge Park and then another at Westport Middle on October 14th. That was an interesting one. What happened at Westport Middle that night was the school board's plan was to give a thirty-minute presentation on what the proposal is, then divide up into groups of eight or ten or twelve people into a room. The board members sent people off into different rooms, which meant nobody could hear what other people were saying. There was no cohesiveness for those who were opposed to this plan, or even for those who might be in favor of it. At Westport we organized that we aren't going to break up into the small groups. We've got seventy-five to one hundred people or whatever it was, we aren't going to break up. We are going to stay right here and we are going to all talk about this together. That just totally blew their minds, they weren't quite sure what to do. So that was kind of the beginning of when the school system finally realized that there was going to be some real opposition to this.

Now, Kevin Cosby, Carmen Weathers, and some others formed a little group which was opposed to QUEST and it was basically an all-black group. Their whole thing was we want to bring our young children back to our bosom and we can take care of them because you white people won't take care of them. Hard to argue with that; white people have not been very good at really taking care of and therefore educating and wanting black children to advance. They were afraid that no white people were going to be able to take care of their black babies. I sympathize with that, but I disagree with it, because you can't do that forever. Our society in 1991 was way beyond that. The workplace was integrated, colleges were integrated by then.

Anyway, we had raised enough sand and had enough strong people like Lyman Johnson and Georgia Powers, well thought of in the white community, in the business community. In the political community, Gerald Neal, who was state senator, was concerned about this. Most of the black community, ministerial, educational, were opposed to this. There was Kevin and Carmen and others who had their well-thought-out reasoning, it's hard to argue with it, but for the most part the black community was very upset by this. So we raised a lot of sand. We got a meeting with the Chamber of Commerce. There was quite a group. It was not just a little committee of some lesser Chamber of Commerce people, it was big time. They basically said, OK superintendent Ingwerson, you've got so much time, you make your presentation. Georgia Powers, your group make a presentation, then we are going to talk about it. It was a closed meeting, no press there, and Ingwerson got up, made his presentation. Georgia got up and gave an introduction and then said, "I'm going to turn it over to my numbers guy," which was me, because I had been the one to go through all the numbers of all the schools and what they were going to look like. I just started going down the list. Such and such elementary, 98 percent black, 2 percent white. Such and such elementary 99 percent white, 1 percent black. Such and such elementary 100 percent white, such and such elementary 100 percent black. Just started going down the list and you should have seen these guys, they had no idea that that was what it was going to mean. They just didn't know that.

We were there two and a half hours or so and finally at one point, Wilson Wyatt, the former mayor of Louisville and esteemed member of this group said, "Superintendent, this isn't going to work. We've got to work on this, or we've got to do something else." I don't remember exactly how he put it. We need to put together a committee, our group needs to put together a committee and get some ideas. So a group of us met every Wednesday morning in David Jones's office in the Humana Building for two or three hours for five to seven weeks. December 18th was the final meeting of that group. So that afternoon we had a press conference, we basically announced that this plan was not good, and in my mind that was the death of it. The Chamber of Commerce, an all-white upper-class group of people wasn't going to support this, it wasn't going to happen. That was really the end of it. Ingwerson had a press conference the next day, I forget what he even said. But without the support of the chamber, he was in trouble.

From there it was just a matter of then working out the details of improving the current plan, but not getting rid of desegregation. So there was a major change, but there was not a major loss of desegregation.

1998–2007: Legal Challenges and Response

In 1984, African American leaders had fought to protect Central High School by ensuring that it had a stable attendance zone from which to draw both black and white students, and they had succeeded. At that time it seemed that the residential zone in the east end and the magnet program that had also been won in negotiations would guarantee the future success of the school. But during the following few years it became obvious that too few white students elected to attend the Central magnet. Because the ratio of black to white had to stay between 15 and 50 percent, black students could not be added to the school if the white numbers did not go up. Consequently, not only were some blacks barred from the school but overall enrollment began to decline, causing African Americans to fear it would be closed. A lenient transfer policy for high school students initiated in 1991 made the situation worse, as white enrollment for Central dropped even further, and black numbers reached the ceiling allowed. The black community began to divide over how to address the problem, specifically whether to do away with the racial balance guidelines and to allow the open enrollment of black students. For example, William E. Summers III, a minister and former participant in the 1960s sit-ins, argued that to do so would be a step backward for integration, while John Whiting, an African American principal formerly at Shawnee and now at Seneca High, insisted that the ratios were wrong and should be ended. The issue resurfaced a few years later when Ricardo X, a teacher at Central High, led a petition drive to ask the school board to exempt Central from the desegregation plan and to allow more blacks to attend. That proposal elicited an emotional response from Lyman Johnson, who said it made him "just want to cry." Meanwhile the school board rejected the petition and reaffirmed its commitment to desegregation. Although this issue ceased to draw the attention of the local media or that of much of the white community, Deborah

Stallworth and a few other black leaders organized Citizens for Equal Assignment to School Environment (CEASE) to pressure the school board for change, and failing that to launch a lawsuit against the restrictions on black enrollment at Central.[21]

In 1998 CEASE hired white attorney Teddy Gordon to represent a group of parents in a suit charging that the racial balance ratio at Central discriminated against African American students by denying them an equal right to admission. In September the U.S. District Court Judge John G. Heyburn II allowed the Fair Housing Council, QUEST, and others, represented by Stephen Porter, to intervene as plaintiffs to argue that the ratios should remain in place. Meanwhile the school board insisted that the plan must remain in place in all schools if it was enforced in any, and that desegregation was a positive good for the community. The case became more complicated in June 1999, when Heyburn decided that the original 1975 court order had never been completely lifted due to ambiguity in Judge Gordon's opinions. If CEASE wanted the black-to-white student ratio changed at Central, it would have to sue to have the whole Jefferson County school system declared integrated and, in light of recent Supreme Court decisions, no longer required to maintain a desegregation program. The organization obliged, marking the first time, as Fran Thomas of the Kentucky Alliance put it, that "Black people sued to get away from white people."[22]

Judge Heyburn's decision in the Central case in June 2000 gave both CEASE and the school board room to celebrate, but it set a precedent that unsettled integration advocates. Heyburn concluded that the racial balance ratio at Central did discriminate against black students and must be eliminated. He determined that Central's magnet program made it unique and that the school delivered an education unavailable elsewhere in the system. Thus, he declared, Central and any other unique magnets must be open to all applicants on an equal basis without regard to race. In the aftermath of the decision the school board identified three other such schools and lifted the ratio from them as well: Brandeis, a math and science elementary; the performing arts magnet at Manual; and the Brown School, which was the only K-12 institution in the system. In a move that caused relief among the board and integrationist parents, however, the judge also declared that the desegregation plan and racial balance could continue in the rest of the schools because the board had made a case for a compelling interest in maintaining diversity in classrooms. In doing so he gave the system more allowance to continue to integrate than was the trend nationally. Members of CEASE felt vindicated and celebrated the opening of Central to more African American students. Civil rights advocates, while appreciative of the room Heyburn gave them, greeted the decision with foreboding. As Suzy Post, the plaintiff in the 1975 court case put it, "I think the whole effort is tragic. It could portend one lawsuit after another lawsuit after another. Everybody is trying to put the best face on it by saying the order could have been worse, but it's a real Pandora's box."[23]

Post's prediction came true just two years later. In 2002 David McFarland, a white parent, filed suit in federal court claiming that student assignment procedures aimed at maintaining a racial balance had denied his two sons admission to two "traditional schools." Jefferson County had set up the traditional schools, which emphasized educational fundamentals, morals, discipline, and parental involvement, at the same time as the magnet school system. Traditionals, however, did not have special academic admission requirements. Students who applied were put on lists by race and gender—one list each for white girls and boys, and black girls and boys—and then admitted by a lottery. McFarland hired Teddy Gordon, who argued that under Heyburn's 2000 decision on unique magnets, the racial balance ratios should be lifted from the traditional schools as well. Other parents whose children were likewise denied entry to traditional schools joined the case, as did Crystal Meredith, whose son had been denied admission to the neighborhood school of her choice. Judge Heyburn waited to hear the outcome in the 2003 *Grutter v. Bollinger* case, in which the Supreme Court upheld the University of Michigan's affirmative action admissions policy, and applied that precedent to McFarland's suit. In June 2004 he ruled that the traditional schools had to go to a single-list lottery. Once again, however, he upheld the desegregation plan for the rest of the system, reasoning that the Supreme Court had shown in *Grutter* that a public educational institution could use race as a factor in admissions in the interest of promoting diversity. Likewise, once again the school board could declare at least partial victory for integration, though they saw their program for ensuring it being nibbled away.[24]

The next, and most damaging bite, came when Gordon and Meredith appealed her part of the McFarland case.[25] Meredith had wanted her son, who was white, to attend Bloom Elementary. He was turned away there because of the need to keep the racial balance in the school and sent to Young Elementary in the west end instead. Meredith claimed that this decision discriminated against her child and hurt his education. The school board defended its policies saying that to lift the ratios would lead to quick and extended resegregation, and that the community had shown its interest in maintaining diversity, most recently in a 2001 poll in which 80 percent of parents supported the desegregation plan. When the Sixth Circuit Court of Appeals upheld the student assignment plan, Meredith and Gordon appealed to the Supreme Court, which accepted the case and combined it with *Parents Involved in Community Schools v. Seattle School District No. 1*.[26]

Because of the national prominence of the case, and the threat it carried not only to the local desegregation plan but also to the cause of integration throughout the country, during the following year the *Meredith* suit, as it was still referred to locally, sparked protest from civil rights groups. The NAACP quickly decried the potential impact of the case and sponsored a series of public forums to raise public attention and concern. Jesse Jackson came to town to urge people to rally to show the Supreme Court that they still supported integration. When the court was in session and hearing the case, the Kentucky Alliance organized a bus load of local parents to go to Washington and protest outside the Supreme Court building against any return to segregation. Throughout the long wait for the case to be heard and decided, local civil rights leaders and representatives of the school system used public appearances to argue for maintaining desegregation. Other voices, including black parents like Deborah Stallworth, questioned whether it was still worth it.[27]

In June 2007 the Supreme Court completed the trajectory it began in the Norfolk case in 1986 and dealt a further blow to efforts by school boards to maintain desegregation. In *Parents Involved in Community Schools* the Court ordered that race could not be the sole factor in student admission decisions. Justice Clarence Thomas's concurring opinion went on to argue that there was no compelling public interest in maintaining integration, cutting off the thin reed of support Heyburn had left Jefferson County for continuing its program. Justice Kennedy offered a small opening, however, arguing that school officials could employ some form of "race conscious" plan to promote diversity. Jefferson County officials hung their response on the latter. Thus while Meredith's supporters celebrated the Supreme Court overturning the system's racial ratios and assignment plan, Jefferson County School officials vowed they would find a way to preserve diversity in the schools.[28] In the following narratives activists and school system staff members describe the legal wrangling over the schools and give their opinion of the outcome.

Carmen Weathers, African American community activist (interview with David Cline, 2005). Weathers is an activist with deep roots in the local community. He is also a graduate of the local schools before desegregation. After a career in coaching at historically black colleges he returned to Louisville in 1972 and became a teacher at Russell Junior High. In succeeding years he taught and coached sports at a number of different schools. He became involved with the monitoring committee set up around the reforms of 1984 and then got active in the effort to protect Central and ultimately to remove it from the desegregation order.

I fought for Central and this is why I fought for Central. I fought for Central, not for Central that was, but for the Central that could be. I see Central with the proper leadership as being the only high school that could adequately deal with the problems present among black students. I see that because other schools are not going to do it. You have to see Central as different and if you don't see it as different, you're either blind or a fool. It's different for any number of reasons. It's different because of its historical mandate and it's also different because of its population. It's also different because of its proximity to the black community. It's also different because of its potential for good and bad. It's not just another Jefferson County public school.

Former Superintendent Ingwerson, to deflect criticism of the plan that came in '84, formed a citizen's committee to monitor the busing program. He put me on there to shut me up. I knew they weren't going to do a damn thing. I got a good friend of mine on the committee, Dr. McMillan, University of Louisville, and I got Dr. Robert Douglas, University of Louisville. We've been friends since the ninth grade in high school. We are best friends, so I got Robert on there. I got him on as a parent. We had kind of a little nucleus. We tried to get them to amend it. We said, look, we know that there are some people, black people in particular, that think integration and progress are the same thing. But why don't you try to do something about Central because of its uniqueness? The board said no, Central's going to do what everybody else does. When I say the board, I mean the central office led by the superintendent. They saw it as bending over or giving in to the direction of a few people that were really opposed to integration in the first place. That was myself and maybe eight or ten or twelve people around town that saw that integration wasn't bad, it was the way it was being implemented that was bad.

We decided to use legal means after about eight years of pleading. I'm certainly far from a lawyer but I felt that black kids in this instance were not being treated fairly on the basis of race. We formed a little committee. We interviewed about five attorneys before we got one and we were quite pleased with Teddy Gordon. Teddy's a good man, civil rights attorney who saw our point as a betrayal of civil rights until I explained it to him that it wasn't a betrayal. It was really about the civil rights of black people. I finally convinced him. He always kids me. He's a very good friend of mine now, but that first day, I called him a bullshit lawyer. [Laughter] He said he laughs about the fact that we didn't start out being friends. I said you ought to stop calling your damn self a civil rights lawyer if you don't see the civil rights that are being abused in this plan. So he called me back the next day, said I'll take the case. That's how we got Teddy Gordon. We interviewed both white and black lawyers. All of them were scared. They didn't want to oppose City Hall, because City Hall gets a lot of mileage out of the fact that we're so integrated. When they try to bring businesses in here, they talk about we're the most integrated school district in the country. We fuck over black children, but that's alright. We're still integrated.

So we filed suit. A lot of people didn't like it, a lot of black people didn't like it, all of the liberal white groups in this town didn't like it. They came together and they got all the publicity. They said that anything that got in the way of integration was bad. We had a judge, a Republican. It was so overwhelming to me. I didn't think we could lose and we couldn't. But the judge rendered his opinion as narrow as he could. He limited it to Central, didn't want to set a precedent.

Deborah Stallworth, African American mother (interview with Tracy E. K'Meyer, 2011). Stallworth was a nurse with a child in the public schools when she got interested in the issue of the racial balance at Central. Although she had had little experience with organizing, she became one of the founders and leaders of CEASE.

The early mid-nineties is when the rumors started about closing Central High School. At that time they were having five to six hundred students in the building. It was big talk out in the community. They couldn't maintain their enrollment. They tried different principals, that type of thing, and none of it was working. So slowly but surely enrollment was dropping. They even had talked about changing the name from Central High School to another name. Of course the voices of the community said no, this is a historically black school, we want to maintain it the way it was, why should we change the name? Well, the reasoning was to get away from that historical piece and maybe add something new where white students would want to go. It had the magnets there but apparently it wasn't attracting the white students to match the black students in order to increase the enrollment. They preferred to go somewhere else. So they did a few things. They kind of beautified the school a bit, kind of did a little touch-up work to it a little bit. I was thinking that they could never close it because Central has a very strong alumni [association] and they would never allow that to happen. But they were on the verge until we decided to start looking into this a little bit deeper.

It's been fifteen years ago now. Everybody seems to think we came out of nowhere and now there's a lawsuit. Long before anything started hitting the papers we started doing meetings. We started having meetings in houses like my house, Fran Thomas's house, Bob Douglas's house, Carmen Weathers's house. Slowly but surely we decided, well, maybe we should do something about it. So we decided to talk to alumni groups, Central High School alumni meetings. We talked to them about what we thought we could do or would like to do to save the school. By then the rumors were getting more specific. The enrollment magic number was five hundred. If you can't maintain five hundred then they close the school. At that time the enrollment was getting there.

We found out there were black children on the waiting list; four hundred kids were on that list because they didn't have a white counterpart. Because of the student assignment plan those four hundred children couldn't get into the building. They can be on the list until one white child decides to enroll. They couldn't allow for more than 50 percent African Americans to be in the building. So this four hundred stayed until a white child came and then one could be pulled off the list.

We decided we'll go out to the school board and ask that Central High School be exempt from the student assignment plan because of the decrease in enrollment. The response was pretty much, this is the student assignment plan, we don't go past that, anything over 50 percent the principal gets in trouble. So we came back home and tried to figure out what we could do to change that mind-set. At that point we decided, well, let's just start asking some attorneys what would happen if we sued them for these four hundred who can't get into the building and get the education of their choice. That is one of the priorities in the school board—we are allowing choice—which isn't true. So when we went to talk to attorneys there wasn't one that said we wouldn't win. Now, they didn't want to sue the school board, but not one attorney said we would not win, which was interesting. At that time we decided to go ahead and form CEASE. I came up with the acronym, which was Citizens for Equal Assignment to School Environment. I liked CEASE, it's like stop this stupid stuff, it's crazy. Then I had to match the words. In fact I laid up all night trying to figure it out. We went and got 501(c) [nonprofit status] so we could start collecting money because we knew eventually we would find a lawyer. One day Dr. Bob Douglas found us an attorney, Teddy Gordon.

Of course we had the NAACP saying, "Heck naw, you're crazy." At the time we formed CEASE Lyman Johnson was still alive. He was always saying that we were rolling the wagon wheel down the hill and we were stupid and crazy, and how dare we after all the work he'd done. The last time I talked with him I said, "I'm one of the people that's crazy, that's rolling the wagon back down the hill, and your work was always, always respected. But your work is not completed. We have to complete the work. You got the wheel here, but what made you think it was at the top of the hill is beyond me, 'cause it ain't. So if it rolls back down it's because it never got there to begin with."

I'll say this because it's over and done with. We met with some people from QUEST at the Urban League with Ben Richmond [of the Urban League], Senator Gerald Neal, and Darryl Owens [a county commissioner]. Senator Neal came to us right before we went to court and says drop the case. He had been meeting with the Board of Education and, "We're going to come up with some things, we're going to do some little tweaking and allow Central High School more African Americans. We're going to look at some of them numbers you've been talking about, flipping so that if you can have 15 percent African American at one school you can have 15 percent white at another," and blah-blah. He did the song and dance. We all just sat there and looked at him like, "No, it's the sink and the baby; we're throwing it all out of the window. Ya'll had your chance at this." He says, "I'll bring the power of my office down on you," and we fell out laughing. He said, "If y'all don't stop this case I'll bring the power of my office down on your ..." I said, "What the hell can your office do?," and just started laughing. Fran's like woo woo. But the men just went—BOOM! [Hitting table loudly] They jump up. I'm like, "Oh, my God, are we going to have to call 911?" They ran over there, boom in the chest. It ain't worth all that. So Darryl Owens says, "Let's get this back together. Let's get this calmed down. Let's get this back down, it ain't worth all that." I'm just telling you the truth, but that's how hot it was. That's how hot it was.

In the trial, Judge Heyburn understood us, but he also understood the community. He did what I thought was a balance with his decision. He understood what we wanted, and what we were trying to do, and he understood the significance. He took the time to understand, not only the legal part which was his responsibility, but also the emotional side and what community we were sitting in and the times that we were sitting in, those types of things. Teddy was able to show that children were being denied, because of the color of their skin, programs that were nowhere else, in the magnet schools. So his decision was on the magnets because those programs existed only in those buildings, nobody could duplicate those programs. So you cannot deny because of the color of skin.

We were happy and that's why you probably won't see CEASE again. We came home with a whole lot of thoughts about creating a foundation, doing a whole lot of work in Central High School, which individual members do every day. Bob Douglas, all of them are down there all the time. Carmen Weathers and Bob Douglas wanted Central to have a stadium. We concentrated on it and got it done. After that it was kind of like our mission was over and that's why energy ran out. It was like this big "phew" for me.

June Hampe, white mother and school staff member (interview with David Cline, 2005).

I was privileged, although some days it didn't feel like much of a privilege, but it was a tremendous privilege as my boss says, to be right where history is in the making, to be on the prep team for both of those lawsuits. It was a phenomenal, phenomenal amount of work, unbelievable amount of work. But I'm proud of the outcome. The first one, which we loosely called the Central lawsuit, was over whether or not we could apply racial guidelines to magnets basically. A lot of the community doesn't see it that way. They see it as "those black people got their school back. Why can't we have a school?" It's really not what was going on. What was going on was to say if a program is unique in this system, which Central is, may you or may you not apply racial guidelines to it.

The courts wound up saying your deseg effort countywide may stay in place. You're doing a good job for the right reasons, but any school that is totally unique in your system, while you may certainly and we hope you will strive for diversity, you can't use the racial guidelines. Go look and see if there are any other schools in addition to Central that you ought to pull the guidelines off of. So we did all that and we wound up with four: Central, Manual, which includes YPAS [Youth Performing Arts School], Brown, and Brandeis Elementary, which is a math-science elementary school. All four of those are pure magnets and all four of those are unique in the system. So we were told to pull the racial guidelines off of those but everything could stay in place, which we saw as a major victory.

A few people on the other side of the lawsuit felt they had won, because Central was no longer under the guidelines. In fact, one of the protagonists shouted across the courtroom at us what fools we were because we were acting like we'd won when we had lost. Were we so stupid we didn't know we had lost? We're sitting here saying fellow, take a look. Except for this many kids, nothing's changed. Indeed, three of the four have continued to stay racially integrated through recruitment practices and selection practices and whatever. Manual's become a little whiter. Brandeis stayed about the same. Brown stayed about the same. They're roughly a third black and this has been through strong recruitment practices. Central has gone to 85 percent African American. I don't think that that's strengthened their program and I don't mean to say that in a racist way at all. Many of our black families do not wish to have their child in a predominately black setting. They don't think that that's the real world and they don't want to do that.

Stephen Porter, white attorney (interview with Tracy E. K'Meyer, 2011).

In my personal opinion the Central case is a case of certain members of the black community remembering how good Central High School was in the thirties, forties, and fifties, and I'm not saying it wasn't. That memory even today survives with people my age, that by golly we had a black school and it was great. I have always understood that philosophy but have disagreed with it; you just have got to come into the real world. You just can't do that anymore. That was what the Central case was all about, certain members of the black community wanted a school they could be strong at, proud of, have leadership in. I'm very sympathetic to that from an empathy standpoint, because I know in our society even in 2011 we are still a racist society.

I represented the Kentucky Fair Housing Council and we were interveners in the Central lawsuit. Our position was the system is still segregated, it's not as bad as it was, but there's still many, many elements of segregation. I remember cross-examining Superintendent Steve Daeschner, who became superintendent in 1993, on the stand, and gave him a picture of all the National Merit Scholars. I said, "Superintendent Daeschner, is that the group of National Merit Scholars from this system?" Yes. How many black faces do you see on that? And there weren't any. I said, "And you're telling me that your system in desegregated? Look at your advanced program, and we had all the numbers, what percentage of your advanced program are black? What percentage are low income?" And the percentages were way different than the actual population. So we tried to make the case that the system should still stay under the court order. But we lost that.

The long-term significance is you've got Central High School, which is predominantly black, and you have the others, which are a pretty good mix and I think that's a shame. But as far as the whole community is concerned there was not a huge impact. We were afraid it would just be a stepping-stone back to something like Ingwerson had wanted, that if you let it happen at a few schools then you could justify it happening everywhere else.

Carmen Weathers, African American activist (interview with David Cline, 2005)

Central can no longer be governed by those ratios, that's what came out of the Central case. Black people said to me, well, it will go back to being all black. That's not a concern of mine. I mean, I'm all black and the black people I'm talking to, I'll say aren't you all black? Are you afraid that somebody might see you as being all black? What's wrong with being all black? If all black is bad, then make it good. It makes sense to me. I don't see anything wrong with being all black. Somebody has told you that all black is something wrong.

June Hampe, white mother and school system staff (interview with David Cline, 2005).

After Central, Teddy Gordon's whole point was he won and where were the white folk and didn't they want to come get him, the great crusader, to do a suit for them so they could win their school? It took three years to recruit somebody, but what he got was a disgruntled parent whose child didn't get into a traditional school, which uses a random draw. Now do you sue the lottery when you don't win? No, but his notion was that we were setting aside seats for black children, and this was wrong, and it kept his child out. They recruited a couple of people that they knew and they had several plaintiffs, there were about five of them, who had all not gotten into traditional school. Well, the goofy thing was that the following year, before this thing actually got to trial, both McFarland children got in on the random draw the next year. Believe me, we didn't contrive that one. Well, did he have the great good sense to drop his lawsuit? No, of course not. "It's the principle of the thing." So the others in the case either got in or I think what they mostly did was they went private and one of them wanted to get us to pay the tuition. Somebody got into an advanced program; he asked for a transfer and got into an advanced program in a school of his choice. We said, you have no standing. You know, this is stupid. But the judge knew that the issue was of such importance that he didn't want to get into the business of disqualifying people, so we went on forward.

We went through this humungous preparation process and I have to give tons of credit to our in-house attorneys, as well as to the external firm that we used, Wyatt, Tarrant, and Combs. They were fantastic. Well, anyway, we presented literally tons of evidence on everything there was to present on. The judge ruled that we could probably do the traditional schools with one list—rather than black boy, black girl, white girl, white boy—that we could probably make it work using one list.

In 2009 Hampe was reinterviewed by David Cline about the outcome of the *Meredith* case and the school board's response.

So Teddy appealed. By this time, you've got the Roberts court, you've got George W. jumping around. So it went to the Supreme Court and the only piece that went was the Meredith piece. When the Bush administration had gotten involved in it, I mean, go figure of course they won. [Laughter] So anyhow, it came down that we couldn't use the racial guidelines. One of the arguments that we used was basically we were doing what the feds told us to do, and now the feds are telling us not to do it. You know, today what we're doing is legal. Tomorrow, it's not, because we have achieved what we were told to achieve. Once we achieved integration and we're declared unitary, and we are patted on the head and told that we had done exactly what we were supposed to do, now we no longer do it and if we continue the same plan, that's bad and wrong. That's what Ruth Bader Ginsburg honed in on. [Laughter] But she didn't carry the day. That wasn't the only thing that we said, but that was one of the things.

As soon as you let your plan go, then it's pfff. The only way to achieve integration was to have a plan, which allowed you to achieve that, and as soon as you let go, bingo, it's gone. It wouldn't take two years and it'd be gone. School system after school system all over the country has been declared unitary and out from under the court supervision, and in most cases, the school systems said, "Oh, thank you, Jesus," and quit. And guess what you've got? Within a couple years, you've got a segregated system again. We had said that's really not what we want to do. We want to keep the mix. And based on housing patterns in this community, ain't going to happen unless we can try.

Justice Kennedy left what we hope is a way out in his ruling in *Meredith*. The way we read the Supreme Court ruling, it was really four, four, and one, and so we took that to be four to five. [Laughter] So Kennedy seemed to leave us a way to devise some kind of a diversity plan. And that's what we did.

Cedric Powell, African American parent and law school professor (interview with David Cline, 2009). Powell is a professor in the University of Louisville Brandeis School of Law who writes on school desegregation and race issues. He is also a parent of children in the public schools. He was interviewed for his expertise on the legal issues in the *Meredith* case.

The Supreme Court always gets in the way. I think one of the things that scholars who are really critical of the *Meredith* decision argue is that the court got involved in a political process that was really working well. Everyone was engaged, embracing diversity, knowing that you had all of these different choices that seemed to be working. Then you have this individualized claim—I want to go to my school—that becomes constitutionalized and the court takes that all the way up. Teddy Gordon got things in motion. To him I think it's a matter of principle, no discrimination, that type of thing, but I don't think he totally looked at the nuance of structural inequality, the history of discrimination, the present-day effects of that, and how you really have to take race into account as one of many factors to change things in the school system.

I think the Supreme Court decision was surprising. We were going along fine. There wasn't any racial turmoil or anything. I think things were working. Then you have, boom, this explosion. I think a number of things were happening across the country. You had places like the Center for Individual Rights litigating and almost threatening colleges and universities: We're going to hit you for reverse discrimination. The Supreme Court has generally been hostile to race-conscious remedies, even when things have been upheld. Justice O'Connor got a lot of credit for being this central liberal who would save affirmative action. But if you look at her opinions they're lukewarm endorsements of race-conscious remedies, so that was a problem. So I think you have this context and then when Justice Roberts becomes chief justice that made the court a lot more conservative. You have this block of five who are generally hostile to race-conscious remedies. I think the court reached out for this case, because, not casting asperities on the way this case was litigated constitutionally, but it was a bare-bones complaint that was drafted by this local attorney and it makes its way up and then the court says OK, this is the case.

People were pretty confident because of *Grutter*. Even though it's in higher education undergraduate and professional schools, people took confidence in that. They said this is the first time that the court actually comes out and says that diversity is a compelling state interest. That's what we're pursuing here, so no problem. But the court reached out and took this case so that they could look at race again. I think that's why there was some surprise. People were relying upon *Grutter* and they were saying, well, even though that is in the professional and graduate school context, and undergraduate schools, those principles are applicable to middle school and high school and elementary school. That's one of the first things that the court says in *Meredith*, this is something different. So I think the court is turning in a way that might place rulings like *Grutter* in jeopardy as well.

Stephen Porter, white attorney (interview with Tracy E. K'Meyer, 2011). In this excerpt Porter advocates a socioeconomically based student assignment plan, which was created by the school board in 2008.

The end result of the *Meredith* case might be better than what we had if they'll stick with it. I've had long talks with Steve Imhoff, the current board chairman about this. He proposed bringing in free and reduced lunch as one of the items in student assignment before the *Meredith* case, before the Supreme Court decision. We had all talked about that over the years. There had been superintendents in Minnesota and other places that had implemented that for a year or two and then got fired and they all went back to neighborhood schools. So it shows that people just weren't ready for it in those systems because they were segregated systems to begin with. Not only were their kids going to have to go to school with black kids but they were going to have to go to school with poor kids. A double whammy, and they just weren't ready for it. I think we are more ready for it because so many of the black kids are poor. They are poor at a greater rate than the white kids are, and so our east end suburban housewives are more used to having poor black kids in their classrooms. They may not have had any poor white kids, but they had poor black kids. So I think we were more ready for it just by virtue of what we've been doing since 1975. So in a way the end result could be very good. It can be a long-run positive because that's how we should be doing it, we should be integrating not only on race.

Pat Todd, white school administration staff (interview with David Cline, 2009). Todd was a teacher in the public schools in 1975. By the period of the lawsuits she had begun working in the system administration and was the director of student placement by the *Meredith* verdict. Here she describes the climate surrounding school desegregation as it stood in 2009 and expresses the uncertainty facing the plan in the future.

We're kind of beginning to feel a little isolated, if you want to know the truth. After the Supreme Court decision, we got busy doing what we thought was a pretty thorough review. We worked with John Powell from the Kerwan Institute at Ohio State, Gary Orfield with the Civil Rights Project, which was at Harvard, now at UCLA and other staff from the NAACP Legal Defense Fund. They were terrific at identifying for us school districts to take a look at and to research. They gave us Cambridge, Massachusetts. Cambridge, of course, is quite unique. I mean, as you can imagine, it's small. Boston is even considerably smaller than we are. But we did interview them extensively and we did learn good things. Then we interviewed Charlotte-Mecklenburg, because back in the seventies, it was Charlotte-Mecklenburg and Wake and Louisville that had similar demographics to one another. We all got into it at about the same time and we had had a history of watching and calling and talking with those two districts. Berkeley was the one that we took the most ideas from.

The reason why I said we're beginning to feel a bit isolated is Charlotte-Mecklenburg rolled back. Richmond rolled back. Oklahoma City rolled back. Seattle, they'd already rolled back before they got in front of the U.S. Supreme Court. Cambridge and Boston were not very aggressive. So Berkeley is continuing to pursue it and Wake is working hard to pursue diversity, but their board elections just elected neighborhood schools folks. So we do think people are kind of looking and watching to see what it is that we do and how we do it, and the more we keep checking around, we find fewer people doing it. Interesting political climate.

■ As Maurice Sweeney complained in 2007, the events in this chapter have been largely forgotten in the community and left out of the dialogue about the *Meredith* decision. There have been no commemorations or retrospective news stories marking the anniversaries of the reforms of 1984 or the victory in preserving desegregation in 1991 to parallel the platform for the remembering of the busing crisis provided by the *Courier Journal* in 1995 and again in 2005. Moreover, in the large body of interviews about the schools conducted since 1975, although interviewers asked questions about the long-term results of desegregation, narrators made only very rare allusions to the changes in the plan over time. While the documentary record amply illustrates the recurring struggles that shaped desegregation in the community, the public memory of local school desegregation simply does not include key turning points and the debates that accompanied them. They loom large, however, in the recollection of those who directly participated, as the narratives here reveal. Thus these interviews fill a lacuna in the story of how the schools got to where they were in 2007, including not only the sequence of events but also the passionately held values about integration and education for African American and white children which shaped the outcome.

Part of the forgotten history includes the results of the revisions of the plans in 1984 and 1991. Commenting on this lack of understanding, June Hampe bemoaned that "a lot of the [people in the community] have not figured out that we don't do what we used to do."[29] Indeed, during the decades following the initiation of countywide school desegregation the plan for accomplishing it was dramatically remade. In 1984 the basis of assignment shifted from the first letter of the last name to residence. At several junctures the board expanded the number of magnet schools and added traditional schools, which were open to students by application. Likewise over time officials redrew boundaries to try to desegregate facilities by including diverse neighborhoods in the residential zone. In 1991 the school board adopted Project Renaissance, which divided schools into clusters and allowed voluntary transfers as long as student populations remained within the prescribed ratio of no more than 50 and no less than 15 percent African American. In doing so, Jefferson County moved away from a mandatory assignment plan and adopted the model of "managed" or "controlled" choice programs that were becoming popular elsewhere.[30] Based on these changes, some narrators or spokespersons associated with the school administration emphasized the difference between the old mandatory busing and the new voluntary assignment, noting that although students were still being transported, they went to institutions that for most of them were chosen by their parents, a distinction sometimes lost in the reaction to the *Meredith* decision.

The forgetfulness about the 1980s and 1990s covers not only the results of reforms but also the values and commitments of the people who shaped them. At each step of the way, in 1984, 1991, and, to a lesser extent around the Central case, there were vigorous community debates about whether and how to change the desegregation plan. These interviews insert the beliefs and experiences of the people who showed up at school board forums, volunteered for oversight committees, or participated in protracted negotiations into the story of school desegregation in the period of federal rollback, refocusing the view away from judges and court-rooms and to community actors. The narrators' stories hint at the turmoil surrounding Superintendent Ingwerson's first ultimately rejected plan to change the system, such as the demonstrations Sherry Jelsma had to navigate outside school board forums in 1984. They reveal the passion of black leaders like Geoffrey Ellis who cried, "Don't bus our babies," and pleaded for a more equitable share of the burden, and the pressure on negotiators like Sweeney who were charged with developing a solution. And they add balance to the story by allowing people on both sides of the debates, like Carmen Weathers and Stephen Porter, to articulate their reasons for and against releasing Central High School from the desegregation plan. Finally, instead of a litany of court battles and judges' decrees, the view from the first-person perspective includes the background organizing that led to lawsuits like the one over Central, making grassroots actions of the black community central to the story.

These oral history narratives, moreover, complicate the understanding of African Americans' attitudes about school desegregation in this period. The local black community was never monolithic on the issue of desegregation and the best path for achieving an equal education for its children. In Louisville, the Black Think Tank, CEASE, and individuals including Joseph McMillan, Kevin Cosby, and Deborah Stallworth reflected the trend observed elsewhere of disillusionment and the rejection of desegregation. But at the same time other leaders persistently and vociferously called for protecting and expanding integration, and not just older civil rights pioneers like Lyman Johnson and Georgia Powers but also those in the next generation like Madeline Hicks. The divide in the black community is illustrated by the Kentucky Alliance, a local civil rights group founded just before busing began in the 1970s. In 1984 the alliance organized transportation for demonstrators to attend school board functions and cry out against Ingwerson's one-way plan, which member, Mattie Jones, called "Jim Crow" and "racism." Alliance leader Fran Thomas later recalled that although standing up to Johnson and telling him he was wrong about the Central case was one of the most traumatic moments of her life, she felt the school should be allowed to resegregate. Finally, a few years later the group again transported demonstrators, this time to protest the *Meredith* case outside the Supreme Court building. In part this trajectory reflects changes in leadership and shifts in individuals' beliefs, but it also demonstrates the mixed feelings about the desegregation plan in the black community, where many people wanted a combination of their own neighborhood institutions and systemwide integration and equity.[31]

In the scholarship on school desegregation since the 1970s, white pro-integrationists fall into the shadows. In Louisville and Jefferson County, there had long been some vocal white activists advocating desegregation of the schools. Stephen Porter, representing these pro-integration activists, articulated the belief that the community simply could not go back to the days of segregation. In addition, prominent white business leaders played pivotal roles in the defense of diversity in the schools, according to Porter because "they did not want to be nationally thought of like the Deep South, wanted to be progressive from a business standpoint."[32] Hampe and Jelsma represent whites who worked within the system; having gotten involved in 1975 through concern for their own children's education, they then continued to plug away at making the desegregation plan work in all its iterations. At times that meant compromising and defending the system and the superintendent during intense community debates. White integrationists could have blinders about the extent of burden on blacks and the reasons African Americans might consider the plan inequitable. But in their narratives they display a commitment to the core values of diversity in the schools, pride in the extent of desegregation accomplished, and a sense of ownership and protectiveness in maintaining it. Whether longtime civil rights activists, defenders of a system they helped create, or just parents who attended a forum and spoke out against the immorality of resegregation, white residents' support represents a side to the debates over desegregation that has been largely lost to both popular and scholarly memory of the period.

In recalling his participation in the 1991 debate to an interviewer, Kevin Cosby asked, "Do you want my thinking at the time, or do you want to know in reflection where I was off?" He proceeded to use his interview to assess and critique his past positions in light of what he has since come to see. Because of this reflective quality, the interviews provide unique information about events and their meaning. With the exception of Sherry Jelsma, whose interview took place in 1988, each of the narrators in this chapter was speaking in the 2000s, and in most cases after the *Meredith* verdict. They knew about developments in the local story, but also about trends in resegregation across the region and the impact of that on black education. Education policy scholars have documented well the lack of desegregation in northern and western cities and the retreat from it in other southern districts. Along with this failure and retreat came an increase in inequity between the educational resources and outcomes of majority-black/Latino schools and majority-white institutions.[33] The awareness of this disparity inspired people like Porter and Hampe to defend programs to maintain a racial and economic balance in the schools, for fear that returning to neighborhood schools in a residentially segregated community would doom the system to persistent inequality. As Ellis put it reflecting on the ultimate result of neighborhood schools, "We knew the resources would become scarce again, and we believed that anyway, and we could not allow the community to become segregated."[34]

At the same time, some of the African Americans who in the 1990s advocated pulling back from the desegregation plan now make the distinction between their goals at that time and what they see as possible in the present. Cosby articulated the Afrocentrism and belief in institution building that inspired him and others to call for black-majority schools in the west end in 1991, but he also discusses where he now thinks he and his supporters were wrong. He and others point out the contemporary lack of facilities and human resources in the west end to sustain the sort of neighborhood schools they both remembered and envisioned. In part the problem was that schools had been closed and would need to be rebuilt. John Whiting added that the supply of black teachers had declined and thus "being a realist, we aren't going to be able to have any type of balance in the teaching staff."[35] These narrators in the end call not for a complete return to neighborhood schools but for choice, a sense of ownership of the schools in black neighborhoods, and a guarantee of an equitable distribution of resources. As Mattie Jones, a longtime Kentucky Alliance activist put it, "I want to see neighborhood schools too, I want to go back home. But when I go back home I . . . want the same quality, I don't want that old bull-jive separate but equal again. I want it equal all the way."[36] Jones's position, and that of other African American narrators, is more complex than a simple rejection or embrace of desegregation, and forces a less binary view of the black community's attitude on desegregation in the schools.

Paradoxically, although most of the narrators were interviewed after the *Meredith* decision, few had very much to say about that case or the community reaction to it. Some had become more involved with their church or moved on to other concerns. A few admitted feeling burned out or seeing others around them withdraw from active participation on this issue. As Hampe recalled, "People just get tired of carrying the banner." Both CEASE and QUEST eventually disbanded after some short efforts to keep them alive. Despite contemporary evidence that there were attempts to organize community concern about the fate of the desegregation plan as first *McFarland* and then *Meredith* wound their way through the courts, these narratives display a lack of sustained attention to those cases. This reflects perhaps that once the question was before the federal courts, local people could do little either for or against desegregation. The seeming futility of action was reflected in an interchange between a reporter and white Kentucky Alliance member Tom Moffett outside the Supreme Court. The reporter asked why bother demonstrating outside the walls where the justices could not hear them, and Moffett wistfully replied, "Who is going to pay attention to us if we don't make this trip?" This sense that matters were out of their hands contributed to the uncertainty that lingers in the narratives of those most directly involved in the school system's desegregation efforts in the wake of *Meredith*.[37]

The immediate response of the school board to the verdict in *Meredith* was to promise to find a way to maintain diversity and to prevent a return to segregated neighborhood schools. As Hampe and Todd reveal, school system staff and board members got to work developing a way to do that by borrowing ideas from other districts still maintaining diversity. During the following year plans centered on the "socioeconomic" approach, drawing on models elsewhere, as well as on ideas that had been floated in Louisville in previous years. In the spring of 2008 the board debated and adopted a new assignment plan that required between 15 and 50 percent of students at all schools to be from neighborhoods with low educational rates, defined as high school plus some college; more than 48 percent minority population; and an average household income of $41,000 or less. The plan also increased the number of magnet schools, reorganized elementary clusters to include more contiguous residential zones, and attempted to reduce transportation times. School officials justified their move in this direction with University of Kentucky polling data that showed more than 90 percent of parents supported racial diversity in the schools and that the majority favored maintaining choice through a more compact cluster plan. The plan went into effect for the elementary level in the fall of 2009.[38]

In the years since *Meredith*, the school board has faced and survived repeated challenges to its response to the Supreme Court order. Teddy Gordon represented different plaintiffs in three suits against the new socioeconomic student assignment plan in three years. Federal judges rejected two of them. A third, in which Gordon argued that an old state law guaranteed enrollment in the school nearest to a student's home, made it to the Kentucky Supreme Court. In September 2012 the justices denied that suit and upheld Jefferson County's assignment plan. Meanwhile, the school board reformed the plan to protect diversity in the schools while addressing parents concerns about long bus rides.[39] Most recently, in the fall of 2012 school board election, supporters of the assignment plan defeated candidates who promised to stop busing and return to neighborhood schools in each of the open seats, reflecting popular support for choice and diversity in education and seemingly protecting integration at least for the immediate future.

At this time of uncertainty about the future of the pro-active efforts to achieve racial and economic mixing in the schools, and in a climate in which leaders from the federal courts down to conservative pundits and politicians have rejected those efforts, it was perhaps easy to forget that for two decades biracial pro-integration coalitions had rallied to buck that national trend, defend the ideal of integration, and work for an equitable way to achieve it. Participants in the debates of the 1980s and 1990s over what to do about desegregation in Louisville and Jefferson County did not forget, however, and their stories of their experiences and beliefs can help us understand how the community's schools got to where they are and can contribute to the dialogue about where they should go next. They reveal the commitment to maintaining equity and protecting desegregation. They unpack the complexity of African Americans' critique of the student assignment plans, pointing not to a simple retreat to neighborhood schools but to a system of choice in which there is equity in resources and parents can feel ownership in the schools. Finally, these narratives illustrate how both blacks and whites have persistently rejected the separation of children into different schools by race and class. The stories that Sweeney complained have been forgotten in the reaction to *Meredith* thus might remind the community of the value of integration and of how men and women in the community, black and white, inside the system and out, have struggled to protect it.

CHAPTER FOUR

Remembering the Meaning and Impact
of School Desegregation

There are many ways to answer the question: What has desegregation meant for individuals, the schools, and the community? Social scientists analyze quantifiable outcomes such as test scores and graduation rates to measure educational achievement or employ an ethnographic approach to document the long-term fruits of an integrated education in individual lives. Oral history interviews can contribute additional information and insight to the assessment of school desegregation. During the interviews used in this book, the interviewers almost invariably asked the speakers to draw conclusions about the meaning of school desegregation. In response, narrators offered mixed appraisals, acknowledging a wide range of both personal and communal consequences. Their stories reveal that individual understandings of the past rarely fall into a stark dichotomy between positive and negative. The nuances in their judgments introduce both balance and complexity to the public memory and discourse about the long struggle for school desegregation in Louisville and Jefferson County.

This chapter differs from the previous ones in both structure and content. The memories shared here center not around a particular set of events or time period, but around questions of what desegregation meant for the narrators, the schools, and the community. Rather than beginning with a contextualizing introduction, the chapter foregrounds the words of the narrators. As the field of oral history has developed, scholars who use and theorize the methodology have invoked the value of yielding some of the interpretive authority in a study of the past to those who lived through it.[1] Historical actors are able to, and almost naturally do, use the formal

149

setting of an interview to draw broader conclusions about the meaning of their own experience. Indeed, the consciousness of recording for posterity and public consumption encourages reflection about the present and about the communal implications of past and personal experience. In a project devoted to documenting and examining the public memory of recent, ongoing, and at times controversial events, it is important to consider how local people remember and explain the significance of those events.

A few caveats: These interviews were conducted at different times, a few as early as 1988, before the most recent reforms in and challenges to the student assignment plan, others late enough for the interviewee to respond to the *Meredith* decision. Thus the narrators assess school desegregation from different points in time and with different amounts of information about the long-term outcome. In oral history the narrators' words do not speak for themselves, unfiltered by the intervention of the scholar. Rather, the interviewers' questions elicited the evaluations, which were then selected, organized, and edited before being presented here. Finally, scholarly studies of the results regionally and nationally provide the reader context for assessing the local impact of desegregation, but such information is not referenced directly by the narrators themselves, who instead derive their conclusions from personal experience and observation.

The narratives that follow are organized into four sections. Relatively few narrators spoke specifically or at length about the conditions in the schools before desegregation. This chapter opens with a couple of those reflections. That is followed by critiques of desegregation that mirror pessimistic declarations of its failure. In contrast, the third section includes remarks from those who emphasize the benefits of desegregation for the community or for themselves, and who insist on memorializing the hard work that went into achieving it. The final and longest set of narratives evaluates the impact of desegregation on schools and the community in ways that blend the positive with the negative, demonstrating the complexity first-person perspectives can bring to the assessment of the past.

Jim Crow Schools

The following narratives describe the conditions in the black schools before desegregation. While the narrators primarily emphasize the inequalities in resources, there are also hints of the less tangible qualities in the black schools under Jim Crow that some African Americans would come to miss after desegregation.

Evelyn Jackson, African American principal during the early years of desegregation in the city schools (interview with Tracy E. K'Meyer, 1999).

When I was a child, the students at Louisville were segregated. They were called colored schools. They were named after well-known celebrities of the black race. Douglass school was for Frederick Douglass. We attended buildings that had been vacated by the whites and had been moved to us. Usually we inherited what the whites discarded. The white schools were provided with the materials and books that they needed, but what they discarded they moved to the colored schools. The state didn't give anything then, you had to buy. My father had six children and a very small salary, but he went to the drugstore or the grocery store to buy secondhand books that had been discarded by the white race. That's the way we got our books. One teacher insisted I have a dictionary, and he did have to buy me a new dictionary. It was just like a Christmas present or something, because I had a new dictionary. When the white schools were given new editions, we were provided with the discarded ones. Materials were provided for the white schools and the colored teachers had to purchase their own. I ran an account at W. K. Stewart's on Fourth Street for years. I bought paper for artwork, a cheap grade of paper I will never forget. It looked as if it had oil in it, but you used that. The poor colored parents had to purchase secondhand books. Nothing was equal. They would say "equal," but nothing was equal. That's a word that has really stuck with me, this "equal."

Sandra Wainwright, African American teacher (interview with Tracy E. K'Meyer, 2000). In this story Wainwright indicates the conditions in black schools in the county, and differences between majority-black and majority-white schools in the city system in the 1960s. Salisbury Elementary, which no longer exists, was in the west end. Due to housing segregation, it remained all black even after desegregation in 1956. Brandeis was a formerly all-white elementary school in the west end. It later became the elementary math, science, and technology magnet. In this story Wainwright refers to herself by her married name, Harris.

Before I got my degree I had to be a student teacher. There was a lady who called the University of Louisville School of Music where I was working on my degree and said that she would accept me as a student teacher for the elementary schools. I had to go to different schools in the county: Berrytown, Griffytown, J-town, and two others, I can't remember what they were. Little bitty schools. I didn't even know we had them. I had to make the fire in the little potbellied stove. This was in the sixties. So I mean, all that marching that we did, it kind of helped a little bit, but didn't help a whole lot because we still had schools that were one room and two room. A couple of schools had first, second and third in that room over there. Fourth, fifth and sixth in this room over there. The best school was, of course, J-town because they had a real school. It was like I was going to some place special. But all the other four schools had just one- or two-room places. It's amazing. It just is. The same thing with the books. Those little schools had used books. In fact, we still had used books when I was teaching at Salisbury Elementary School.

I was to be the first black teacher at Brandeis. They called me in and said, "Now we would like for you to go to Brandeis Elementary School." He said, "It's going to be a white faculty and you're going to be teaching mostly white people. Are you willing?" I said, "I can do it." I was not supposed to go there until they finished the new building. They had a new section that they were adding on to Brandeis, where I was supposed to go. So I had to teach at Salisbury for half a year. From September to December. I want you to know, at Salisbury I can remember wanting scissors, plain old scissors to have children make cutout things. We would have to write a note to the office. Tell the office what day and what time we wanted to borrow the scissors. They gave us like, fifteen or twenty paperclips, fifteen or twenty thumbtacks. In that day we had jars of paint. We would go down into the basement and each teacher was allowed two tablespoons of white, two tablespoons of blue, green, orange, and purple. You would put them in your little cups and take it upstairs and the children would paint. All those kinds of things when I was at Salisbury.

When I moved to Brandeis, I had a telephone in my room. I could not believe it. I said, "Ohhhh." This is at Brandeis, in the new section. I go to Brandeis and I get on the phone because it's almost art time and I want to have some scissors because I didn't have any in my classroom. They said when you want something from the office you just pick up the telephone and call. I said, "Ohhh, this is great." So I get on the phone and I say, "This is Ms. Harris, Room 3 (whatever it was). I would like to borrow twenty-eight, no, make it twenty-nine, because I want to have a pair of scissors for me. And I would like fifteen thumbtacks, and twenty paperclips." And the lady said, "What are you saying?" I said, "Well, I need some scissors and I'll have them back to you by"—because we had to have them back. If we said we wanted them from 1:00 to 2:00, we had to have them back at 2:00. I was telling her about the paint. I said, "I don't know where I'm going to get the paint. So if you tell me where to get the paint and I can bring some baby food jars from home." She said, "Ms. Harris, write down what you need." I couldn't believe it. I said, "I need thumbtacks, paperclips, paint, I need construction paper." I wrote down all this stuff. They did not only send me twenty-eight, they sent me thirty-six pairs of scissors. And they said they are yours for the year. They gave me a whole box of paperclips. A whole box of tacks. Erasers, chalk, crayons. I thought I was in heaven. And then, on top of that, all those books that we had at Salisbury. Those old raggedy books. I had brand-new books at this new white school.

Clint Lovely, African American teacher and coach (interview with Elizabeth Gritter, 2005). Although acknowledging some financial disparity, Lovely focuses not on the imbalance in resources with the white schools but on the strength of the teaching and sense of community that existed at the black schools before desegregation.

The teachers were very strict, demanding and no nonsense. They demanded that we get in there and learn and try to do the best we could do academically as well as socially. They didn't have any problem with taking a ruler to our hand. If we got out of line they would discipline us with a quickness. They kind of put the fear of God in us, and I guess at that time you could do that. So the education we got was pretty good. As far as I knew we had the same books that everyone else did. Now I didn't know and I still don't know to this day whether we did or didn't. I know we had the Dick and Jane books, the *Weekly Readers*. I think that we had the same advantages as far as materials. Financially though, no.

At Central, we had an awful lot of pride in our school. It was the place we wanted to be. It was the focal point of our black community because it was the only school there, and it was our entertainment. We looked forward to the football games on Friday nights. We looked forward to the basketball games in the winter. We lived and died Central High School. It was everything to us.

Academically we had different levels of education at Central when I was there. We had what we called the College Preparatory, we had General Education, and we had the people that were in the Vocational Education. We were a comprehensive high school, we had everything in there. We prepared people for every field. We had auto body, auto mechanics, tailoring,

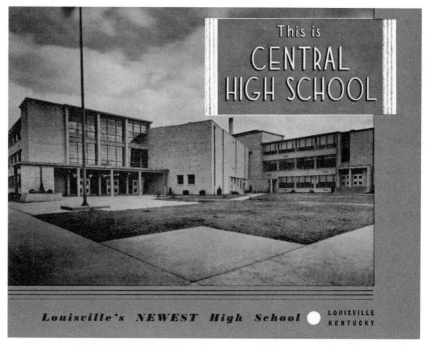

*"This is Central High School," 1952. Commemorative program
celebrating the opening of the new Central High in 1952. (Courtesy of the
Jefferson County Public Schools Archives)*

cooking, and cosmetology. Most of the older people who are in the areas of
cooking or tailoring came out of Central. Most people employed by these
department stores through the town are Central graduates. Those do the
seamstress and tailor work. Over half of them graduated from Central High
School, because that's what we did, we turned out tailors.

Shelby Lanier, African American policeman and activist (interview with
Tracy E. K'Meyer, 1999). Lanier attended Central before 1956. Here he
describes the disparate treatment of the school, even after the early wave
of desegregation.

I graduated from Central High School in 1954. I played football and baseball
at Central. While at Central we didn't even have a field, a football stadium.
When I first started I went into old Central, and they had a stadium there
right at the school. So then they built a new Central, the present Central
High School. When they built that school we were supposed to have a

stadium and it was supposed to have a swimming pool and all those kind of things. But when they built it they didn't do that! Then you'll find out how long it even took before they finally built the pool and they never built the stadium. In other words, it was like every time that we got something which we were supposed to have anyway—every school had a stadium—it was always something that we were denied or it had to be like it's something special and we've had to struggle to get it! That's where that racism comes in big time and it still exists. In other words, OK, if you get a new school, then what happens is there's something that you we're going to shortchange you in the deal and then you're going to have to struggle for it to get it.

Critiques of Desegregation

By the time of the interviews, some black community leaders had become disillusioned with integration in principle and called for the end of programs to achieve it. This section contains a sampling of those voices critiquing the assumptions behind desegregation, the reasons they believed it failed, and what was lost in the process, as well as representative whites who either opposed the desegregation plan all along or have come to doubt its effectiveness.

Carmen Weathers, African American community activist, leader in the effort to release Central from the desegregation plan (interview with David Cline, 2005).

This is beginning to go into the third generation of this social experiment that has not yielded any progress to black people. It would seem to me, just as an educator, you would want to amend this process, change it, tweak it, do something to it other than say continue to get on this bus, come out here, and go back just as ignorant as you were when you got on the bus. Black people still believe that somehow or another at the end of that bus ride, with no evidence to support it, that they're better. They say things like, "Well, it teaches you to get along with other people." That's the most ridiculous thing I've ever seen in my life. If you are a human being and I'm a human being, I don't need to get on a damn bus to learn how to get along with you. That implies that wherever I come from, we don't teach how to get along.

The real world is this ghetto that you live in. That's the real world that 90 percent of the black people who are in Jefferson County live, where they see each other; that's the real world. I mean, if you respect people and you see the larger society has certain rules and these rules operate whether you're in the black or the white part of town, you're courteous to people, you're considerate. If those rules are enforced, it doesn't matter where you wind up. To suggest that you have to be in proximity to white people in order to be prepared for this new world is ludicrous. It's saying that you have nothing in your experience or culture that equips you to deal with the real world. Therefore, I must compensate for this cultural deficit that you have and now you're ready. Now that's ludicrous.

Georgia Eugene, African American community activist, volunteer in 1975, and later staff with school system (interview with David Cline, 2005). Eugene refers to Morris Jeff, who was a local leader of black power–oriented organizations.

I still think we have not managed desegregation, and I don't see where it has been managed anywhere in the country. I remember Morris Jeff saying to us, "It's only peers that integrate." So I have to accept that you're a peer of mine and you have to accept it for us to truly integrate. Just because we're in the same space at the same time doesn't mean that integration occurs. We have not yet managed in this country to truly integrate, except in isolated cases.

What we really tried to implement, in my opinion, is the melting pot theory. I mean that you melt us all down and we all become "American" and forget everything else. That's not a realistic goal. We all need to learn to exist with one another and accept one another as we are. I think that's the true aim of integration and, yes, I think it's a worthy goal. But it's how we get there that we're not doing a very good job of.

See, I don't think school busing was set up to be that goal. I think that school busing was set up to bring about dispersal. It was to make people move. I call it white flight and black pursuit. They fly and we follow, and they fly and we follow. But then what we do, what we leave behind is a remnant and the remnant we left behind we don't leave the sustenance with it. We need to learn to make where we are better. I think that we would have done better with, rather than desegregate, to deal with the issue that first brought us to court in this country. The issue was black kids having to go past all-white schools to get to school. So the solution became sending white and black kids past schools. That doesn't make sense. You changed the problem and then you wonder why it didn't solve the original problem. You never tried to solve the original problem. When the case was taken to court, it was that there was an unequal share of resources given to white and black schools. The solution came to bus kids. What somebody said is that this country would not support putting more money into black schools, so we will make no schools black. We changed the problem; we keep doing that. We keep doing that and then we wonder why stuff doesn't work.

Benetha Ellis, African American mother and founder of United Black Protective Parents (interview with David Cline, 2004).

I don't see any benefits of busing because most of those kids that went to school with my children, they're either on drugs or they're alcoholics. They didn't finish school. They don't have any jobs. They're wanting to be drug dealers or tried to be drug dealers or they're dead. I just don't see the benefits. They weren't used to that hostility that they encountered and a lot of them couldn't take it. They said the heck with it. What am I going out here to be treated like this for? They don't want me out here. I don't want to be out here. So a lot of them took other turns in life, where they could have been very, very smart. I'm lucky because my children did fine. I have one, she's an accountant. My son is vice president of operations of Coca Cola. My daughter is twenty years in the military. So I'm lucky.

But I don't think that riding the bus has helped any. I think it is a waste of taxpayer's money. There should have been a better way of doing it. At first we were saying bus the teachers, upgrade the schools. I think it was all a plan because there are no schools in the west end anymore. All of them are closed. They are apartment buildings or condos or whatever you want to call them. We don't have any schools in the west end, very few. So now they don't have any choice but to bus them because there ain't nowhere to go in the neighborhood. I think they should have upgraded what we had and held the teachers to a higher standard. Get the right materials in the schools that we had, because we had good schools. We had good teachers.

Some attitudes changed. With my son, I could see the change when he started going to PRP [Pleasure Ridge Park]. He had a lot of white friends because he played basketball and he would stay all night with them and the parents were very supportive. So I think everybody just tried to start accepting the fact that that was the way it was going to be. So they just make the best out of a bad situation. But, if you go to Central right now there will blacks at one table and whites at the other. There's not a lot of intermingling because I think it's by choice. I don't think it has anything to do with racism or whatever. I guess it's the neighborhood you live in, the friends you have, and I think that they have a right to do that. If they have white friends, they have white friends. If they have black friends, they have, but don't try to force it because if you force it, it ain't going to fit.

Jean Ruffra, white mother and leader of Save Our Community Schools (interview with Ethel White, 1988).

I really think that was one of the worst five or six years in the history of the Jefferson County school system. I don't think busing has done what the experts thought it would do. I think it has destroyed our neighborhood school concept. The thing that bothers me the most is what has happened to students that were caught up in those early years of busing when you did have inadequate teachers. You had personnel that were there to draw a paycheck and they could have cared less what happened to those students in that school. Those youngsters during those years they missed so much. We had to stop a lot of the football games. We had to stop a lot of basketball games because of financial problems, and I haven't even touched on the finances. The busing for desegregation that first year cost us millions of dollars that could have gone into educational needs, teachers' salaries, this type of thing, but it went for other things! Those youngsters lost so much.

Sandra Wainwright, African American teacher (interview with Tracy E. K'Meyer, 2000).

I think we're going to look down fifty years from now and say I can't believe they had children riding for an hour, an hour and a half, to go to a school when they had schools in their neighborhood. What I liked about King School—my kid acted up, I would say, "Hey, sit there. We're going to walk home together today." You can't do that with busing. You see your parents maybe on conference day or you get on the telephone and call. I had problems with us moving out of the community. See, I could walk into a store and see some kid doing something wrong and I'd say, "Hey, you know better than that. You better put that back there." Just like that. You better not tell somebody's child that nowadays. But when you lived in the neighborhood, they all knew my husband was a teacher. They also knew he was a coach. When you go in the community they knew you because you were the one that was teaching their children. Now, I can see why we would have to go and probably do what we had to do. Yeah, we needed it. But no, I didn't want to leave my neighborhood.

Frances Bloom, white teacher in city and then county schools (interview with Elizabeth Gritter, 2005).

I questioned the need for such wholesale busing because it was a huge expense. I'm not sure that I saw major changes in the academic performance other than the kids were spread out. I think they had more educational opportunities because everybody wasn't at the same level. They would see kids that were performing much better and maybe strive a little harder, some kids would. Others would just totally give up. I think it had its successes, but I think busing also had some failures to it. I think it was a colossal amount of money that was spent on transportation that could have better been spent providing in the schools. If you want to spend that money, maybe put extra teachers in and make the classes smaller so we can give more individual attention. I've always been a believer in a smaller class; you get more attention from the teacher than you do in a larger class. If you can give more personal attention to a child, they're going to do better in school.

I think the goal of busing was to provide an equal education opportunity for every child. The courts, who I guess made the decision, or the people who started the lawsuit, saw the county schools as having more opportunities than the inner-city schools had. They wanted to equalize that. I think that's where it began, wanting those equal opportunities for their kids. I think for some kids, it probably did that. I think for some kids, they would have fallen through the cracks no matter where they were. I think it's hard to take kids out of their neighborhood. It decreases the opportunity for a parent to become involved in the school, and I think that's a major factor in a child's success, is how involved the parent is. If parents aren't involved, the kids are going to be less inclined to achieve at a high level. Transportation was a major problem for most parents of the inner-city schools. They depended on public transportation and if it took too many bus changes to get out to the school where their child was, they just wouldn't show.

I think I was probably more optimistic initially, that yeah it would equalize things. I think over time, I've maybe moved back toward the middle, like I'm not sure it did. Looking back, I'm not sure it really did equalize things. I think certainly it gave some opportunities to kids that they might not have had to see other neighborhoods. A lot of the kids that went out to affluent schools that had never been out of their own neighborhoods to see what the possibilities are there. They lived very sheltered lives. I think the biggest success that I can see from busing is there's probably a lot more acceptance of other races and equality in hiring, or it's more readily acceptable to have friends of other races, whereas they may not have had it not been for busing.

Desegregation Success Stories

As Bloom hints in her final words, alongside this critique was another appraisal, one that on balance emphasized the constructive outcomes of desegregation. Some narrators talk about the broader social benefits for the community, while a few mention the gains in their own lives. Often narrators display a consciousness that this is not a common memory of school desegregation, and they take the opportunity to insist not only that the gains be acknowledged but also that credit be given to the unheralded men and women who made it happen.

June Key, white mother and school volunteer (interview with Ethel White, 1988). This interview was conducted before many of the later reforms and challenges to the desegregation plan.

There was an article just last week that expressed the feeling that when you walked into a school there's still the isolation there. I thought the most articulate statement in the whole article was from a black parent who said, "We didn't start out to just bring black children and white children and adults together socially." Anybody that thought that never grasped the idea! This happened to bring equal educational opportunities, the same kind of schools for white children as for black children. The same kind of materials and equipment in the schools no matter where you walked in—whether it was an urban area, the black community or white—the science labs were equipped the same. The books were just as new in one and just as bad in one as in the other, they had a mix of both. The teachers in one could have taught at any other school. That's what it was all about! We want what is best for our children and we don't think they're getting it and if it takes desegregating the schools and our children having to go to school with white children or vice versa to bring that about then that's what we have to do. And there truly were differences. Anybody that wants to be honest, there were differences. Buildings were older in the older communities and so there were differences and they did need to change. I don't buy that a black child necessarily learns better because they sit next to a white child. I think a black child can learn no matter where if they got a good teacher and they got equipment and they got materials and the help that they need just the same, the white child needs that same kind of help. That's what it was all about is to try to equalize opportunity. I just think our progress is tremendous.

I feel like that a lot of people painted some very dark pictures of what had happened—anything that happens that's wrong, any child that gets hit by a rock or any policeman, as one did, gets his eye put out and you had burnings and you had buses being rocked and those kind of things, and the slurs from both black and white people being hurled at children, children having to lay down on the buses with the rocks. Those are things none of us are proud of. There's many things that I'm not proud of about Louisville and Jefferson County that happened in those early days. But what I am proud of so outweighs it that it's hard for me to dwell on the negative. I think this school system has pulled itself together. I would put this school system against any in the country. I think we're one of the most progressive, one of the best school systems in the country. It's sort of like the phoenix coming from the ashes. I think we have just risen out of the despair and out of many concerns and we have become a much, much, much better school system. Some people will still say they don't believe in what happened. Of course they're entitled to that, but I personally believe we are much better people. I think the system is much better and the community is much better for what we've gone through.

Pat Todd, white teacher and then administrator for the school system (interview with David Cline, 2009).

I think that the federal deseg order, while it was highly problematic in its initial few years of implementation, has really strengthened the school system and the community vision over time. I'm not saying we don't have our problems. I'm not saying that we are not threatened now with rollback. But when you talk to civic leaders, what you hear a great deal of is that there does seem to be more common interest and common vision, because whatever's happening in the schools in the inner city, you can have suburban children sitting in those schools. And whatever's happening in the suburban schools, you've got inner-city kids sitting there. So it has created more of a sense of unity and common vision from a community development—and frankly, I mean, from an economic development—perspective. I believe that most of our business leaders here in town are very concerned about the quality of the workforce, both in terms of organically growing up our own industries, but also in attracting others from other parts of the country or even internationally. They take a look at Chicago and they see what's going on in the inner city of Chicago or even Nashville or Indianapolis or Cincinnati, and they think, "If we're not careful, we could have a large demographic group of our children looking more like that." While it's not perfect and the school system has a long way to go, we think it's better than having them isolated in schools of color and poverty.

June Hampe, white mother, school volunteer, and participant in reform processes of the 1980s and 1990s (interview with David Cline, 2005).

Why has our deseg plan worked and no place else that we can point to in the country, who had a sizeable district, has it worked? We went to court to keep it. So many other places, it's the district going to court to get rid of it. Well we went to court to say we have to continue to do this. Why does it work here and it hasn't worked other places? I think there are several factors but one factor is commitment on the part of the school administration to make it work. Are all of our administrators gods? For heaven's sake no. Have they been for thirty years? For Pete's sake no. But the school board and the upper administration has [sic] remained true to the notion that the judge said we have to. That's what's carried it through, tremendous respect for the court ruling. What we have done every time we've adjusted the plan, '84, '91, '96, 2001, it's always been to make it easier for everybody to live with. Keep the same goals, and smooth off the rough stuff, and try to keep it easier. Now is it hard to administer? You'd better believe it. But by and large, it works very well most of the time for most people. I think that it's been a tremendous commitment on the part of the school district. The religious community has been really fairly supportive. The business community as a whole has been supportive. I think the university's been supportive. We don't have major anybodies out in the community jumping up and down and saying, get rid of this stupid thing. The community has really been supportive.

Does that mean everybody loves the plan? Absolutely not. Are there things I'd do differently? Yes, a lot more balance to it. But then that's one of the advantages of old age; you get to look back, you have perspective which you don't have when you're young and that's probably a good thing because it gets you up and out in the morning and chug, chug, chug. Somebody's got to get out there and be on the battlement or behind the scenes doing the stuff, and you can't do that if you don't believe in what you're doing.

Sherry Jelsma, white parent and human relations volunteer in 1975; school board president in 1984 (interview with Ethel White, 1988).

During that period [1975] there were people whose whole lives were consumed with trying to ensure safety and quality in the schools. They really had to do that for about a year and then gradually it got more normal. But the first year if we hadn't had people in the schools volunteering the way we did I don't think we could have made it. I think the people in the schools were heroes. The principals and the teachers and the parents were the ones that—and the kids—pulled it through, white and black.

Ken Miller, white national guardsman (interview with Elizabeth Gritter and Timothy P. McCarthy, 2004).

I like now to identify myself with [busing] because I'm a history teacher. I risked my life to help the schools. Bull cheese. [Laughter] I'm just trying to jump on board, grab a hold of somebody else's bravery. The true story there, in my opinion, is the people, especially African Americans, that put their kids on those buses, those were the brave ones. They were dreaming the American Dream that if there's a place where there is a neutral zone in America it's got to be a school. If it isn't a school, where is a place in this country that we can go feel that we're on level playing ground? I mean that's the whole premise behind public schools, that something good can happen there and the cycle that your parents went through, we could break the cycle. Education is a dream factory, and so those are the heroes that risked their kids, dreamed dreams that it would hold together; and it did.

Edith Yarborough, African American student during initial busing years and later teacher (interview with David Cline, 2009).

Through busing, I think I've gleaned many blessings. I really have. Initially, you look at it as, oh, I'm being bused and others were too. We were being placed in schools where we're not wanted, and it's uncomfortable. But, it was for the bigger cause, and we need to advance that cause. We need to advance the cause of exposing children to other opportunities. I would take any opportunity. I don't care if I had to travel five hundred miles away to get there, if that's going to advance us as a people; I don't mean collectively as blacks, but as a people. Blacks, whites, Latinos. If that's going to help my community, if that's going to help my state, if that's going to help us as a people, then we need to stop looking at what's uncomfortable, because that's what they did in the past. Your grandmother, your parents did that. It's not about me, me, me, me, me.

We'd be foolish to say there haven't been gains, because there have been gains. I think we should always be thinking ahead, and trying to make the best culture, to make our communities better. I mean, it's uncomfortable, but so what? If my grandmother can do it, and my daddy endured it, so what? I can do it. To whom much is given, much is required. You just can't keep taking and not give back.

Bonita Emerick, white student who participated in 1975 school boycott (interview with Elizabeth Gritter, 2005).

Looking back, I now believe that busing was a necessary evil. It is now common to see interracial groups of friends in restaurants, in the workplace, and on campus. When I was young, this would not have been common or accepted. I think that busing helped bring black and white children together, and it educated them of their cultural differences and taught them that these differences were OK. I've learned that you have to be open, to accept people for who they are because if everybody acted and behaved in the same way, there would be no diversity and just everybody going about like as a machine and not accepting that black people can like their clothes and their music and still live next to you. That if you can learn to accept that, you can grow and have a lot of new friends and appreciate a lot of different things that the world has to offer.

Clint Lovely, African American teacher and coach at Central High (interview with Elizabeth Gritter, 2005).

Personally for me desegregation has been a success. For me it has because I never would have gotten to experience some of the things I have experienced had it not been for integration. It worked for me. I can't speak for everybody else. I think it has been successful and I also think it has not been a success; it is both sides of that coin. If thirty years ago you told me you wanted to integrate I would say I am against it, I'm totally against it. But it would be all for selfish reasons, all because I was an athletic coach and I wanted to maintain that power I had athletically. I am just going to be honest; I wanted to maintain that power that we had at Central. I didn't want anyone else to have that power. We were black and proud and I wanted to maintain that power. Now, it's more than sports. Sports are still the focal point of my life, but there is more to it now. It's about getting these kids educated and having them be able to have a dream. Have them be able to have a dream and be able to try and obtain something for themselves. That is the most important thing now. I am a strong supporter of integration because I have seen and experienced for myself the doors that it can open.

Finding the Middle Ground

The narratives in this final section illustrate how complicated first-person retrospective assessments of school desegregation can be. During what were at times multihour interviews, narrators came back to the question of the results of busing and desegregation from many different angles and made an effort to give a complete and balanced answer. They mourn the damage it caused while listing its accomplishments. They critique the way it was carried out, while concluding it was good for society. In short, they seek, as Robert Cunningham put it, a "middle ground" from which to view the long-term consequences for the community.

Robert Cunningham, African American community activist (interview with Tracy E. K'Meyer, 1999; interview with Elizabeth Gritter, 2004).

I think there's a lot of good things that have come from [school desegregation]. Getting to know each other, getting to understand one another, all of that has been good. But there have been a lot of losses. I don't know what the loss was in the majority community. I'm not sure what their loss has been if any, but I do know in the black community there has been loss of things that black kids probably don't even realize because they weren't here, they didn't see it. I'm often called by young black folk to talk about the early black community because they know nothing about the vibrancy that was there. Oh, they hear about the music and maybe a few other things, but they don't know about what was there that was so rich, the culture that was so rich that was there, that we were proud of.

I think school desegregation in a way was one of the main reasons for that loss. It was greatly responsible for the cessation or death of the culture within the black community. I don't think it was deliberately done. There wasn't too much in the black community that the majority community saw worth salvaging. Our books were handed down from the white school system. The books that white kids had last year we got next year. But there was a feeling of solidarity that was within the black school that made the school ours. If it didn't have a chemistry lab it was still ours. If I didn't make As and Bs, this was still mine. I was a part of this. I felt as though we saw some of that taken away when we began to go into white schools. I guess what I'm saying is, I don't think we in the black community felt like it was that bad before desegregation. Being together meant a lot for us because there was a lot that we had that we understood that we gave one another. Not having whites in the classroom wasn't something that we were concerned about. Although we knew that we went to an inferior school system, which was one of the very reasons for people like myself to push for integrated schools. So that was one of the things that I felt even at that time. We may not have had that state of art gymnasium or science center or whatever, but we had some more things that we felt were worth preserving.

Those of us who were somewhat pro-desegregation, have to now look back and say, "Wait a minute, has it been worth that?" One of my greatest concerns was black kids taken into a white environment that is unfriendly and would mess them up psychologically, and I think it has in many ways. So I was concerned about that. I saw black kids being brought into a society, into a setting that now told them they didn't look right, they didn't see themselves in the book any place, you don't talk right. That can wound you, and I think that happened.

There is probably a black child on some street corner today, right now, who we have given up on who probably has a mind that has in it the answer for cancer or AIDS that will never get to a medical school. There's probably some Thurgood Marshall standing on one of these corners right now that we have given up on just by looking at him or her, that will never make their way to a law school because we don't see the value in helping them and how much that's going to help all of us. I think in many ways that happened. I don't think it was the intent. I do think that school desegregation or busing, if we want to call it that, was a good intention. It was supposed to have been a remedy for something that was terrible, which was school segregation. I just think it didn't work well because there were those that didn't see the value of it or didn't help it to work well, including some of the elected officials at that time that were here and some of the people whose voices could have meant something.

It's hard for me to sit in a room now and discuss this with people and know what side to be on. I hear those guys who say, "I've always said we never could go to school with white kids." So I can't say he's wrong. And this other guy says, "I think a lot has come out of this." I can't say that he's wrong because a lot has come out of it. So I try to find a middle ground and say that it has helped because it has brought these kids physically together, it has made that white kid go home and say, "No, all those black kids are not dumb. There's a kid next to me that makes straight As." It has made black kids see white kids. My granddaughter even now, she comes home and tells me about something that happened in school. I used to, in my old way of thinking, ask, "Was he black or white?" And she'll look at me—and she's twelve years old, thirteen now—she says, "Well, I didn't even notice." She doesn't even notice it. The point I'm making is I think it has done something because it has brought these kids together. There's a lot of white folks now and a lot of black folks that are with one another because they met in school that wouldn't have met. Where would they have met, church? They don't go to church together. Church is not nearly as integrated as school is. So I think it has brought that. I think that knowing one another has helped a lot. Those are the positive sides of it. When I see black kids and white kids who I know are dedicated to helping one another and doing things together, even businesses together, it does something for me because I know that wouldn't have happened in my day. So I think for the things that were lost, it may have been worth it.

Phil Mahin, African American teacher assigned to county schools after busing (interview with Elizabeth Gritter, 2005).

What I didn't like about desegregation was that you lost the teachers who cared about students. Because when you have to have so many black teachers teach out in the county, there's not that many of us. So maybe you might have one or two black teachers in each school. So therefore, you don't have a lot of students, black students, who said, "Well, I can identify with these teachers." I've been in teaching thirty-some-odd years, and there are good white teachers and there are good black teachers. But my sense of it is that quite a few of the white teachers didn't want to be involved. They weren't concerned because first of all they were being forced to teach these kids, and they just didn't want to; there was no connection there. You got a kid coming all the way from the west end going all the way out in the county, whereas you got schools right here in the city he could go to. That just wasn't good, in my opinion. I think we could have gotten them just as good of an education if not better if we stayed the way we were.

The problem was the distribution of the books and the distribution of all the quality of the other schools. That's what the problem was. Whatever the county got or whatever the other schools got, you got to make sure every-body gets it. That wasn't happening. So that was the main problem to me. As I see it, these "predominantly black schools" weren't getting the same facilities that the predominantly white schools were getting. But as far as teaching-wise, they probably were getting a better quality of teachers, in my opinion, because to me to be a teacher, you got to care. If you don't care, you're a dead duck. I don't care if you're white, purple, green, or blue, you got to care about all the kids. I think when you're forced to do something, I think that's what a lot of white teachers had a problem with. When you're forced to teach another race or whatever, they didn't take kindly to that, quite a few didn't. I'm not saying all of them. I don't want to characterize every single one of them. That's just my own personal opinion.

The main benefit I see out of school desegregation is that it stepped up the quality as far as materials. In other words, some schools were getting a lot more quality of equipment—books and so on and so forth, whereas other schools were being neglected out in the west end or the southern part of Louisville, central part of Louisville. So that was the main purpose of the desegregation plan was that they tried to make things equal. As far as integrating the whites and blacks, I think there's some good that there's an inter-meeting of white and black because it's going to have to happen sooner or later in the real world and the career life; you're going to have to deal with it.

But I don't think you have to have it in schools. I feel like let a kid choose wherever he wants to go. If it happens to be a predominantly black school, fine. If it happens to be a predominantly white school, fine. If it happens to be half and half, fine. I understood why they forced the issue, though, be-cause there was too much disparity as far as the dispensing of equipment, the dispensing of material things. So if you force it and you make whites come and blend with blacks you're going to have this gap closing. I see that as a positive. But, why don't you just make it equal without saying I'm going to bus you from the furthest part of Louisville all the way thirty miles to go to school out here?

Also, the whites didn't always come, so that's another problem. The whites who lived out in the county, they're not coming into the west end of

Louisville. You see they were busing the blacks out there to make the quota correct. The blacks were being bused out and the whites were staying. I didn't like that part of it. Matter of fact, I hated that part of it because you're losing your community. You're losing your community base. You're saying your school is better than my school, and I say bullcrap. I say the schools like Central and DuValle and Virginia Avenue, they were all black schools, they were good schools. Let's put us on equal footing. Now if whites want to come to Central, fine. You go where you want to go but don't say that we're inferior to you as far as teacher quality. The only difference is you might have better equipment than we had. So that's the only difference. I think that's what desegregation did. It brought facilities that should have been at Central and should have been in the west end. They should have gotten them in the first place. There shouldn't have to be a blending of two races, so we can have these facilities.

To summarize, the good parts of desegregation were the facilities, that was the good part. And it probably was a good part that you had mixing of the white and black, so you understand what blacks go through and vice versa, you understand whites. That's probably good; eventually it turned out to be good. I believe to this day that's what should have happened. I think we've come through it OK. I think Louisville has evolved. We got a lot more growing to do, especially education-wise, and that's another story. But I think it's gotten better. I think relationships have gotten better between white and black, but we still have a ways to go. But we'll get there. Hopefully they'll get there before my lifetime is over.

Dan Withers, African American teacher who taught at both city and county schools (interview with David Cline, 2004).

It looked like we lost a generation of black kids academically. When I was at Shawnee there were a lot of excellent students. When I went to PRP, the black kids were still in their academic mode. They had not been taught not to be good academic students. They did very well, extremely well at PRP when I was there. But when I got to Fairdale, out of eleven hundred total students, three hundred black students, it was less than ten who were on the honor roll, and it was that way for the entire time I was there. I was there for about eight years. I said, we're losing a generation. Where are our good black students going? I hope they were someplace, because they did have magnet programs that they could volunteer to go to. I was hoping that if they weren't at Fairdale, they would still be at other schools in the system.

That's one reason I was pretty much anxious to come to Central, because I just knew that a lot of good black students were going to Male, Manual, and Central. So I said well, I have an opportunity to go back to Central, which was historically a black school, where I graduated, where I'm still having black kids who are doing extremely well. But either at Fairdale they were just transferring out because they didn't like the reputation that Fairdale had, or we just lost them someplace in the school system before they got to high school. Was it in elementary during the busing years, or was it in middle school during the busing years, or they just chose not to go to Fairdale— they had an opportunity to go to Manual or one of the magnet schools and they transferred out? I couldn't tell you. My experience at Fairdale was that we had lost a lot of our minority students.

But I think desegregation has helped society. It's been a struggle, but I think it has helped society because I think that now white folks who thought of blacks as being inferior or being bogey bears, realize that black kids aren't all that way, or most of them are not that way. They realize that black kids are human just like they are. The black kids who've developed their biases because they lived in isolated communities realized that all white folks aren't bad. So I think it has opened up society in terms of allowing blacks and whites to accept one another and to integrate. I think society is much better off for it, in my opinion. You would have people who would disagree with me adamantly probably, black and white people. I think it has helped society, but I think that it's been a struggle and I think we lost some black kids in the process.

Joe McPherson, African American principal at Central (interview with David Cline, 2004).

The Central staff was well integrated before forced busing. I'd say the staff at that time might have been about seventy-thirty, 70 percent black teachers and white teachers 30 percent. But then when busing was forced on us, well, let's don't say forced on us. Let's say when busing came about. Our staff had already been integrated. I remember one of the supervisors came by and asked me and another teacher, who was our best English teacher, if we wanted to go to Atherton to teach and we said no because we said the kids here at Central need us. Thelma Lauderdale was [one of] our better teachers and she said Mac, they came over and asked me if I wanted to go to Atherton. I said they asked me the same thing. So we figured we needed to stay there with our kids because they needed us, so we declined to go.

*Joe McPherson (right) with Robert Moore and B. Edwards of the
Central High School Band. (Courtesy of the* Louisville Defender *Collection,
Special Collections, University of Louisville)*

But they systematically took the black teachers out and sent them out to
different schools like Butler and Eastern, one here and one there.

Now traditionally, when they merge the systems, the inner-city schools
are either torn down or transferred into elementary schools or junior high
schools. There was one time when the merger first started in '75 we had a
huge assembly. The county parents, the white parents came to Central just
to look around to see if it was a real school. Some of them were amazed
and they said, "Well, this is better than where our kids go." The word was
out that they came down there to change the name of the school. Some
of the Central High School older alumni were there to check to see what
I was going to say or do about it. So my speech to the audience was don't
come down here trying to talk about changing the name of the school
because we're not going to change it. The word was out they were going
to call it River City High School or River Glen, something like that. But I
told the people, no, we're not going to change the name of Central High
School. We've been here too long. Our tradition is stronger than most other
schools because they came along after Central. Central has been there a
hundred years. So instead of talking about changing the name and closing
the school down they decided, well, we'll come in and do some cosmetic

work. Some of the things were really needed. Our class offerings changed because they had to reflect the offerings at the other schools. For example, if Eastern taught Latin 4, and some of those kids were at Central, we had to offer Latin 4. If we did not have enough calculus or trigonometry, advanced classes, we had to put those classes in.

The good part about it was the academic part where you would have an expanded curriculum. You would have more offerings. We had a lot of good students at that time. We had students who were [National] Merit finalists. In fact, at one time we had more of the higher academic kids than the other schools in our cluster. The other school principals couldn't understand it. They used to tease me and say, well, you got those kids from us. Well, that's fine but they belong to us now. Resources, supplies, and things like that had to improve because if your expanded curriculum required you to have those higher academic classes you had to have the supplies and the books to go with it. Our PTA flourished a little bit more then than it normally had. We had some parents who were in the know at the board. We had one of the little state senators who treated the super-intendent like he was a kid. When we needed something we'd approach them and let them go after the Board of Education to get the supplies. So the supplies and the equipment was [sic] increased. The chemistry lab, [we] tore the whole lab out and refinished it. The language labs, we had to redo those.

One of the negatives that came out of forced busing at Central High School was no school spirit. We had a school song. The kids that were bused there said, we don't want to learn a school song. We won't be here but two years. Kids were spread out all over town back in those days and kids came to Central, a lot of the athletes. We had guys walking the hall at six-six that wouldn't play basketball. Our football team went down. Athletics went down, both participation-wise and spectator-wise. We didn't hardly have anybody that would show up for games, basketball or football, because the kids lived in the Ballard area, Eastern area, Waggener and Atherton area, they didn't want to come to Central. They wouldn't come back at night. It's still that way. The school spirit never came back really.

Clint Lovely, African American teacher and coach at Central High (interview with Elizabeth Gritter, 2005).

The thing that I loved about Central, and everybody loved about Central, was that it represented the black community. Now, I don't think we have a high school that represents the black community anymore. I don't think we have a focal point. Our focal point now has gone to the University of Louisville for whatever reason. Most of the brothers rally behind the University of Louisville because we see that as being a black situation.

At the time when I was teaching school at Central, everything was Central. That's why we had some good things going on at Central because the emphasis was on Central High School and its blackness. But now it's not. Even though it's pretty much black again, it's not the same. We have had two or three decades of going to other schools like PRP [Pleasure Ridge Park], Eastern, other places like that. Our allegiance is not at one school anymore, it's spread out. We are everywhere, instead of being in just some places, we are everywhere. So, I guess in that vein it's good. But, I hate losing what we had, the community and spirituality. It was almost spiritual, if you understand what I mean. If we lost, we cried because it hurt. When we won, the whole community was happy.

On the other hand, after merger and desegregation I saw more parental involvement. I saw better treatment for the athletes that were injured. We had doctors all of a sudden. We had one of the greatest orthopedic teams in the world. They volunteered their services. We didn't have that before. Those are the kinds of doors that were opened up to us. I remember one year I had a parent to pay for my football banquet at the end of the season. Do you know that everybody at that banquet, about sixty of us, had a big steak, a baked potato, salad, dessert, and tea. They were big sirloins on that plate. We had it made! That was fantastic! She saw to that, she took care of that because she wanted to take care of her son. She wanted to make sure her son didn't have his banquet in the cafeteria. Those are the kinds of things I am talking about, things coming to us that ordinarily we wouldn't have had coming to us.

And, looking back, the white kids who came down to Central during that time are far richer and better human beings than the kids who didn't. I run into them daily and they all tell me what a great experience they had and how they wouldn't trade it for anything in the world. So, it was good because it let people know people. It got us to the point where we could talk to each other. But we did lose something at Central. I guess with change something has to happen, it couldn't stay the same. We loved that bond we had with the high school, but we don't have it anymore. Now, all of our kids are at PRP or Ballard, Wagner, or at Eastern, they are all over. Central now is gradually becoming black again, and if we are not careful we are destined to relive this, maybe not in my lifetime, but in the next one hundred years or so, if we are not careful.

Do we want to go back? That is the question. Knowing what I know now, we don't need to go back. I don't want white people to have anything I can't have, and the only way I can have it is to be out there with them. If somebody had asked me if I was for integration in 1975 I would have said no because I liked things the way they were. But you have to change. Like I said, we lost a lot, but we did gain. We as a people gained and some white people gained as well. So it was a win-win situation, I guess, for both people.

■ Did school desegregation fail black students and their communities, or did it equalize resources and generate better interracial understanding? Just as local people disagree about the ultimate answer to the question of the impact of school desegregation, so have a generation of social scientists. For more than forty years scholars have sought to answer that question using a variety of methodologies and interpretive approaches. The conclusions of these studies have often been contentious; the sheer volume and disparate findings providing fodder for arguments both for and against school desegregation. Those who take a dim view of the results assert that there have not been significant improvements in black achievement and that any gains need to be weighed against the social costs of court-ordered busing. Moreover, historians and sociologists point to the losses suffered by African Americans with the closing or decline of schools in their communities.[2] In the past decade, however, a growing consensus, or as one author put it, a "preponderance" of scholarship, has formed to support the conclusion that desegregated school environments improve quantifiable measures of achievement for minority and poor students and benefit long-term life and career experiences for both blacks and whites.[3] Oral history adds additional evidence and insight to this debate, not only corroborating social scientists' conclusions in a more personal, human way but also creating a model for a more balanced public dialogue about school desegregation.

Scholars, school officials, and pundits most commonly measure the educational impact of desegregation with comparisons of test scores in reading and math. While the gap between the scores of whites and blacks has not disappeared, investigations in communities across the country demonstrate that it narrows in desegregated settings. One study, for example, examined twenty-two thousand schools and found that black and Hispanic students posted more gains in math when they attended diverse institutions, rather than racially or ethnically isolated ones. Studies that take a broader and more qualitative view produce consistently positive findings about the impact of school desegregation on career trajectories and changed attitudes. Black graduates of racially mixed schools are more likely to go to college, especially an integrated one, and work in professional and integrated environments later. In addition, graduates of all races of desegregated schools are more racially tolerant and comfortable in mixed settings. On the other hand, in the wake of Supreme Court decisions rolling back desegregation, scholars have traced the harmful impact of the return to racial and economic segregation. A close examination of the Norfolk, Virginia, schools, for example, revealed that "none of the promises attached to the return to neighborhood schools came true." White flight did not reverse and parental involvement did not increase, but the educational gap between whites and blacks widened.[4] In short, although school desegregation never achieved all that its proponents hoped for, it produced better outcomes than the alternative. The predominant conclusion of this body of scholarship thus belies the political narrative of school desegregation's failure, instead demonstrating its relative success as a social policy both quantitatively and qualitatively.

Although no scholars have completed a thorough review of the educational results of school desegregation in Louisville or Jefferson County, extant evidence indicates that outcomes there mirror national trends. In the first decade following the 1975 busing order, the gap between the test scores in both math and reading for whites and blacks narrowed dramatically, as African American students began to catch up with their white counterparts. Yet that gap began widening again after 1985. After 1996 the differences in reading scores stabilized, but the gap on math tests fluctuated widely from year to year without a consistent pattern. On another measure, ACT results, African American student scores climbed throughout the 1980s and 1990s, while the gap between black and white results narrowed. The gap also remained smaller than that in a national sample, indicating that Jefferson County was doing a comparably better job of reducing inequalities between white and black student achievement. These patterns were replicated for SAT scores. Despite these gains on standardized pre-college tests, however, a 2008 study of test scores in primary and secondary grades revealed persistent racial differences in both the state and county. Some schools in Jefferson County do substantially better than others in narrowing that gap, however, resulting in differences between white and black reading scores at some high schools as low as three or four points and at others as high as twenty-six or thirty.[5] Thus while differences in achievement persist, the educational experience and results depend to a great extent on the individual school setting.

Amy Wells of Columbia University Teachers College and her research associates used qualitative methods to assess the long-term impact of desegregation in Louisville for an amicus brief in the *Meredith* case. Reflecting findings elsewhere, members of the 1985 and 1986 graduating class of Jefferson County schools reported to Wells's research team that going to integrated schools made them more open-minded, more racially tolerant, and more comfortable in diverse settings. They also asserted that because of residential segregation, school was their only opportunity to get to know someone of another race. They recalled challenges such as problems with transportation and racial tension within the schools and admitted that being the first generation to go through county-wide desegregation required sacrifices. But they also emphasized the changes in their worldview that served them well after graduation, in particular in the contemporary integrated workplace. More recently, education policy scholar Gary Orfield conducted an opinion survey of current students in the Jefferson County Public Schools and their parents. These students, like the alumni of a generation earlier, spoke well of their experience, citing their feeling of being prepared to go into a "rapidly diversifying society."[6] Thus the county's public schools have shown gains in test scores in the initial post-desegregation period, and signs of some improvement in standardized tests more recently, but also persistent inequality in other educational measures. On the other hand, local graduates like those in national studies laud the less quantifiable changes that enriched their lives. In short, in Jefferson County there has been an incomplete transition to educational equity, but one that has had widely acknowledged individual and societal benefits.

When concluding their own story, or commenting on the impact of the long struggle over school desegregation in Jefferson County, narrators do not cite statistics, scholarly analyses, or even public surveys; nor do they often talk about trends in test scores or short-term educational gains. Instead they assert what they know from their own experience and observations, and elaborate the way desegregation affected them as individuals or their community. Reflecting pessimistic conclusions about desegregation from scholars and commentators, some narrators saw little progress for black students individually and little value resulting from whites and blacks going to school together. They regret the black children who fell through the cracks, largely due to the lack of support for them in the desegregated schools. They lament the lost sense of pride, belonging, and community that sustained young African Americans. While education policy investigations rarely measure or account for this sense of what was lost, it has been documented in a growing body of historical work that explores how African Americans remember their segregated schools. In these studies historians have examined African Americans' memories of caring and qualified teachers, high expectations, plentiful extracurricular activities, and parental and community support for students and schools.[7] The memory of Central as such a school helps explain the deep attachment to the institution and the determination of the local black community to protect it in subsequent years.

These memories of what was lost provide an opportunity for understanding how African Americans view the impact and process of desegregation. Both scholars and the public must be wary of romanticizing the past; there were dramatic class and resource differences between black schools throughout the region before desegregation. But the memories of these schools cannot simply be dismissed as nostalgia either. Most of the interviews that support this body of scholarship, like the local oral histories presented here, took place years after desegregation and thus were influenced by and reflect the speaker's experience—either as an individual or as a part of the community—with the process. In interviews African Americans acknowledge what their schools lacked, and they discuss how the absence of labs or their out-of-date books circumscribed their education, especially in comparison to the white schools. In the Louisville interviews, for example, Evelyn Jackson and Sandra Wainwright paint clear pictures of the inequality masked by "separate but equal." African Americans went into desegregation looking for the resources to equalize education for their children. But when those children encountered hostile teachers, ostracism from activities, and new barriers to parental involvement, they missed those less tangible elements that they had experienced in their all-black schools. As Barbara Shircliffe concluded from her examination of nostalgia in black memories of segregated schools, this did not mean that segregation was good or that African Americans opposed desegregation, but that they use their interviews to criticize how the latter was accomplished.[8]

But for every story about the damage to black students and their community, others document the benefits of school desegregation. The oral histories contain positive assertions that affirm much of the evidence from the social science scholarship. The narrators recall how desegregation equalized facilities and resources, minimized the differences between schools, and opened up doors of opportunity, for which they are grateful. Most important, many narrators assert that school desegregation facilitated better race relations as black and white students got to know each other, overcame biases, and embraced diversity. This benefited not only

Black and white children play together in a sixth-grade volleyball tournament at the formerly all-white Waller Elementary School, 1976. (Courtesy of Jefferson County Public Schools Archives)

individuals, insist the narrators, but the larger society as well, because it helped integrate other aspects of life and made Louisville a more united community. Finally, the interviews reflect pride in the success of the district. Narrators used the interviews to praise the people who did the day-to-day work of making integration happen and sustaining it, insisting that the accomplishment and hard work that went into it be part of the public memory of school desegregation.

Most often, however, narrators make a point of enumerating both the positive and negative results of desegregation. Disappointed black parents and activists conclude that desegregation did not help their community and was a failure, but some, like Benetha Ellis, concede that their own children were helped or that attitudes did change. Ardent supporters like June Hampe and Pat Todd admit that school officials made mistakes in the implementation of busing. Black teachers worry about a lost generation of African American youth but conclude that overall society improved. Black students admit to suffering but feel it was worth it for the personal and communal gains. Central High lost its spirit but gained in resources and curriculum. These interviews demonstrate how people see many sides of an issue, assess the past in light of different and sometimes contradictory values, and stand back and take a larger view of the communal, as well as the personal, impact. Narrators in an interview setting are conscious of their responsibility to speak to an unseen audience and to posterity. People frequently respond to this responsibility with efforts to be clear, broad-minded, and inclusive of all points of the story, and to step out of their own experience and speak for the community.[9] Because they do so, the narratives provide a nuanced, multilayered, and, most important, balanced perspective on the past and present. These voices can remind us that for all the weaknesses in the process of desegregation and the losses that it caused, it also improved schools and enriched lives, not only in quantifiable ways measured by social scientists but also in intangible ways understood best through the stories of people who experienced it.

desegregation, but so are the individual acts that can inspire action toward a better future.

Much about the story of school desegregation in Louisville and Jefferson County can lead to dispiriting conclusions about the effort's futility. Rigid housing segregation undermined the success of the 1950s integration plan based on residence, while white flight to the suburbs soon caused resegregation and rolled back its limited results. Many of the pioneering black students—unwelcome in the high schools, barred from activities, accused of theft and cheating, and expected to fail—became bitter. The next generation of black students was bused far from home into white-dominated schools where they faced violence, openly racist rhetoric from antibusing demonstrators, and simmering hostility from teachers and white classmates. The uneven burden of busing and the apparent damage desegregation caused to African Americans' academic achievement and sense of self-esteem led some blacks to reject the ideal of integration and embrace neighborhood schools. Forty years after *Brown*, African American community activists seemed to give up on integration when they asked the federal district court to release Central High School from the desegregation plan.

Such stories in communities throughout the country contribute to a public dialogue that characterizes school desegregation as a social policy that "everyone knew" had failed and that should be abandoned.[2] Social scientists have analyzed this dialogue, revealing how a once robust and two-sided debate gave way to a pessimistic tale with debilitating policy implications. The ideology of modern conservatism shifted attention away from racial discrimination as a cause of educational inequality and toward individual responsibility, while conservative rhetoric fueled an ever growing hostility to collective solutions rooted in government action. Since the Nixon administration the federal government has turned against busing and school desegregation, a process that culminated in Supreme Court reversals of desegregation rulings. Local civil rights advocates have found these political trends increasingly difficult to buck. Meanwhile, the demographic transformation and economic decline of American cities and the concomitant underfunding of their public schools made desegregation and educational gains harder to achieve and engendered pessimism about the whole endeavor. Opponents repeat claims that busing and desegregation did nothing to help African Americans, despite a growing consensus in a large body of scholarship that proves otherwise. As political scientist Roslyn Arlin Mickelson demonstrates, federal judges have often disregarded social scientific evidence when overturning desegregation court orders, relying instead on personal experience or their moral or ideological positions. Much of the public has followed suit. As scholar Richard Pride argues, people believe the stories they hear, and those with negative experiences are more likely to talk, especially when the dominant narrative reinforces their views. But this chorus of condemnation eclipses a more hopeful narrative of desegregation and obscures evidence of the ways resegregation has eroded public education.[3]

Rather than letting this false discourse incapacitate us, we should seek to discover what went wrong with the implementation of school desegregation and heed the voices of those who lived through it to make it right. Any effort to achieve equality in the schools must begin with an understanding of the racist structures and assumptions that limited and undermined integration. In Louisville and Jefferson County, even those who with good intentions tried to implement *Brown* in the 1950s failed to address or even recognize how racial discrimination shaped housing patterns and limited the success of residence-based desegregation. Aside from a few individuals in the civil rights community, whites assumed that desegregated schools must be majority white; indeed they considered a school to be resegregated and in danger of decline when it attracted too many blacks. Even the most ardent integrationists took for granted that black students would bear the burden of busing by being transported for more years than whites, and they rarely appreciated that something of value might be lost with the end of black-led institutions. Most important, white hostility and assumptions about the ability and character of black students engendered disillusionment and alienation among young African Americans, and allowed too many of them to suffer the consequences of low expectations. Thus much of the worst in the history of school desegregation was rooted in the racism that many whites at the time could not see, and which too many in our "post-racial" nation still fail to acknowledge.

To correct the past failures of school desegregation, we must find ways to confront and overcome this persistent racial divide. During these oral history interviews, many of the narrators mused on how to do that. People on all sides of the debates of the 1990s and after have reached the consensus that the community cannot simply adopt neighborhood schools. Such schools, they believe, would inevitably be segregated and unequal. Some activists conclude that the best way to achieve equal education is to end the housing segregation by race and class that undermines school integration. Other participants in post-*Meredith* debates insist on preserving some parental choice of schools because it promotes political investment in quality education throughout the county. African American activists, meanwhile, call for strengthening the institutional foundations of education in west end neighborhoods by building new facilities, recruiting black teachers, and increasing minority authority and agency within the school system. Finally, narrators conclude that there must be an equal distribution of resources among all schools. Community activists insist that whites would choose integrated schools if all schools were equal, and the success of some downtown and west end magnets in attracting white students bears this out. As Mattie Jones proposes: "If you make my neighborhood comparable to the east end, make it comfortable, and have the same opportunities, [you] don't have to bus whites down here, they're gonna come."[4] Despite incomplete and discouraging results from past efforts, these narrators draw lessons from the long struggle for school desegregation and present a vision for schools in which equality in resources, respect, and authority would promote diversity and truer integration.

As Zinn suggests, remembering the historical moments when people strove to achieve, support, and defend school desegregation can give us the energy to enact this vision today and in the future. The oral histories collected here comprise an alternative narrative of school desegregation that restores to public memory and to the public dialogue the stories of local people dedicated to building equal education and better human relations. In Louisville that dedication showed in 1956 when policy makers rejected the path of massive resistance and opted for a peaceful implementation of *Brown*. Principals, teachers, and community members quietly prepared for mixed schools by encouraging students and parents to understand and accept each other. Although limited and short lived, this first wave of integration in the city schools gained national praise and bolstered the fledgling local civil rights movement. It also became a point of pride that inspired a later generation to try again.

In 1975, at the time of virulent and violent opposition to desegregation, people staffed rumor hotlines, restocked inner-city libraries, arranged meetings among black and white parents, organized school human relations groups, sponsored rallies to denounce racism, and stood up to the Klan. Others acted by merely putting their children on the bus or by holding their classes as usual. As the open opposition on the streets declined, pro-desegregation activists continued to monitor the treatment of black students and the funding of schools in the west end. These often quiet, behind-the-scenes actions do not fit the dominant narrative of the white backlash against federal government intervention on behalf of civil rights, but they laid the groundwork for ongoing endeavors to ensure equal education, and they remind us that many local people chose—and can choose—options other than unremitting opposition.

In the mid-1980s, when the federal court-led rollback of school desegregation began throughout the country, grassroots community activists
in Louisville and Jefferson County rallied against school officials' efforts
to shift the burden of busing to black families. In 1991 the same activists
fought plans to kill the desegregation plan in the elementary schools. In
both cases, they achieved compromises that preserved the ideal of integration and improved the implementation of it. The groups involved
in these efforts—the NAACP, the Fair Housing Council, the League of
Women Voters, religious organizations, and business leaders—shared the
belief that desegregation was working and was good for the community.
Their achievements revealed the extent to which that sentiment still enjoyed broad-based support at the dawn of the new century. Indeed, the
desegregation of the Jefferson County public schools did not lose ground
until it was challenged in a federal district court in the Central High case,
which opened the door to ongoing litigation. Before that, as long as the
local community controlled decision making about the schools, abandonment of the desegregation plan was not inevitable. Scholars' focus on the
trajectory of the court decisions that dismantled desegregation obfuscates
the grassroots push back against the threat of resegregation, and thus hides
the stories that can inspire community agency.

This narrative of pro-desegregation activism reveals the extent to which
the battle over the schools was inextricably linked to the long struggle for
civil rights, particularly in the eyes of those who participated in it. Even
before *Brown*, black leaders saw the schools as an important step in their
campaign to open tax-supported facilities. Local people remember the
campaign for racial equality in the schools as a natural progression after
victories against Jim Crow in libraries and city government in the preceding
years, and civil rights activists looked to success in the schools as justification for moving on to open accommodations. The interracial alliance that
worked for desegregation in 1975 had its roots in the open housing movement. Whites who joined PIE or other integrationist groups that opposed
the antibusing movement saw it as a way to stand up against racism. For
Suzy Post, the white plaintiff in the case that led to the 1975 busing order,
the ACLU's and other organizations' monitoring of equal rights within the
schools in the wake of busing proved that the civil rights movement was
not dead.[5] During the defense of desegregation and busing plan reforms
in the 1980s and 1990s, many members of the pro-busing coalition explicitly invoked the need to defend the gains of the civil rights movement and
carry them forward. Finally, people retrospectively expressed pride that
the small part they played in bringing about school desegregation "helped

to bring down some of the barriers that separated our community" and to broaden access to the American Dream.[6]

The connection participants saw between the struggle for school desegregation and the civil rights movement becomes most clear when they assess the results and meaning for the community. Although inequities persisted, desegregation brought additional money to previously black-majority schools, equalizing teacher pay and augmenting other resources. Black students recognized the doors of opportunity that opened to them, particularly their access to broader curricula, programs, and activities that had not existed at inner-city and west end schools. Individuals also recall the personal changes they experienced as a result of encountering newly mixed racial environments. Yet the most striking result of school desegregation was how it helped young students meet people different from themselves and overcome their biases. Several narrators commented that over time, teachers and students alike no longer saw people as black or white, contributing to better relations within the schools, which in turn benefited the whole community. Even those who worried about the cost or doubted the educational benefits of desegregation, particularly for black students, admitted that attitudes did change and that on balance, as Robert Cunningham put it, "for the things that were lost, it may have been worth it."[7] Thus many local people regard school desegregation in Louisville and Jefferson County as a success because it furthered the aims of the civil rights movement, enhancing resources and opportunity for minority students, while forging better human relations.

A little more than fifty years after *Brown*, the Supreme Court attempted to end the struggle for school desegregation by declaring even voluntary efforts to accomplish it unconstitutional. That battle remains unfinished, however, because *Brown*'s goals—equality in education and an equal and just society—are undermined by persistent racism and the retreat from pro-active steps to overcome it. What we remember about the history of desegregation shapes debates over how to complete the task of achieving those goals. The story recalled here is not about numbers and court cases; it is instead a diverse and multifaceted human tale that forces us to recognize the complexity of the long struggle for school desegregation. One narrative, reinforced by contemporary conservative political discourse, recalls only the worst in the history of school desegregation, a tale marked by opposition, failure, and abandonment. But another and more hopeful story of school desegregation highlights how for decades blacks and whites struggled magnificently to achieve both equity and interracial understanding, their large and small actions reminding us how positive change takes

Pleasure Ridge Park High School yearbook, 1980. School human relations committees provided opportunities for students to work together to address issues of race relations. (Courtesy of Jefferson County Public School Archives)

place. Those interested in securing the promise of *Brown* must heed the memory of what went wrong—and of what went right—and the lessons about what minority and poor children still lack in our schools. Most important, this other story should inspire a renewed commitment to bringing young people of different race and class together in equal and supportive schools.

APPENDIX

Interviewees

Interviews are located either in the Southern Oral History Collection, Southern
Historical Collection, Louis Round Wilson Special Collections Library, at the University
of North Carolina–Chapel Hill (SOHC) or at the Oral History Collection, University
Archives, Ekstrom Library, at the University of Louisville (OHC). The interviews in the
SOHC are listed with their identification number.

Frances Bloom (interview with Elizabeth Gritter, August 3, 2005, U-0084 SOHC). White
   elementary school teacher; in 1975 was transferred from a black school in the west
   end to a formerly white county school.
Anne Braden (interview with Tracy E. K'Meyer, March 22, 2001, OHC). White mother
   and civil rights activist.
Rev. Kevin Cosby (interview with Tracy E. K'Meyer, April 7, 2011, in author's possession).
   Minister of St. Stephen's Church in the west end and leading exponent of returning
   to neighborhood school assignment in 1991.
Raoul Cunningham (interview with Tracy E. K'Meyer, August 24, 1999, OHC). African
   American student in newly desegregated city schools after 1956; leader of student
   sit-ins in 1961.
Robert Cunningham (interview with Tracy E. K'Meyer, September 1, 1999, OHC;
   interview with Elizabeth Gritter, October 16, 2004, U-0024 SOHC). African American
   civil rights activist; leader of Parents for Quality Education in 1975, active in
   Kentucky Alliance.
Benetha Ellis (interview with David Cline, October 16, 2004, U-0101 SOHC). African
   American mother, leader of United Black Protective Parents in 1975.
Geoffrey Ellis (interview with Tracy E. K'Meyer, March 22, 2011, OHC). African
   American minister; staff member of Kentucky Commission on Human Rights, chair
   of the education committee for the NAACP, and member of the citizens' advisory
   committee on the desegregation plan reform in 1984.
Bonita Emerick (interview with Elizabeth Gritter, August 2, 2005, U-0086 SOHC). White
   student who in 1975 was removed from school by her parents, opponents of the
   busing program.
Georgia Eugene (interview with David Cline, August 5, 2005, U-0102 SOHC). African
   American mother, PTA volunteer, and community activist; school staff member in 1975.
Darnell Farris (interview with David Cline, December 5, 2004, U-0144 SOHC). African
   American student who was bused to formerly white county school in 1975.
Dawne Gee (interview with Elizabeth Gritter, December 9, 2004, U-0026 SOHC). African
   American student who lived in the county in 1975 and attended a formerly white
   county school.

Michael Gritton (interview with David Cline, October 15, 2004, U-0103 SOHC). White student who attended formerly white county school during the 1975 busing crisis.

June Hampe (interview with David Cline, August 2, 2005, and October 15, 2009, U-0145 and U-0460 SOHC). White mother and volunteer in the schools in 1975; in 1984 member of the citizens advisory committee; school system staff during the legal challenges to the desegregation plan.

Madeline Hicks (interview with Tracy E. K'Meyer, April 1, 2011, OHC). African American mother and dentist; during debate over desegregation plan in 1991 she helped found the pro-integration organization QUEST; daughter of Milburn Maupin.

Ruth Higgins (interview with Darlene Eakin, 1973, OHC). White principal of newly desegregated elementary school in 1956. This interview, like all those conducted by Eakin, have only the year conducted indicated in the material in the archives.

Todd Hollenbach (interview with Ethel White, July 12, 1988, OHC). White Jefferson County judge executive in 1975.

Evelyn Jackson (interview with Darlene Eakin, 1973, OHC; interview with Tracy E. K'Meyer, December 3, 1999, OHC). African American principal of newly desegregated elementary school in 1956.

Sherry Jelsma (interview with Ethel White, May 16, 1988, OHC). White mother and human relations volunteer in 1975; president of school board in 1984.

June Key (interview with Ethel White, August 9, 1988, OHC). White mother, PTA volunteer, and member of the Community Consensus Committee in 1975.

Laura Kirchner (interview with Elizabeth Gritter, December 8, 2004, U-0087 SOHC). White teacher in majority-black and high poverty school in west end in 1975.

Shelby Lanier (interview with Tracy E. K'Meyer, September 29, 1999, OHC). African American policeman and activist.

Clint Lovely (interview with Elizabeth Gritter, August 4, 2005, U-0028 SOHC). African American teacher and football coach at Central High School in 1975.

Phil Mahin (interview with Elizabeth Gritter, August 1, 2005, U-0088 SOHC). African American teacher transferred to formerly white county school in 1975.

Milburn Maupin (interview with Darlene Eakin, 1973, OHC). African American teacher in 1956; later promoted to principal and became first black deputy superintendent in the local school system.

Joe McPherson (interview with David Cline, December 9, 2004, U-0104 SOHC). African American principal at Central in 1975.

Ken Miller (interview with Elizabeth Gritter and Timothy P. McCarthy, December 8, 2004, U-0089 SOHC). White national guardsman assigned to ride on the buses for protection in 1975.

Louis Mudd (interview with Tracy E. K'Meyer, August 21, 2000, OHC). African American student in newly desegregated city schools after 1956.

Sterling Neal (interview with David Cline, May 16, 2005, U-0155 SOHC). African American student in the newly desegregated city schools after 1956.

Henry Owens (interview with David Cline, May 31, 2006, U-0156 SOHC). African American student in the newly desegregated city schools after 1956.

Roy Owsley (interview with Darlene Eakin, 1973, OHC). White administrative assistant to Mayor Charles Farnsley in 1956.

Mrs. James Pate (interview with Darlene Eakin, 1973; OHC). White parent and PTA leader during the 1956 desegregation of schools. All extant information regarding this interviewee lists only her married name.

Josephine Trowel Patterson (interview with Darlene Eakin, 1973, OHC). African American teacher in the city schools in 1956.

Stephen Porter (interview with Tracy E. K'Meyer, March 9, 2011, OHC). White attorney; founder and leader of QUEST during the 1991 debates over the desegregation plan; attorney for intervening plaintiffs in the Central case.

Suzy Post (interview with Timothy P. McCarthy, December 7, 2004, U-0178 SOHC; interview with Sarah Theusen, June 23, 2006, U-0178 SOHC). White civil rights activist, mother, and plaintiff in the lawsuit that lead to busing for desegregation in 1975.

Cedric Powell (interview with David Cline, October 6, 2009, U-0461 SOHC). Professor in the University of Louisville Brandeis School of Law. He was interviewed for his expertise on the legal issues in the *Meredith* case.

Diane Robertson (interview with Joe Mosnier, August 1, 2005, U-0176 SOHC). White east end student bused into inner-city school in 1975.

Marcella Robinson (interview with Ethel White, September 8, 1990, OHC). White school bus driver in 1975.

Ken Rosenbaum (interview with Elizabeth Gritter, December 7, 2004, U-0091 SOHC). White former teacher, curriculum coordinator, and president of the newly merged teachers' union in 1975.

Jean Ruffra (interview with Ethel White, August 15, 1988, OHC). White mother and leader of Save Our Community Schools in 1975.

Harvey Sloane (interview with Ethel White, December 1, 1988, OHC). White mayor of Louisville in 1975.

Deborah Stallworth (interview with Tracy E. K'Meyer, March 4, 2011, OHC). African American mother; founder of CEASE, the organization that supported the lawsuit to end the desegregation plan at Central High in the 1990s.

Charles Summers (interview with Elizabeth Gritter, August 3, 2005, U-0092 SOHC). White principal at county high school in 1975.

Maurice Sweeney (interview with Tracy E. K'Meyer, December 2, 2011, in possession of author). Staff member of Kentucky Commission on Human Rights and president of the NAACP in 1984.

Deanna Tinsley (interview with David Cline, August 3, 2005, U-0146 SOHC). African American student in the newly desegregated schools after 1956.

Pat Todd (interview with David Cline, October 15, 2009, U-0462, SOHC). White teacher in the public schools in 1975; staff member in central administration of the schools, responsible for student assignment by the time of the *Meredith* verdict.

Sandra Wainwright (interview with Tracy E. K'Meyer, March 16, 2000, OHC). African American teacher in the city schools before 1975; transferred to formerly white county school in 1975.

Morton Walker (interview with Darlene Eakin, 1973, OHC). White president of school board in 1956.

Carmen Weathers (interview with David Cline, August 3 and 4, 2005, U-0147 SOHC). African American teacher, coach, and activist; organizer of lawsuit to remove Central High School from the desegregation order.

Gerald White (interview with Tracy E. K'Meyer, August 29, 2000, OHC). African American student in the newly desegregated schools after 1956 and later teacher at Shawnee High School.

John Whiting (interview with Tracy K'Meyer, March 30, 2011, OHC). African American principal at Shawnee High School in 1975; advocate of return to neighborhood schools and the end of desegregation order for Central High School in the 1990s.

Dan Withers (interview with David Cline, October 15, 2004, U-0148 SOHC). African American teacher who was transferred from west end school to a county school in 1975.

Edith Yarborough (interview with David Cline, October 17, 2009, U-0463 SOHC). African American student who was bused from west end high school to a county school in 1975.

Notes

Introduction

1. The round table was "State of the Field: School Desegregation and White Flight," Annual Meeting of the Organization of American Historians, Seattle, March 28, 2009. For a sample of such reviews of school desegregation, see Bankston and Caldas, *Troubled Dream*; Clotfelter, *After Brown*; Orfield and Eaton, *Dismantling Desegregation*; Patterson, *Brown v. Board of Education*.

2. See Bartley, *Rise of Massive Resistance*; Gates, *Making of Massive Resistance*. Later works that focus on this early period include Lassiter and Lewis, *The Moderates' Dilemma*; Anderson, *Little Rock*.

3. On the busing crises of the 1970s and the post-1968 story of school desegregation, see Mills, *Busing U.S.A.*; Formisano, *Boston Against Busing*; Taylor, *Desegregation in Boston and Buffalo*; Pride and Woodard, *The Burden of Busing*; Pratt, *The Color of Their Skin*. On the link between opposition to school desegregation and the new conservatism, see Lassiter, "The Suburban Origins of 'Color-Blind' Conservatism."

4. In addition to the studies mentioned above, see Gaillard, *The Dream Long Deferred*; Jacobs, *Getting Around Brown*; Monti, *A Semblance of Justice*; Dougherty, *More Than One Struggle*; Daugherity and Bolton, *With All Deliberate Speed*.

5. Klarman, *Brown v. Board of Education and the Civil Rights Movement*; Lau, *From the Grassroots to the Supreme Court*; "Round Table"; Burton and O'Brien, eds., *Remembering Brown at Fifty*.

6. Theoharis, "'We Saved the City'"; Hall, "The Long Civil Rights Movement and the Political Uses of the Past."

7. Baum, *Brown in Baltimore*; Pratt, *The Color of Their Skin*; Lassiter, *The Silent Majority*.

8. The Jefferson County Public Schools were given credit for leading Kentucky toward its status as the most integrated state in the nation in Frankenberg, Lee, and Orfield, "A Multiracial Society with Segregated Schools."

9. The phrase and inspiration are both drawn from Dittmer, *Local People*.

10. I am most influenced here by Frisch, *A Shared Authority*. For other discussions of this theme in oral history, see Portelli, *The Death of Luigi Strastulli*; Perks and Thomson, *The Oral History Reader*; and Charlton, Myers, and Sharpless, *Handbook of Oral History*.

11. For more on the Long Civil Rights Movement project, see https://lcrm.lib.unc.edu/blog/.

12. These debates are summarized in Elinor A. Maze, "The Uneasy Page: Transcribing and Editing Oral History," and Richard Candida Smith, "Publishing Oral History: Oral Exchange and Print Culture," in Charlton, Myers, and Sharpless, *Handbook of Oral History*. For those interested in unedited versions, the archives contain both the raw recordings and the unedited transcripts.

13. On demographic characteristics of the school districts, see Thompson, "School Desegregation in Jefferson County"; and Brady, "Community Influence on Urban School Desegregation."

14. On the development of segregation in Louisville, see Wright, *Life behind a Veil*. Employment statistics are from *Population and Housing Statistics for Census Tracts Louisville, Ky. and Adjacent Area*.

15. Wright, *A History of Blacks in Kentucky*, 104–5, 144–6; Wilson, *A Century of Negro Education in Louisville, Kentucky*, 131–35.

16. For more on the Louisville context, see K'Meyer, *Civil Rights in the Gateway to the South*, introduction and chap. 1.

17. I borrow this metaphor from one of those activists, Anne Braden. See, *The Wall Between*.

18. C. W. Anderson Jr., to Milton R. Kovitz, March 2, 1944, NAACP microfilm series 3B role 12 location 585; Charles W. Anderson to Roy and Thurgood, March 16, 1944, NAACP microfilm series 3B role 12 location 595; "Anderson's Bill Would Save State $1,000,000; At Terrific Cost to Colored Youth," *Louisville News*, March 11, 1944, clipping in NAACP microfilm series 3B role 12 location 577–78; "Straining at a Gnat and Swallowing the Old Camel," *Louisville News*, March 11, 1944, clipping in NAACP microfilm series 3B role 12 location 580; Karelen Isom, "Kentucky Senate Defeats Bill to Admit Negro Students to White Colleges," clipping, March 16, 1944, NAACP microfilm series 3B role 12 location 596–97; Hardin, *Fifty Years of Segregation*, 75–76.

19. "Committee Favors Ending of Segregation in Schools," *Courier Journal*, September 19, 1951; "Mayor's Group Approves Segregation Law Change," *Courier Journal*, December 11, 1951; "Mayor's Committee Would Amend Day Law," *Defender*, December 15, 1951; "Pitt Proposal Seems Doomed," *Defender*, February 9, 1952.

20. For the story of the legislative effort to overturn the Day Law in spring 1954, and a detailed treatment of early school desegregation in Louisville, see K'Meyer, *Civil Rights in the Gateway to the South*, chap. 2.

Chapter One

1. Interview with Barry Bingham by Ethel White, March 17, 1988, Oral History Center, University Archives, Ekstrom Library at the University of Louisville.

2. "NAACP Will Ask City to End Park Segregation," *Courier Journal*, May 19, 1954; "What Louisvillians Think of the Supreme Court Decision," *Defender*, May 20, 1954; "City, County are Planning Integration," *Courier Journal*, May 18, 1954; Frank L. Stanley, "Being Frank about People, Places, and Problems," Defender, June 17, 1954; "Will Kentucky Be Last?," *Defender*, June 17, 1954.

3. "City, County Are Planning Integration," *Courier Journal*, May 18, 1954; Hugh Morris, "Decision Voids State's Day Law," *Courier Journal*, May 18, 1954.

4. Hugh Morris, "Decision Voids State's Day Law," *Courier Journal*, May 18, 1954; Allan M. Trout, "Desegregation Delayed in State," *Courier Journal*, June 18, 1954; "City Schools to Continue Segregation This Autumn," *Courier Journal*, July 27, 1954.

5. "Desegregation Study Asked by Carmichael," *Courier Journal*, November 2, 1954; "Ask Discussion on School Integration," *Defender*, November 4, 1954; "School Desegregation

Held Needing Five Years," *Courier Journal*, February 14, 1955; Jean Howerton, "September, '56 Is Still Integration Target Here," *Courier Journal*, June 1, 1955; "Twenty Demand Integration Here Now," *Courier Journal*, July 22, 1955.

6. "Desegregation Plan for City Provides for Redistricting 'Without Regard to Race,'" *Courier Journal*, November 22, 1955; "High Schools May Avoid Need of Redistricting," *Courier Journal*, February 7, 1956; "Pupil-Transfer Plan Criticized, Defended," *Courier Journal*, November 23, 1955. The plan and Carmichael's justification for it are covered at length in Carmichael and James, *The Louisville Story*, 79–91.

7. K'Meyer, *Civil Rights in the Gateway to the South*, 50.

8. "Citizens' Views on Carmichael Desegregation Plan," *Defender*, December 1, 1955.

9. "Segregation Called 'Burden upon Spirit' by Church Women," *Courier Journal*, September 9, 1954; "High School Youth Speaks on Integration," *Courier Journal*, January 18, 1955; Marion Porter, "'Climate of Approval' Is Called Key to School Desegregation," *Courier Journal*, January 20, 1955; "County Group Publishes Data on Integration," *Courier Journal*, April 3, 1955; "Stand of KEA Group on Integration Praised," *Courier Journal*, April 17, 1955; "Desegregating Teachers Association," *Defender*, September 29, 1955. A list of similar community forums can be found in Carmichael and James, *The Louisville Story*, 65–70.

10. For comparisons to other border cities and states in the Deep South, see Taggart, "The Failure of Apparent Successful School Desegregation"; Berkowitz, "Baltimore's Public Schools in a Time of Transition," 415; Baum, *Brown in Baltimore*; Monti, *A Semblance of Justice*.

11. On massive resistance, see Bartley, *The Rise of Massive Resistance*; Anthony Badger, "*Brown* and Backlash," in Webb, *Massive Resistance*, 39–55. On the link to anticommunism, see Lewis, *The White South and the Red Menace*.

12. See letters to editor of *Courier Journal* from J. A. Hess, May 24, 1954, Mayme Rawlings, May 25, 1954, James R. Parr, May 26, 1954, Frank H. Miller Sr., June 1, 1954, and William Hass, June 3, 1954; Carmichael and James, *The Louisville Story*, 51–53; "Questions on Integration Fired by White Parents," *Courier Journal*, April 27, 1955.

13. "109 File Suit to Keep Segregation," *Defender*, May 3, 1956; "Millard Grubbs— September 8, 1956," and Federated Press Release, September 9, 1956, in box 53, file 16 of the Anne and Carl Braden Papers, State Historical Society of Wisconsin, Madison (hereafter cited as Braden Papers); "Citizens' Council Organized Here," *Defender*, June 28, 1956; "Citizens' Council Files Suit against City's Board of Ed," *Defender*, August 23, 1956; "First Regular Term Integration Begins," *Courier Journal*, September 11, 1956; "Phone Callers Urging School Boycott," *Courier Journal*, September 28, 1956; "City School Officials to Rule Today on Admitting Foe of Integration," *Courier Journal*, November 29, 1956; "Segregationist Gains Admission to Male," *Defender*, January 10, 1957; Philip Harsham, "Segregationist Seized Trying to Oust Chief," *Courier Journal*, January 17, 1957; "Kasper, Grubbs, Branham Harangue Fifty Persons," *Defender*, December 20, 1956.

14. Louisville ex-defendants to friends in Brooklyn, December 15, 1956, box 9, file 7, Braden Papers; Braden, *The Wall Between*, 291.

15. "Parents Told What Schools Children to Attend in Fall," *Courier Journal*, March 6, 1956; "Integration to Be Less Than Slated," *Courier Journal*, April 3, 1956; "School Survey Prompts 'Limited Integration,'" *Defender*, April 5, 1956; Stanley, "Being Frank about People, Places, and Problems," *Defender*, September 6, 1956; "School Choice Survey Should

Not Limit Integration," *Defender*, April 5, 1956; "Estimates Seem Awry on Integrated Classes," *Courier Journal*, September 6, 1956.

16. "First Regular Term Integration Begins"; Carmichael and James, *The Louisville Story*, 97–100; Benjamin Fine, "Segregation End Here a Landmark, Fine Says," *Courier Journal*, September 11, 1956 (reprinted editorial from *New York Times*); "Louisville Undergoes Changes in Education," *Defender*, September 6, 1956; Anne Braden, "Draft Report on School Desegregation in Kentucky," [1956], box 12, file 53, Braden Papers; "73.6 Percent of City Pupils Integrated," *Courier Journal*, October 23, 1956.

17. "Carmichael's Repeated Attacks," *Defender*, October 18, 1956; "Negroes Hear Carmichael Reaffirm Competence View," *Louisville Times*, October 30, 1956; "Carmichael Says No Ridicule Intended," *Courier Journal*, October 31, 1956; Stanley, "Being Frank about People, Places, and Problems," *Defender*, November 8, 1956; "Carmichael Says White People Not Ready," *Defender*, July 10, 1958; "Whites Not Opposed to Negro Teachers," *Defender*, July 31, 1958; "City Schools Begin Teacher Integration," *Courier Journal*, September 10, 1959; "Board Votes to Integrate Teachers in Fall," *Defender*, August 6, 1959; "School Board Takes Next Logical Step," *Defender*, August 6, 1959.

18. Charles H. Parrish was an African American sociologist and the first black faculty member at the University of Louisville.

19. Cunningham later became an officer in the local NAACP and a staunch defender of the later county-wide desegregation plan.

20. Interview with Ruth Higgins by Darlene Eakin, 1973, OHC.

21. See chapter 4 for a discussion of a similar issue in African American assessments of schools before and after desegregation.

22. "73.6 Per Cent of City Pupils Integrated," *Courier Journal*, October 23, 1956; "Pupils in Integrated Schools Gain Here," *Courier Journal*, October 2, 1957; "On Desegregation, Surprising Statistics," *Courier Journal*, June 30, 1959; "Louisville Undergoes Changes in Education," *Defender*, September 6, 1956; "Officials Say Integration Has Gone Smoothly," *Defender*, November 8, 1956. For a review of the school integration statistics, including the impact on teachers, see Thompson, "School Desegregation in Jefferson County," 53–60.

23. On the failure of southern districts to make progress, see Cascio, Gordon, Lewis and Reber, "From Brown to Busing."

24. The results of the Kemper and Associates survey are reprinted in Carmichael and James, *The Louisville Story*, table 1; J. Michael McElreath, "The Cost of Opportunity: School Desegregation's Complicated Calculus in North Carolina," in Daugherity and Bolton, *With All Deliberate Speed*, 22.

25. "Protest Demonstration Failed to Materialize as Expected," *Defender*, September 13, 1956; "13 Negroes Keep Citizens' Council from Meeting—Until They Leave," *Courier Journal*, October 4, 1957; "Biased Woman Faces Court Order," *Defender*, December 20, 1956; "Parents, Foes of Integration Face Trial," *Courier Journal*, January 15, 1957.

26. Benjamin Fine, "Louisville Takes Bias End in Strike," *New York Times*, September 12, 1956; "Integration Runs Smoothly in City Schools; Report Only Two Conflicts," *Defender*, September 13, 1956; Tom Karsall, "It's Elementary to First Graders," *Courier Journal*, April 15, 1957.

27. "City's Integration Will Be Filmed," *Courier Journal*, April 19, 1957; "School Integration Success Has Put Louisville on Map, South African Says," *Courier Journal*, November

20, 1956; Robert L. Riggs, "Ike Lauds City's Desegregation," *Courier Journal*, September 12, 1956; "Sharing the Credit," *Defender*, September 20, 1956; Jean Howeton, " 'Quiet Heard around the World'—School Integration in Louisville," *Courier Journal*, January 28, 1957; K'Meyer, " 'Gateway to the South.' "

28. For a fuller discussion of this phenomenon, see chapter 4.

29. Carmichael and James, *The Louisville Story*, 129–36.

30. "Officials Say Integration Has Gone Smoothly," *Defender*, November 8, 1956; Anne Braden, "Draft Report on School Desegregation in Kentucky," box 12, file 53, Braden Papers; Stanley, "Being Frank about People, Places, and Problems," *Defender*, July 3, 1958.

31. This story is told is detail in Thompson, "School Desegregation in Jefferson County," 86–112, and *Report on Public Schools in Louisville, Kentucky, 1956–1971*. For a comparison of Louisville to the broader impact of *Brown* on teachers, see Fulz, "The Displacement of Black Educators Post-*Brown*," especially 28–29.

32. "City, County Are Planning Integration," *Courier Journal*, May 18, 1954; "Louisville Undergoes Changes in Education," *Defender*, September 6, 1956; Hardin, "Race, Housing," 76–78, 82–83; Lyne, *Schoolhouse Dreams Deferred*, 28–29; Thompson, "School Desegregation in Jefferson County," 66.

33. "County Will Desegregate Schools by '56," *Defender*, July 7, 1955; "Van Hoose's Proposals Due Study," *Courier Journal*, January 1, 1956; "Majority of County Pupils Now Integrated," *Defender*, September 28, 1958; Thompson, "School Desegregation in Jefferson County," 77–82.

34. Mark V. Tushnet, "The Supreme Court's Two Principles of Equality: From *Brown* to 2003," in Lau, *From the Grassroots to the Supreme Court*, 340–60.

Chapter Two

1. For an introduction to the busing story and case studies of similar cities to Louisville, see Mills, *Busing U.S.A.*; Pride and Woodard, *The Burden of Busing*; Gaillard, *The Dream Long Deferred*; Pratt, *The Color of Their Skin*.

2. Thompson, "School Desegregation in Jefferson County," 120–32; "Emotion Not the Answer," *Defender*, July 29, 1971; "Blacks Still Dissatisfied with Newburg Busing Plan," *Defender*, August 5, 1971; "Van Hoose Must Stand Tall," *Defender*, August 5, 1971; "Newburg Children—the Real Victims," *Defender*, July 12, 1971; "County School Board Elects to Defy HEW," *Defender*, August 12, 1971.

3. "Redistricting Asked for Newburg Schools," *Defender*, September 3, 1971; "Report of the KCLU-LCLU Committee on Proposed Louisville School Desegregation Suit," box 6, file "Desegregation Suit History," Progress in Education (PIE) Papers, University of Louisville Archives (hereafter cited as PIE Papers); Linda Raymond, "US Court Asked to Order City School Desegregation," *Louisville Times*, June 23, 1972; "Three Suits Filed," *Defender*, June 29, 1972.

4. "A Dead End?" *Defender*, December 7, 1972; James Nolan, "School Desegregation Suits in Louisville Area Dismissed," *Courier Journal*, March 9, 1973; James Nolan, "Louisville Area Schools Told to Draft Desegregation Plan," *Courier Journal*, December 29, 1973; Susan Brown, "City Board Won't Appeal Decision," *Defender*, January 10, 1974; "Act Illegally," *Defender*, February 7, 1974.

5. Jason Williams, "School Boards Petition to Stay Desegregation," *Defender*, September 5, 1974; Sedler, "The Louisville–Jefferson County School Desegregation Case."

6. "Chronology of Merger Plans, 1975," box 4, file "Brown School Ad Hoc Committee on School Merger," PIE Papers; Priscilla Hancock, "Finances Force City BofE to Seek Merger with County," *Defender*, February 28, 1974; "Third Party Needed to Arbitrate Merger," *Defender*, May 16, 1974; Jason Williams, "City Schools Try to Force Merger with County," *Defender*, November 14, 1974; Jason Williams, "County Board of Education Denies City's Merger Request," *Defender*, November 28, 1974; Jason Williams, "Louisville School Board Ends Years of Educating," *Defender*, April 3, 1975. On black resistance to the idea of merger, see "Where Are Black Leaders?," *Defender*, January 27, 1972; "State Black Legislators Needed in School Struggle," *Defender*, February 3, 1972; Anne Braden to SCEF Board and Staff, May 3, 1972, in box 6, file "Desegregation Suit History," PIE Papers; "Pan Hellenic Forum Fails to Agree on City-Cty [County] School Merger," *Defender*, June 22, 1972.

7. "Jetting Plan Unworkable," *Defender*, March 9, 1975; Jason Williams, "New County Desegregation Plan," *Defender*, April 3, 1975; Jason Williams, "Community and Schools Prepare to Implement Peaceful Desegregation Plan," *Defender*, April 24, 1975; "Plantation Mentality Afflicts Judge Gordon," *Defender*, June 12, 1975; Jason Williams, "School Desegregation," *Defender*, July 24, 1975; Jason Williams, "Gordon's Desegregation Plan Has Special Requirements for Black Students," *Defender*, August 7, 1975.

8. Cecil Blye, "Mixed Feelings in Newburg; Blacks Differ over Busing," *Defender*, July 29, 1971; "Blacks Still Dissatisfied with Newburg Busing Plan," *Defender*, August 5, 1971; Meryl Thornton, "LUL Presents Its Views on School Desegregation," *Defender*, February 28, 1974; Jason Williams, "Seeks Desegregation Positive Safeguards," *Defender*, March 21, 1974; Jason Williams, "Busing Favored by Most Blacks; Some Gripes," *Defender*, March 7, 1974; Priscilla Hancock, "Racial Balance in Schools Draws Criticism from Blacks," *Defender*, April 11, 1974; Notice about Meeting, March 28, 1974, in box 4, file "West End School Committee," PIE Papers; James Parks, "Panthers Prepare to Protect Community, *Defender*, August 28, 1975; Phyllis A. Mitchell, "Rachelle Edmondson Starts Anti-busing School," *Defender*, December 12, 1974.

9. "Busing Brainwash," *Defender*, March 2, 1972; "Black Leaders Oppose Nixon's Busing Edict," *Defender*, March 23, 1972; "Urban League Takes Busing Stand," *Defender*, May 18, 1972; "New Desegregation Plan Offers Great Challenges," *Defender*, April 18, 1974; "Black Parents, Youth Hear Speakers Ask Support of Integration Plan," *Courier Journal*, August 20, 1975; "Open Letter to Parents," *Defender*, September 4, 1975; ad featuring Ann Elmore, *Defender*, August 28, 1975.

10. On the movement of the 1960s in Louisville, see K'Meyer, *Civil Rights in the Gateway to the South*. On the homeowners' rights movements, see Meyer, *As Long As They Don't Move Next Door*, chap. 10. On tensions in local race relations, see Roper Research Associates, *A Community Study among Whites and Negroes in Louisville, Kentucky*.

11. On the antibusing movement, see K'Meyer, *Civil Rights in the Gateway to the South*, chap. 8.

12. Draft of pamphlet, 1972, in Social Action File 1: "Ad Hoc Committee for School Integration," in the State Historical Society of Wisconsin, Madison. For a fuller description of white involvement in open housing movement, see K'Meyer, "Well, I'm Not Moving."

For a fuller description of the defense of the Black Six and pro-integration response in the 1970s, see K'Meyer, *Civil Rights in the Gateway to the South*, chaps. 6 and 8.

13. The inept deputy in the Andy Griffith Show.

14. Hall, "The Long Civil Rights Movement and the Political Uses of the Past," 1255–58.

15. This began with attention to the opposition in Boston, which focused on the latter's race, class, and ethnic roots. See Formisano, *Boston against Busing*. Similar themes on the relationship between the white antibusing movement and conservatism were identified in Durr, *Behind the Backlash*; McGirr, *Suburban Warriors*; Gray, "To Fight the Good Fight." Others have put more emphasis on the interplay of race and opposition to the changes wrought by the civil rights movement. See, for example, Causey, "The Long and Winding Road"; Andrews, "Movement-Counter Movement Dynamics and the Emergence of New Institutions"; Lassiter, *The Silent Majority*. For an overview of the educational literature, see Rossell, Armor, and Walberg, *School Desegregation in the Twenty-First Century*. For discussion of what was lost in black communities during desegregation, see chapter 4.

16. See for example, Formisano, *Boston against Busing*; and Durr, *Behind the Backlash*.

17. Diane Aprile, Mike Wines, and Ira Simmons, "At Fairdale High, a Quiet Day Turned Sour Near the End," *Louisville Times*, September 5, 1975; Martin E. Biemer, "Officials Thankful Pupils Left before Riot Began," *Louisville Times*, September 6, 1975; Judy Rosenfield, "Everyday People . . . ," *Louisville Times*, box 5, file "Anti-Busing Activity, September 1975," PIE Papers.

18. "Mothers Admit Sin in Sending Youth to School," *Courier Journal*, September 16, 1975; *NARPF Newsletter* untitled notice, October, 1975; "Tools of Learning; Reefers, Con Games," *NARPF Newsletter*, November 23, 1975; "In Our Schools," *NARPF Newsletter*, March 9, 1976, all in box 4, file "National Association to Restore and Preserve our Freedom," PIE Papers; Robert L. Quire to editor, *Courier Journal*, October 23, 1975. For more on this, see K'Meyer, *Civil Rights in the Gateway to the South*, 275.

19. Sue Connor testimony in U. S. Commission on Civil Rights, *Hearing before the U. S. Commission on Civil Rights*, 34; Joseph A. Ratterman to editor, *Courier Journal*, February 1, 1975; Glenn L. Head to editor, *Courier Journal*, August 9, 1975.

20. For a summary of continued housing segregation, see K'Meyer, *Civil Rights in the Gateway to the South*, 142; for a more detailed account of this incident, see ibid., 271–72.

21. Theoharis, " 'We Saved the City' "; Hall, "Long Civil Rights Movement and the Political Uses of the Past," 1255–58.

22. Ben Johnson, "Black Parents, Youth Hear Speakers Ask Support of Integration Plan," *Courier Journal*, August 20, 1975.

23. Interview with Mattie Mathis by David Cline, May 15, 2006, (U-0153) Southern Oral History Collection, Louis Round Wilson Special Collections Library, at the University of North Carolina–Chapel Hill.

24. On negative assessments of school desegregation fifty years after *Brown*, see the introduction. On Louisville as a case study, see Arnez, "Implementation of Desegregation as a Discriminatory Process."

25. Sheldon Shafer, "Fewer Blacks, 49%, Now Support School Busing," *Courier Journal,* April 20, 1977.

26. Wells, Holme, Tijerina Revilla, and Atanda drew a similar conclusion about the prevalence of individual assessments about personal growth in *Both Sides Now.*

27. "Memories of 1975 Still Vivid in Minds of the Participants," *Courier Journal,* September 4, 1995.

Chapter Three

1. Maurice Sweeney, "School Assignment Challenges," *Courier Journal,* June 14, 2007.

2. Orfield and Eaton, *Dismantling Desegregation,* 9.

3. Ibid., 17–18.

4. Ibid., 115.

5. Hall, "The Long Civil Rights Movement and the Political Uses of the Past," 1255–57. On the success of southern desegregation, see Boger and Orfield, *School Resegregation,* introduction.

6. On the Norfolk case, see Susan Eaton and Christina Meldrum, "Broken Promises: Resegregation in Norfolk, Virginia," in Orfield and Eaton, *Dismantling Desegregation,* 115–41.

7. Orfield and Eaton, *Dismantling Desegregation,* xxiii; Erwin Chemerinksy, "Segregation and Resegregation of American Education," in Boger and Orfield, *School Resegregation,* 38–41.

8. For discussion of the social science scholarship on the impact of desegregation, see chapter 4. On the court's role in school desegregation, see Wilkinson, *From Brown to Bakke;* Lau, *From the Grassroots to the Supreme Court;* Daugherity and Bolton, *With All Deliberate Speed;* Burton and O'Brien, *Remembering Brown at Fifty.*

9. "White Flight in Jefferson Ended in 1978, Study Shows," *Courier Journal,* July 13, 1979; Carolyn Colwell, "School Board Decides to Bus Whites in Consecutive Years," *Courier Journal,* February 26, 1980; Elinor J. Brecher, "Boundary Changes Proposed for High, Middle Schools," *Courier Journal,* April 12, 1980; Michael Day, "Students Voluntarily Queue Up for Busing to Central and Butler," *Courier Journal,* February 15, 1981.

10. Throughout the years there was much confusion over whether the Jefferson County Public Schools were still under federal court order. Gordon's initial declaration in 1978 that the case was closed contained ambiguities in the legal language, and almost immediately some aspects of the busing plan—such as the question of busing first graders— were taken back to court. In September 1980 Gordon again ruled the case ended and the schools desegregated. At first, civil rights lawyers did not object. But after the 1984 reforms, they asked the courts to review the changes, muddying the picture of whether the system was under court supervision. In fall 1985, the district court judge Thomas Ballantine ruled that the Board of Education no longer had to get court approval for changes to the plan. Finally, in 2000, another district court judge, John Heyburn, declared the schools desegregated, creating an opening for legal challenges to the assignment plan.

11. Leslie Scanlon, "School Board Hopes to Reduce Busing for Desegregation," *Courier Journal,* January 21, 1983; Saundra Keyes, "Committee Named to Consider Changes in

School Busing," *Courier Journal*, April 22, 1983; Saundra Keyes, "No School Closings Are Foreseen If Busing Plan Is Revised Next Year," *Courier Journal*, August 26, 1983; interview with John Whiting by Tracy E. K'Meyer, March 30, 2011, OHC; Saundra Keyes, "Blacks on Panel Question Options for Desegregation," *Courier Journal*, December 4, 1983; Saundra Keyes, "Busing Blacks Eleven Years Is Too Much, Panel Says," *Courier Journal*, December 11, 1983; Saundra Keyes, "School Officials Tie Geographic Plan to Long-Term Busing," *Courier Journal*, January 11, 1984.

12. [Untitled block summary of details of Ingwerson Plan], *Courier Journal*, February 14, 1984; Saundra Keyes, "Blacks Criticize Ingwerson's Plan, Threaten Lawsuit," *Courier Journal*, February 14, 1984; Leslie Scanlon and John C. Long, "Advisory Panel Greets Plan with Wrath, Pleasure," *Courier Journal*, February 14, 1984; Saundra Keyes, "Black Ministers Plan Petition Drive against Busing Plan," *Courier Journal*, February 22, 1984; Alan Judd, "Group Makes Its Voice Heard on Busing Plan," *Courier Journal*, March 6, 1984; Leslie Scanlon and Saundra Keyes, "Impact on Students," *Courier Journal*, March 9, 1984; Saundra Keyes and Leslie Scanlon, "Groups Pressure School Board to Delay Vote on Busing," *Courier Journal*, March 23, 1984; Saundra Keyes, "Majority of Ingwerson's Committee Urges Withdrawal of Busing Plan," *Courier Journal*, March 24, 1984.

13. Saundra Keyes and Leslie Scanlon, "Compromise Offer on Busing Plan Getting Hard Look," *Courier Journal*, March 30, 1984; Leslie Scanlon, "Cautious Optimism Greets Announcement of Negotiated Busing Plan," *Courier Journal*, March 31, 1984.

14. Not the same John Heyburn as the later judge.

15. Scott Wade, "New Jefferson Policy on Transfers May Upset Schools' Racial Balance," *Courier Journal*, June 10, 1991; Scott Wade, "Jefferson Might Halt Elementary Busing," *Courier Journal*, September 24, 1991.

16. Sugrue, *Sweet Land of Liberty*, 488–92. See, for example, Bell, "Serving Two Masters."

17. Mark E. McCormick, "Think Tank Tries to Soothe Ills of the Black Community," *Courier Journal*, January 14, 1991; interview with Kevin Cosby by Tracy E. K'Meyer, April 7, 2011, in possession of the author; Leslie Scanlon, "Reaction Mixed to Proposed Desegregation Changes," *Courier Journal*, September 24, 1991; Wade, "New Jefferson Policy on Transfers May Upset Racial Balance"; Scott Wade and Leslie Scanlon, "Boysen Says Jefferson Need Not Stop Busing," *Courier Journal*, September 25, 1991; Scott Wade, "Fifteen Black Leaders Support Plan to End Elementary School Busing," *Courier Journal*, October 2, 1991.

18. Jim Adams, "Battle-Weary Rights Activist Blasts Plan to End Busing," *Courier Journal*, September 26, 1991; "Ex-Senator Schedules Forum to Fight Plan to End Busing," *Courier Journal*, September 29, 1991; Scott Wade and Leslie Scanlon, "Forum of Protest: School Plan to End Busing Called Racist," *Courier Journal*, October 4, 1991.

19. Scott Wade, "Blacks, Whites Tell School Board How They Feel about Busing Plan," *Courier Journal*, October 8, 1991; Scott Wade, "Meeting's Speakers United in Support for End to Busing," *Courier Journal*, October 11, 1991; Scott Wade and Rick McDonough, "Chorus Urging Delay of Vote Grows," *Courier Journal*, October 11, 1991; Andrew Wolfson and Cynthia Wilson, "Blacks' Old, New Guards Emotionally Torn over School Plan," October 13, 1991; Scott Wade and Patrick Howington, "Revisited: Angry Parents Say Forums Designed to Stifle Debate," *Courier Journal*, October 15, 1991; Patrick Howington, Scott Wade, and David Goodwin, "Parents, Frustrated with Board Demand Delay of Busing

Vote," *Courier Journal*, October 16, 1991; Scott Wade, "Ingwerson Delays Busing Plan Vote," *Courier Journal*, October 19, 1991; Stan MacDonald and Scott Wade, "Bluegrass State Poll: Blacks, Whites Divided over Plan to End Forced Busing," *Courier Journal*, October 27, 1991. For a summary of polling data on black opinion on busing, see Orfield, "Public Opinion and School Desegregation," 661–62.

20. Scott Wade, "Citizens Panel to Look at Ingwerson Busing Plan," *Courier Journal*, November 8, 1991; Scott Wade, "Business Leaders Join Study of Schools' Plan to End Busing," *Courier Journal*, November 16, 1991; Scott Wade, "Ingwerson Defends Student Assignment Plan in TV Forum," *Courier Journal*, November 23, 1991; Patrick Howington and Scott Wade, "Revised School Plan Approved: Sets New Racial Balance; Decision Decried as Hasty," *Courier Journal*, December 20, 1991; interview with Madeline Hicks by Tracy E. K'Meyer, April 1, 2011, OHC; Interview with Stephen Porter by Tracy E. K'Meyer, March 9, 2011, OHC.

21. Wade, "New Jefferson Policy on Transfers May Upset Racial Balance"; Nikita Stewart, "Central High's Road to Racial Harmony Remains Bumpy," *Courier Journal*, September 3, 1994; Beverly Bartlett, "Central Racial Limits Spur Emotional Debate; School Board Also OKs Tax Increase," *Courier Journal*, October 25, 1994; interview with Deborah Stallworth by Tracy E. K'Meyer, March 4, 2011, OHC.

22. Michael Jennings, "Schools' Integration Tested," *Courier Journal*, April 13, 1999; Michael Jennings, "Suit over Central Goes to Trial," *Courier Journal*, April 14, 1999; Harold J. Adams, "Jefferson Schools Remain under 1975 Integration Order," *Courier Journal*, June 11, 1999; Thomas Nord, "Judge Allows More Time in Suit over Central High," *Courier Journal*, July 13, 1999; "Settlement in Central Case Looks Unlikely," *Courier Journal*, March 28, 2000; Andrew Wolfson, "Schools and Race: Attitudes Changing," *Courier Journal*, June 25, 2000.

23. Chris Poynter, "School Desegregation: Court Decree Dissolved," *Courier Journal*, June 21, 2000; Jim Adams, "School Decree Dissolved; Order Creates Uncertainty for Jefferson District," *Courier Journal*, June 21, 2000; Wolfson, "Schools and Race: Attitudes Changing."

24. Chris Kenning, "Jefferson Schools' Quotas Challenged," *Courier Journal*, November 3, 2002; Chris Kenning, "Jefferson Suit Is Expected to Proceed," *Courier Journal*, June 24, 2003; Chris Kenning, "School Desegregation Plan on Trial," *Courier Journal*, December 8, 2003; Chris Kenning, "School Racial Plan in Louisville Upheld," *Courier Journal*, June 30, 2004.

25. Neither the attorney Teddy Gordon nor the plaintiff Crystal Meredith could be interviewed. Efforts to find contact information for Meredith were unsuccessful, and Gordon declined to be interviewed.

26. Chris Kenning, "Judges Back Jefferson Desegregation Plan," *Courier Journal*, July 22, 2005; Chris Kenning, "Parent Pursues Race Bias Suit," *Courier Journal*, January 22, 2005; Chris Kenning, "Supreme Court to Hear Jefferson's School Suit," *Courier Journal*, June 6, 2006.

27. Chris Kenning, "NAACP Backs Race Factor in School Assignment," *Courier Journal*, June 24, 2006; Chris Kenning, "Jackson Urges Race-Based School Rally," *Courier Journal*, June 28, 2006; Chris Kenning, "Jefferson School Policy Attacked," *Courier Journal*, August 26, 2006; Chris Kenning, "School Racial Plan Defended," *Courier Journal*,

September 8, 2006; Andrew Wolfson, "Louisvillians to Rally in DC," *Courier Journal*, December 4, 2006.

28. Nancy Rodriguez, "Supreme Court Desegregation Decision; Plaintiffs: Act Now, District: Not Yet," *Courier Journal*, June 29, 2007; Antoinette Konz, "Supreme Court Desegregation Decision; New School Chief Sees No Return to Segregation," *Courier Journal*, June 29, 2007.

29. Interview with June Hampe by David Cline, August 5, 2005, (U-0145) SOHC.

30. For a review of the relative benefits of managed choice versus mandatory assignment and voluntary plans, see Rossell, "Controlled Choice Desegregation Plans"; Rossell and Armor, "The Effectiveness of School Desegregation Plans, 1968–1991."

31. Leslie Scanlon, "Despite Critics' Comments Some Believe Ingwerson's Plan Is More Reasonable Approach to Busing," *Courier Journal*, February 14, 1984; Alan Judd, "Group Makes Its Voice Heard on Busing Plan," *Courier Journal*, March 6, 1984; Interview with Fran Thomas by Todd Read, March 26, 2011, OHC; Wolfson, "Louisvillians to Rally in DC."

32. Interview with Stephen Porter by Tracy E. K'Meyer, March 9, 2011, OHC.

33. Case studies illustrating this retreat are included in Orfield and Eaton, *Dismantling Desegregation*. For an examination of the impact of the return to neighborhood schools on black and Latino students, see Goldring, Cohen-Vogel, Smrekar, and Taylor, "Schooling Closer to Home."

34. Interview with Geoffrey Ellis by Tracy E. K'Meyer, March 22, 2011, OHC.

35. Interview with John Whiting by Tracy E. K'Meyer, March 30, 2011, OHC.

36. Interview with Mattie Jones by Todd Read, March 1, 2011, OHC.

37. Wolfson, "Louisvillians to Rally in DC."

38. "Jefferson Officials Discuss School Assignment Plan," *Courier Journal*, February 5, 2008; "Poll: Parents Back Diversity in Schools," *Courier Journal*, April 15, 2008; "School Board OKs Assignment Plan," *Courier Journal*, May 29, 2008.

39. "Public School Assignments Back in Court," *Courier Journal*, July 27, 2007; "Schools' Course since Race Ruling Ok'd," *Courier Journal*, August 3, 2007; "Judge to Hear Challenge to JCPS Plan," *Courier Journal*, February 29, 2003; "Second Parent Asks to Join Student Assignment Suit," *Courier Journal*, July 23, 2009; "Family Asks Judge to Rethink Ruling on School Assignment," *Courier Journal*, August 14, 2009; "JCPS Student Assignment Plan Challenged in New Suit," *Courier Journal*, June 17, 2010; "School Assignment Case Tossed Out," *Courier Journal*, August 13, 2010. For example, in June 2012 the board increased the number of clusters and decreased the number of schools per cluster, with the aim of achieving shorter ride times.

Chapter Four

1. Early influential discussions of the concept of sharing interpretive authority include the essays in Frisch, *A Shared Authority*, and Katherine Borland, " 'That's Not What I Said': Interpretive Conflict in Oral Narrative Research," in Gluck and Patai, *Women's Words*. For a recent discussion among oral historians about shared authority and collaborative oral history research, see the essays in the special issue "Shared Authority" of the *Oral History Review*.

2. The leading scholars in advancing and summarizing the view that school desegregation did not bring enough gains to be worth the cost are Christine Rossell, David Armor, and Raymond Wolters. See Rossell, Armor, and Walberg, *School Desegregation in the Twenty-First Century*; Armor, *Forced Justice*; and Wolters, *Race and Education, 1954–2007*. The scholarship on black communities and schools has been led by Walker with *Their Highest Potential*.

3. For two recent reviews of this literature, which argue that the most recent and methodologically sophisticated studies support this consensus, see Mickelson, "Twenty-First Century Social Science on School Racial Diversity and Educational Outcomes"; Linn and Welner, *Race Conscious Policies for Assigning Students to Schools*.

4. For summaries of the literature, see Mickelson, "Twenty-First Century Social Science on School Racial Diversity and Educational Outcomes"; Linn and Welner, *Race Conscious Policies for Assigning Students to Schools*; and Orfield and Frankenberg, *Diversity and Educational Gains*. See also Wells, Holme, Tijerina Revilla, and Atanda, *Both Sides Now*; Susan Eaton and Christina Meldrum, "Broken Promises: Resegregation in Norfolk, Virginia," in Orfield and Eaton, *Dismantling Desegregation*, 115–41; Godwin, Leland, Baxter, and Southworth, "Sinking *Swann*"; Mickelson, "The Academic Consequence of Desegregation and Segregation"; Goldring, Cohen-Vogel, Smrekar, and Taylor, "Schooling Closer to Home."

5. Innes, *How Whites and Blacks Perform in Jefferson County Public Schools*; information on test scores of black and white students provided by Robert Rodosky of Jefferson County Public Schools; Aubespin, Clay, and Hudson, *Two Centuries of Black Louisville*, 246.

6. Wells, Duran, and White, "Refusing to Leave Desegregation Behind"; Orfield and Frankenberg, *Experiencing Integration in Louisville*.

7. Sowell, "Black Excellence"; Irvine and Irving, "The Impact of the Desegregation Process on the Education of Black Students"; Walker, *Their Highest Potential*. See also, Cecelski, *Along Freedom Road*; Noblit and Dempsey, *The Social Construction of Virtue*.

8. Dougherty, "From Anecdote to Analysis"; Morris and Morris, *The Price They Paid*; Shircliff, " 'We Got the Best of That World.' " I am indebted to Jack Dougherty for sharing with me his paper, "More Than One Memory."

9. Schrager, "What Is Social in Oral History?"

Conclusion

I thank John Dittmer for bringing Howard Zinn's words to my attention as part of a lecture he presented at the Filson Historical Society in Louisville on May 18, 2012.

1. David L. Kirp, "Making Schools Work," *New York Times*, May 20, 2012.

2. Susan Eaton and Christina Meldrum, "Broken Promises: Resegregation in Norfolk, Virginia," in Orfield and Eaton, *Dismantling Desegregation*, 115.

3. Saatcioglu and Carl, "The Discursive Turn in School Desegregation"; Pride, "Public Opinion and the End of Busing"; Mickelson, "Twenty-First Century Social Science on School Racial Diversity and Educational Outcomes," 1176–77; Pride, *Political Use of Racial Narratives*, chap. 10.

4. Interview with Mattie Jones by Todd Read, March 1, 2011, OHC.

5. Interview with Suzy Post by Sarah Theusen, June 23, 2006, (U-0178) SOHC.

6. Unidentified bus driver quoted in "Memories of 1975 Still Vivid in Minds of the Participants," *Courier Journal,* September 4, 1995; Interview with Ken Miller by Elizabeth Gritter and Timothy P. McCarthy, December 8, 2004, (U-0089) SOHC.

7. Interviews with Robert Cunningham by Tracy E. K'Meyer, September 1, 1999, OHC, and by Elizabeth Gritter, October 16, 2004, (U-0024) SOHC.

Bibliography

Archival Collections

Louisville, Ky.
    University of Louisville Archives
        Progress in Education Papers
Madison, Wisc.
    State Historical Society of Wisconsin
        Anne and Carl Braden Papers
        Social Action Files
Washington, D.C.
    Library of Congress, Manuscript Division
        National Association for the Advancement of Colored People Papers,
            microfilm edition

Newspapers and Magazines

Courier Journal
Defender
Louisville Times

Unpublished Sources

Brady, Darcell Yvette. "Community Influence on Urban School Desegregation." Ph.D.
    diss., University of Illinois-Chicago, 1999.
Dougherty, Jack. "More Than One Memory: Contested Histories of Segregated
    Schooling in the North and South." Paper presented at the History of Education
    Society Annual Meeting, Chicago, October 30, 1998.
Thompson, John Marshall. "School Desegregation in Jefferson County, Kentucky,
    1954–1975." Ph.D. diss., University of Kentucky, 1976.

Published Sources

A Community Study among Whites and Negroes in Louisville, Kentucky. New York: Roper
    Research Associates, 1969.
Anderson, James, Dara N. Byrne, and Tavis Smiley, eds. *The Unfinished Agenda of Brown
    v. Board of Education.* New York: Wiley and Sons, 2004.

Anderson, Karen. *Little Rock: Race and Resistance at Central High School*. Princeton: Princeton University Press, 2010.

Andrews, Kenneth T. "Movement–Counter Movement Dynamics and the Emergence of New Institutions: The Case of White Flight Schools in Mississippi." *Social Forces* 80 (March 2002): 911–36.

Armor, David J. *Forced Justice: School Desegregation and the Law*. New York: Oxford University Press, 1995.

Arnez, Nancy L. "Implementation of Desegregation as a Discriminatory Process." *Journal of Negro Education* 47 (Winter 1978): 28–45.

Aubespin, Mervin, Kenneth Clay, and J. Blaine Hudson. *Two Centuries of Black Louisville: A Photographic History*. Louisville: Butler Books, 2011.

Bankston III, Carl, and Stephen J. Caldas. *Troubled Dream: The Promise and Failure of School Desegregation in Louisiana*. Nashville: Vanderbilt University Press, 2002.

Bartley, Numan V. *The Rise of Massive Resistance: Race and Politics in the South during the 1950's*. Baton Rouge: Louisiana University Press, 1969.

Baum, Howell S. *Brown in Baltimore: School Desegregation and the Limits of Liberalism*. Ithaca: Cornell University Press, 2010.

Bell, Derrick A. "Serving Two Masters: Integration Ideals and Client Interests in School Desegregation Litigation." *Yale Law Journal* 85 (March 1976): 470–516.

Berkowitz, Edward. "Baltimore's Public Schools in a Time of Transition." *Maryland Historical Magazine* 92 (Winter 1997): 412–32.

Boger, John Charles, and Gary Orfield, eds. *School Resegregation: Must the South Turn Back*. Chapel Hill: University of North Carolina Press, 2005.

Braden, Anne. *The Wall Between*. Knoxville: University of Tennessee Press, 1999.

Burton, Orville Vernon, and David O'Brien, eds. *Remembering Brown at Fifty: The University of Illinois Commemorates Brown v. Board of Education*. Urbana: University of Illinois Press, 2009.

Carmichael, Omer, and Weldon James. *The Louisville Story*. New York: Simon and Schuster, 1957.

Cascio, Elizabeth, Nora Gordon, Ethan Lewis, and Sarah Reber. "From Brown to Busing." National Bureau of Economic Research Working Paper Series, no. 13279, July 2007, 1, http://www.nber.org/papers/w13279.

Causey, Virginia. "The Long and Winding Road: School Desegregation in Columbus, Georgia, 1963-1997." *Georgia Historical Quarterly* 85 (January 2001): 398–434.

Cecelski, David. *Along Freedom Road: Hyde County, North Carolina, and the Fate of Black Schools in the South*. Chapel Hill: University of North Carolina, 1994.

Charlton, Thomas L., Lois E. Myers, and Rebecca Sharpless. *Handbook of Oral History*. New York: Altamira Press, 2006.

Clotfelter, Charles T. *After Brown: The Rise and Retreat of School Desegregation*. Princeton: Princeton University Press, 2006.

Daugherity, Brian J., and Charles C. Bolton. *With All Deliberate Speed: Implementing Brown v. Board of Education*. Fayetteville: University of Arkansas Press, 2008.

Dittmer, John. *Local People: The Struggle for Civil Rights in Mississippi*. Urbana: University of Illinois Press, 1995.

Dougherty, Jack. "From Anecdote to Analysis: Oral Interviews and New Scholarship in Educational History." *Journal of American History* 86 (September 1999): 712–23.

———. *More Than One Struggle: The Evolution of School Reform in Milwaukee*. Chapel Hill: University of North Carolina Press, 2004.

Durr, Kenneth. *Behind the Backlash: White Working Class Politics in Baltimore, 1940–1980*. Chapel Hill: University of North Carolina Press, 2003.

Formisano, Ronald P. *Boston against Busing: Race, Class, and Ethnicity in the 1960s and 1970s*. Chapel Hill: University of North Carolina Press, 1991.

Frankenberg, Erica, Chungmei Lee, and Gary Orfield. "A Multiracial Society with Segregated Schools: Are We Losing the Dream?" Civil Rights Project, Harvard University, January 2003.

Frisch, Michael. *A Shared Authority: Essays on the Craft and Meaning of Oral and Public History*. Albany: State University of New York Press, 1990.

Fulz, Michael. "The Displacement of Black Educators Post-*Brown*: An Overview and Analysis." *History of Education Quarterly* 44 (Spring 2004): 11–45.

Gaillard, Frye. *The Dream Long Deferred: The Landmark Struggle for Desegregation in Charlotte, North Carolina*. 3rd ed. Columbia: University of South Carolina Press, 2006.

Gates, Robbin L. *Making of Massive Resistance: Virginia's Politics of Public School Desegregation, 1954–1956*. Chapel Hill: University of North Carolina Press, 1964.

Gluck, Sharon Berger, and Daphne Patai, eds. *Women's Words: The Feminist Practice of Oral History*. New York: Routledge, 1991.

Godwin, R. Kenneth, Suzanne M. Leland, Andrew D. Baxter, and Stephanie Southworth. "Sinking *Swann*: Public School Choice and the Resegregation of Charlotte's Public Schools." *Review of Policy Research* 23 (September 2006): 983–97.

Goldring, Ellen, Lora Cohen-Vogel, Claire Smrekar, and Cynthia Taylor. "Schooling Closer to Home: Desegregation Policy and Neighborhood Contexts." *American Journal of Education* 112 (May 2006): 335–62.

Gray, Julie Salley. "To Fight the Good Fight: The Battle over Control of the Pasadena City Schools, 1969–1979." *Essays in History* 37 (1995), www.essaysinhistory.com/articles/2012/119.

Hall, Jacquelyn Dowd. "The Long Civil Rights Movement and the Political Uses of the Past." *Journal of American History* 91 (March 2005): 1233–63.

Hardin, John. *Fifty Years of Segregation: Higher Education in Kentucky, 1904–54*. Lexington: University Press of Kentucky, 1997.

Innes, Richard G. *How Whites and Blacks Perform in Jefferson County Public Schools*. Bowling Green, Ky.: Blue Grass Institute for Public Policy Solutions, 2008.

Irvine, Russell, and Jackie Irving, "The Impact of the Desegregation Process on the Education of Black Students: Key Variables." *Journal of Negro Education* 52 (Autumn 1983): 410–22.

Jacobs, Gregory S., *Getting Around Brown: Desegregation, Development, and the Columbus Public Schools*. Columbus: Ohio State University Press, 1998.

Klarman, Michael J. *Brown v. Board of Education and the Civil Rights Movement*. New York: Oxford University Press, 2007.

K'Meyer, Tracy E. *Civil Rights in the Gateway to the South: Louisville, Kentucky, 1945–1980.* Lexington: University Press of Kentucky, 2009.

———. " 'Gateway to the South': Regional Identity and the Louisville, KY, Civil Rights Movement." *Ohio Valley History* 4 (Spring 2004): 43–60.

———. "Remembering the Past and Contesting the Future of School Desegregation in Louisville, Kentucky, 1975–2012," *Oral History Review* 39 (Summer/Fall 2012): 230–57.

———. "Well, I'm Not Moving: Open Housing and White Activism in the Long Civil Rights Movement." *The Sixties: A Journal of History, Politics, and Culture* 2 (June 2009): 1–24.

Lassiter, Matthew D. *The Silent Majority: Suburban Politics in the Sunbelt South.* Princeton: Princeton University Press, 2006.

———. "The Suburban Origins of 'Color-Blind' Conservatism: Middle-Class Consciousness in the Charlotte Busing Crisis." *Journal of Urban History* 30 (May 2004): 549–82.

Lassiter, Matthew D., and Andrew B. Lewis. *The Moderates' Dilemma: Massive Resistance to School Desegregation in Virginia.* Charlottesville: University Press of Virginia, 1998.

Lau, Peter F., ed. *From the Grassroots to the Supreme Court: Brown v. Board of Education and American Democracy.* Durham: Duke University Press, 2004.

Lewis, George. *The White South and the Red Menace: Segregationists, Anticommunism, and Massive Resistance.* Gainesville: University of Florida Press, 2004.

Linn, Robert L., and Kevin G. Welner, eds. *Race Conscious Policies for Assigning Students to Schools: Social Science Research and the Supreme Court Cases.* Washington, D.C.: Committee on Social Science Research Evidence on Racial Diversity in Schools, National Academy of Education, 2007.

Lyne, Jack. *Schoolhouse Dreams Deferred: Decay, Hope, and Desegregation in a Core-City School System.* Phi Delta Kappa International, 1998.

McGirr, Lisa. *Suburban Warriors: The Origins of the New American Right.* Princeton: Princeton University Press, 2001.

Meyer, Stephen Grant. *As Long as They Don't Move Next Door: Segregation and Racial Conflict in American Neighborhoods.* Lanham, Md.: Rowan and Littlefield, 2000.

Mickelson, Roslyn Arlin. "The Academic Consequence of Desegregation and Segregation: Evidence from the Charlotte-Mecklenburg Schools." *North Carolina Law Review* 81 (2003): 1513–62.

———. "Twenty-First Century Social Science on School Racial Diversity and Educational Outcomes." *Ohio State Law Journal* 69 (2008): 1173–1228.

Mills, Nicholaus, ed. *Busing U.S.A.* New York: Teachers College Press, 1979.

Monti, Daniel J. *A Semblance of Justice: St. Louis School Desegregation and Order in Urban America.* Columbia: University of Missouri Press, 1985.

Morris, Vivian Gunn, and Curtis L. Morris. *The Price They Paid: Desegregation in an African American Community.* New York: Teachers College Press, 2002.

Noblit, George W., and Van O. Dempsey. *The Social Construction of Virtue: The Moral Life of Schools.* Albany: State University of New York Press, 1996.

Orfield, Gary. "Public Opinion and School Desegregation." *Teachers College Record* 96 (Summer 1995): 654–70.

Orfield, Gary, and Susan E. Eaton. *Dismantling Desegregation: The Quiet Reversal of Brown v. Board of Education.* New York: The New Press, 1996.

Orfield, Gary, and Erica Frankenberg. *Diversity and Educational Gains: A Plan for a Changing County and Its Schools.* Civil Rights Project, University of California–Los Angeles, 2011.

———. *Experiencing Integration in Louisville: How Parents and Students See the Gains and Challenges.* Civil Rights Project, University of California–Los Angeles, 2011.

Patterson, James T. *Brown v. Board of Education: A Civil Rights Milestone and Its Troubled Legacy.* New York: Oxford University Press 2002.

Perks, Robert, and Alistair Thomson. *The Oral History Reader.* New York: Routledge, 1998.

Population and Housing Statistics for Census Tracts Louisville, Ky., and Adjacent Area. Washington, D.C.: United States Government Printing Office, 1942.

Portelli, Alessandro. *The Death of Luigi Strastulli and Other Stories: Form and Meaning in Oral History.* Albany: State University of New York Press, 1991.

Pratt, Robert A. *The Color of Their Skin: Education and Race in Richmond, Virginia, 1954–1989.* Charlottesville: University Press of Virginia, 1992.

Pride, Richard A. *Political Use of Racial Narratives: School Desegregation in Mobile, Alabama, 1954–97.* Urbana: University of Illinois Press, 2008.

———. "Public Opinion and the End of Busing: (Mis)Perceptions of Policy Failure." *Sociological Quarterly* 41 (Spring 2000): 207–25.

Pride, Richard A., and J. David Woodard. *The Burden of Busing: The Politics of Desegregation in Nashville, Tennessee.* Knoxville: University of Tennessee Press, 1985.

Report on Public Schools in Louisville, Kentucky, 1956–1971. Louisville: Commission on Human Rights, Commonwealth of Kentucky, 1971.

Rossell, Christine H. "Controlled Choice Desegregation Plans: Not Enough Choice, Too Much Control?" *Urban Affairs Review* 31 (September 1995): 43–76.

Rossell, Christine H., and David J. Armor. "The Effectiveness of School Desegregation Plans, 1968–1991." *American Politics Quarterly* 24 (July 1996): 267–302.

Rossell, Christine H., David J. Armor, and Herbert J. Walberg, eds. *School Desegregation in the Twenty-First Century.* Westport, Conn.: Praeger, 2002.

"Round Table: *Brown v. Board of Education,* Fifty Years Later." *Journal of American History* 91 (June 2004): 19–118.

Saatcioglu, Argun, and Jim Carl. "The Discursive Turn in School Desegregation: National Patterns and a Case Analysis of Cleveland, 1973–1998." *Social Science History* 35 (Spring 2011): 59–112.

Schrager, Samuel. "What Is Social in Oral History?" *International Journal of Oral History* 4 (June 1983): 76–98.

Sedler, Robert A. "The Louisville-Jefferson County School Desegregation Case: A Lawyer's Perspective." *Register of the Kentucky Historical Society* 105 (Winter 2001): 3–32.

"Shared Authority." Special issue, *Oral History Review* 30 (Winter-Spring 2003).

Shircliff, Barbara. " 'We Got the Best of That World': A Case for the Study of Nostalgia in the Oral History of School Segregation." *Oral History Review* 28 (Summer-Autumn 2001): 59–84.

Sowell, Thomas. "Black Excellence: The Case of Dunbar High School." *Public Interest* 35 (Spring 1974): 1–21.

Sugrue, Thomas. *Sweet Land of Liberty: The Forgotten Struggle for Civil Rights in the North*. New York: Random House, 2008.

Taggart, Robert. "The Failure of Apparent Successful School Desegregation: Wilmington, Delaware, 1954–1978." *American Educational History Journal* 32 (January 2005): 94–101.

Taylor, Steven J. L. *Desegregation in Boston and Buffalo: The Influence of Local Leaders*. Albany: State University of New York Press, 1998.

Theoharis, Jeanne F. " 'We Saved the City': Black Struggles for Educational Equality in Boston, 1960–1976." *Radical History Review* 81 (Fall 2001): 61–93.

U. S. Commission on Civil Rights. *Hearing before the U.S. Commission on Civil Rights: Held in Louisville, Kentucky, June 14–16, 1976*. Washington, D.C., 1976.

Walker, Vanessa Siddle. *Their Highest Potential: An African American School Community in the Segregated South*. Chapel Hill: University of North Carolina Press, 1996.

Webb, Clive, ed., *Massive Resistance: Southern Opposition to the Second Reconstruction*. New York: Oxford University Press, 2005.

Wells, Amy Stewart, Jacquelyn Duran, and Terrenda White. "Refusing to Leave Desegregation Behind: From Graduates of Racially Diverse Schools to the Supreme Court." *Teachers College Record* 110 (December 2008): 2532–70.

Wells, Amy Stuart, Jennifer Jellison Holme, Anita Tijerina Revilla, and Awo Korantema a Atanda. *Both Sides Now: The Story of School Desegregation's Graduates*. Berkeley: University of California Press, 2009.

Wilkinson, J. Harvie. *From Brown to Bakke: The Supreme Court and School Desegregation, 1954–1978*. New York: Oxford University Press, 1978.

Wilson, George D. *A Century of Negro Education in Louisville, Kentucky*. Louisville: Louisville Municipal College under the auspices of the Work Projects Administration, 193[6].

Wolters, Raymond. *Race and Education, 1954–2007*. Columbia: University of Missouri Press, 2008.

Wright, George C. *In Pursuit of Equality, 1890–1980*. Vol. 2 of *A History of Blacks in Kentucky*. Frankfort: Kentucky Historical Society, 1992.

———. *Life behind a Veil: Blacks in Louisville, Ky, 1865–1930*. Baton Rouge: Louisiana State University Press, 1985.

Index

Note: Page numbers in italic type refer to illustrations or the map.

success, 46–47, 162–63; and busing, 60–61, 73–80, 79, 100–102; persistence of, 107, 141–47, 184–86; 1981–2007, 107–8, 112–13; white, 144

Progress in Education (PIE), 60, 78–79, 101–2, 185

Project Renaissance, 120, 142

Public opinion: on desegregation, 1, 46, 120, 129; on busing, 1, 54; on choice, 146–47; on diversity, 146–47

Quality Education for All Students (QUEST), 120–21, 123, 125–26, 128, 134, 145

Quality of education, 57, 63, 101, 120

Race-conscious remedies, Supreme Court approval of, 139

Racial balance in schools, 52, 54, 111–12, 120–21, 127–38, 145

Racially identifiable/polarized schools, 51, 52

Racism: of teachers, 34, 37, 42–44, 49, 83–84, 92; students' experiences of, 36–37, 39–44; antibusing and, 60, 70–71, 98–100; of parents, 66–67, 86, 98–99; empathy for victims of, 71; structural, 99–100, 139; unacknowledged, 183

Rehnquist, William, 108

Religious community, 11, 18, 60, 111, 112, 116, 119, 123, 162, 185

Residential clusters, 107, 120, 124, 142, 146

Ricardo X, 127

Richmond, Ben, 134

Richmond, Va., 2, 3, 141

Roberts, John, 138, 139

Robertson, Diane, 94–95, 104

Robinson, Marcella, 68–70, 98–100

Rockford, Ill., 109

Rosenbaum, Ken, 83–84

Roundtree, Rita, 63

Ruffra, Jean, 62–63, 158

Rumor-control hotline, 76

St. Louis, Mo., 18, 50

Salisbury Elementary School, 151–52

Sampson, F. G., 122

Save Our Community Schools, 59, 62–63

Schaffner Elementary School, 62–63

Scholarship: on desegregation, 2–3, 45, 109, 144, 174–76, 181–85; on busing, 2–3, 61, 97–98, 100–101, 104; on civil rights, 4, 6

School and classroom experiences: after desegregation, 33–49; violence in, 49, 59, 72, 79, 89, 91, 95–96, 99; busing's impact on, 80–96, 102–4; before desegregation, 150–55

School Board. See Jefferson County Board of Education; Louisville Board of Education

School spirit. See Community/school spirit

Seattle, Wash., 141

Segregation, 8–11, 49–51, 58–60, 97, 99–100, 138, 150–55, 182, 183, 185

Senate Bill 6 (1953), 12

Shawnee Junior and Senior High School, 42, 72–73, 96, 116, 169

Shircliffe, Barbara, 177

Sixth Circuit Court of Appeals, 55–56, 129–30

Sloane, Harvey, 62

Smoketown neighborhood, 9

Social mixing of blacks and whites, 18–19, 41, 93–94, 98, 164, 167

Socioeconomic factors in student assignment, 64, 71–72, 140, 146

Southern High School, 59, 69, 91–92

Southern Oral History Program (SOHP), 6

Spond, Joyce, 63

Stallworth, Deborah, 127–28, 130, 132–35, 143

Stanley, Frank, 57

State Guard, 99

States' rights, 18

State troopers, 91–92

Steele, Charles, 16

Student assignment plans, 7, 111–12, 128–38, 140, 142, 146–47. See also Alphabet plan

Students. *See* African American students; White students

Summers, Charles, 71–72, 99

Summers, William E., III, 127

Suspensions of African American students, 71–72, 78–80, 99

Swann v. Charlotte-Mecklenburg Board of Education (1971), 54

Sweeney, Maurice, 107, 112, 115–18, 143

Teacher desegregation: firing of black instructors, 12, 45; post-*Brown*, 18; resistance to, 21–22, 51, 52; personal recollections of, 31–33

Teachers: salaries of, 9, 11, 83; school and classroom experiences of, 24–26, 29–30, 32–33, 44, 47, 81–88, 151–53; role of, in desegregation, 24–26, 35; racism of, 34, 37, 42–44, 49, 83–84, 92; transfer of, 81–83, 86–88, 96, 167–68, 170–71; supply of black, 145, 167–68

Test scores, 174–75

Theoharis, Jeanne, 2–3, 100–101

Thomas, Clarence, 130

Thomas, Fran, 128, 133–34, 143

Tinsley, Deanna, 36–38, 48, *119*

Todd, Pat, 140–41, 146, 161–62, 178

Traditional schools, 129, 137–38, 142

Transfer option, 17–18, 20, 28–30, 38, 45, 49, 50

Truancy, 67, 81

Union Labor Against Busing, 59

Unitary status, 109, 118, 138

United Black Protective Parents, 57, 78–80, 101–2

United Church Women of Kentucky, 18

U.S. Commission on Civil Rights, 99

U.S. Health, Education, and Welfare (HEW) Department, 52, 54–55, 62–63, 97

U.S. Justice Department, 108

U.S. Supreme Court, 108–9, 118, 128, 130, 138–40, 182, 186

University of Kentucky, 12, 119

University of Louisville, 12

Urban League, 24, 112, 134

Urban renewal, 51

U.S. News and World Report (magazine), 32

Valley High School, 59, 65, 73

Van Hoose, Richard, 16, 52

Violence: associated with busing, 3, 5, 58, 59, 61, 64, 66, 68–69, 71–73, 78–79, 88, 91–92, 97–99, 161; associated with housing segregation, 20, 100; in schools, 49, 59, 72, 79, 89, 91, 95–96, 99; threats of, 71, 76, 78, 91, 114; attributed to African Americans, 99

Virginia Avenue Elementary School, 20, 29, 33

Voluntary desegregation, 1, 3, 109, 111, 121

Wade, Andrew and Charlotte, 19–20

Wainwright, Sandra, 87–88, 151–53, 158–59, 177

Wake County (N.C.) Public School System, 141

Walker, Morton, 17, 22–23, 30, 47

Waller Elementary School, *178*

Weathers, Carmen, 126, 130–33, 135, 137, 143, 155–56

Wells, Amy, 176

West Chestnut Baptist Church, 119, 123

West end neighborhood, 9, 36, 42, 51, 56, 59, 71–73, 93–94, 101, 111, 113, 117, 122, 145, 157, 168–69, 183–84

Western Elementary School, 37

Western Junior High School, 36–38

Wetherby, Lawrence, 16

White, Ethel, 6

White, Gerald, 42

White Citizens' Council, 18

White flight, 7, 51, 108, 113, 175, 182

White Power, 98

Whites: attitudes of, toward desegregation, 18, 120; reactions of, to busing, 54, 58–60, 97 (*see also* Busing: opposition to); support for